STUDIES IN GERMAN LITERATURE,
LINGUISTICS, AND CULTURE
Vol. 67

Ursula Sampath

Kaspar Hauser:
A Modern Metaphor

CAMDEN HOUSE

Copyright © 1991 by
CAMDEN HOUSE, INC.

Published by Camden House, Inc.
Drawer 2025
Columbia, SC 29202 USA

Set in Garamond and printed on acid-free paper.
Binding materials are chosen for strength and
durability.

ISBN: 1-879751-05-4

Library of Congress Cataloging-in-Publication Data

Sampath, Ursula, 1937–
    Kaspar Hauser : a modern metaphor / Ursula Sampath.
      p. cm. -- (Studies in German literature, linguistics, and
culture ; v. 67)
    Includes bibliographical references and index.
    ISBN 1-879751-05-4
    1. German literature--20th century--History and criticism.
2. Hauser, Kaspar, 1812–1833, in fiction, drama, poetry, etc.
I. Title. II. Series.
PT405.S287 1991
830.9'351--dc20   91-29137
                                                           CIP

Table of Contents

Preface

My FIRST ENCOUNTER WITH Kaspar Hauser goes back to my school days in Ansbach, Germany, where on a mandatory class outing to the local *Heimatmuseum* the sudden confrontation with the faded relics of the murder brought the mystery of 1833 poignantly alive for me. I remember that the 'why' and 'how' of the sad story preoccupied me for a long time. But it was not until many years later, and in a different setting, that I began to notice how many modern writers were concerned with Kaspar Hauser, and the questions 'why' and 'how' took on other, literary dimensions. The dissertation which grew from this research forms the basis of this book.

It gives me great pleasure to acknowledge my debt to all those who contributed to the preparation of the manuscript. First of all, I would like to thank Memorial University of Newfoundland for granting me leave of absence to do the necessary research, and for supporting this project.

I would like to express my sincere gratitude to the supervisor of my original thesis, Mr. Gilbert McKay (St. Peter's College, Oxford) for his expert guidance and unfailing encouragement; to Dr. David Constantine (The Queen's College, Oxford) for his helpful comments and for his own contribution to the literature in question; and also to Professor Siegbert Prawer, whose enthusiastic approval of my project in its early stages made all the difference, and meant a great deal to me. The helpful and friendly staff at the Taylor Institute, Oxford, at the National Archives in Marbach am Neckar, and at the City Archives in Ansbach, all made research a pleasure.

Furthermore, I would like to thank the authors who very kindly took the time and trouble to answer my queries, and in some cases volunteered helpful hints or even material, namely: Jürg Amann, Wolf Biermann, Dieter Forte, Sibylle Gielen, Peter Härtling, Walter Kempowski, Reinhard Mey, and Guntram Vesper. I am also very grateful to Janet Brooks Gerloff for allowing me the use of her drawing of Kaspar Hauser, and to Peer Baedeker, Thilo Jörger, Ulrike Leonhardt, as well as Johannes Wacker of the Württembergische Landesbühne, whose information helped me to close some gaps in my research. A special thank you also goes to my fellow Kaspar-Hauser-enthusiast, Ulrich Struve of Princeton University, for a lively exchange of ideas in the recent years, and for generously informing me of some of his latest discoveries. Several of my colleagues undertook the bothersome task of proofreading, and I really appreciate their help.

Last, but not least, I want to thank my husband, Hugh, without whose patience and support I could not have completed this project.

Introduction

ALMOST SIXTEEN DECADES HAVE passed since the death of
Kaspar Hauser, the young foundling of Nuremberg, whose mysterious
past and tragic fate engaged the attention of his contemporaries to such
an extent that he became known as the "Child of Europe." During much
of the nineteenth century, a multitude of sensationalized accounts of his
story and speculations about his origin and murder kept the youth in
the limelight. Literary interest was less pronounced, but it, too, centered
almost exclusively upon Kaspar Hauser's surmised abduction from a
noble family. Only two nineteenth-century contributions can be said to
be of more serious intent: Karl Gutzkow's novel *Die Söhne Pestalozzis*
(1870), and Paul Verlaine's poem "Gaspard Hauser chante" (1881).

In the course of the twentieth century, the flood of polemics concerned with the ancestry of the youth has dwindled to a trickle in the
absence of any fresh and solid evidence. But the memory of Kaspar
Hauser has not faded. On the contrary, there has been a marked revival
of interest in the figure in recent years. Several books have appeared on
the German market which retell the story based on the documented
facts.[1] Feuerbach's detailed account of 1832[2] is still reissued periodical-
ly, photographs of relevant sites, artifacts, and portraits have been
compiled, and drawings about the foundling exhibited.[3] In Switzerland,
a journal with humanistic ideals made its (temporary) appearance under
the title *Kaspar Hauser*. There is even work on a Kaspar Hauser opera
in progress, with as yet uncertain results.[4] In the scientific community,
psychologists are familiar with the "Kaspar Hauser syndrome," a term
coined by Alexander Mitscherlich to describe the consequences of
emotional deprivation during childhood, and members of the medical

---

[1] See, e.g., Hans Scholz, *Kaspar Hauser: Protokoll einer modernen Sage* (Munich:
Wilhelm Heyne, 1985; orig. publ. Hamburg: Campe, 1964); Kurt Kramer, *Kaspar
Hauser: Kein Rätsel unserer Zeit* (Ansbach: Ansbacher Verlagsgesellschaft, 1978);
Marcus Conradt, *Fünfeinhalb Jahre unter Menschen* (Stuttgart: Ernst Klett, 1983);
Ulrike Leonhardt, *Prinz von Baden, genannt Kaspar Hauser* (Reinbek bei Hamburg:
Wunderlich, 1987).

[2] Anselm von Feuerbach, "Kaspar Hauser: Beispiel eines Verbrechens am Seelenleben
des Menschen," reprint in Jochen Hörisch, ed., *Ich möchte ein solcher werden wie ...*
(Frankfurt a. M.: Suhrkamp, 1979; orig. publ. Ansbach: J. M. Dollfuß, 1832). All future
references to Feuerbach's work are taken from the latter reprint.

[3] The annotated photo documentary by Johannes Mayer and Peter Tradowsky, *Kaspar
Hauser: Das Kind von Europa* (Stuttgart: Urachhaus, 1984), gives a good general
overview. With regard to artwork, see e.g. the series of drawings and paintings on
Kaspar Hauser by Janet Brooks Gerloff (1986).

[4] Music by Walter Haupt, libretto by Gerd Uecker. If this project comes to fruition, it
will be produced by the Bayerische Staatsoper, Munich.

profession are speculating anew about the physiological implications of the boy's long-term confinement.[5]

As a source of literary inspiration for works which go beyond the historical controversies, the foundling did not really come into his own in Germany until the beginning of the twentieth century, when both minor and major writers began to use aspects of the story in various ways and in different genres. Since that time, Kaspar Hauser has transcended the traditional boundaries of literature (prose, poetry, and drama), and has made his appearance in modern media, such as radio plays, films, and even some songs of the postwar *Liedermacher*.

This phenomenon strongly suggests that Kaspar Hauser is more than a literary anachronism. If we accept the truism that all artistic endeavor relates to and depends on its historical context, and that artists can be seen as seismographs for the moods and problems of their era, we have to suspect that the figure has emblematic significance, and acts as a catalyst for contemporary concerns.

To find out what exactly Kaspar Hauser stands for in the twentieth century, and to ascertain patterns of continuity and change, is the main purpose of this study. As for the time frame of this investigation, the twentieth century up to the present virtually selects itself as a natural choice of period. As mentioned above, the turn of the century marked a turning away from the preoccupation with historical facts and rumors, and the beginning of the figure's popularity for conveying other, more abstract concerns. Furthermore, the chosen span of time coincides with what is often loosely referred to as *Die Moderne*, a useful, if somewhat vague, collective term which has come to denote "alle neueren ... Literaturströmungen."[6] The label signals a new beginning, while sidestepping the still controversial formal distinctions between often overlapping literary movements which need not concern us in the given context.

The adjective *German* in the title should be interpreted as 'in the German language', as the investigation also includes works from Austria and Switzerland. The manifestations of interest in Kaspar Hauser in international literature — such as, for example, Melville's comparison of the figure to his Billy Budd in the nineteenth century, or two recent

---

[5] See "Ödipus und Kaspar Hauser: Tiefenpsychologische Probleme in der Gegenwart," *Der Monat* 3, no. 25 (Oct. 1950): 11–18; and Günter Hesse, "Kaspar Hauser und sein Schlüssel," *Deutsches Ärzteblatt: Kulturmagazin* 81, no. 6 (10 Feb. 1984): 365–68.

[6] *Metzler Literatur Lexikon*, ed. Günther and Irmgard Schweikle (Stuttgart: Metzler, 1984), 289. The general acceptance of the term *Moderne* in this sense is shown by the use of headings such as Herbert A. and Elisabeth Frenzel's "Junge Moderne der Gegenwart," *Daten deutscher Dichtung: Chronologischer Abriß der deutschen Literaturgeschichte*, vol. 2, 11th edition (Munich: Deutscher Taschenbuch Verlag, 1975; orig. publ. Cologne: Kiepenheuer & Witsch, 1953); or, more up-to-date, Hans-Henrik Krummacher, Fritz Martini, and Walter Müller-Seidel, *Zeit der Moderne: Zur deutschen Literatur von der Jahrhundertwende bis zur Gegenwart* (Stuttgart: Alfred Kröner, 1984).

poems by contemporary English poets[7] — cannot be considered here, although it could be a rewarding task to draw broader comparisons.

The term *literature* referred to in the title also needs clarification. For the purpose of this thematic analysis, I have excluded material which merely reviews the known historical events and speculations. This type of writing, informative as it may be on occasion, cannot really contribute to our understanding of Kaspar Hauser's contemporary significance. My focus is on a selection of works with at least some fictional or subjective ingredients. Regardless of whether a work incorporates historically accurate material or merely hints at elements of the Kaspar Hauser story in an oblique manner, the main criterion for its inclusion was a tangible concern with matters beyond the factual background.

The perimeter for this type of material has been drawn rather widely to encompass examples of both traditional and modern media, as long as they meet the above requirements. It has been recognized for some time, with approval or disapproval, that the concept of literature has undergone an irrevocable expansion. As Gerhard Kaiser remarks: "Über die Notwendigkeit, den eng gefaßten Begriff von Literatur fallenzulassen, gibt es inzwischen keine Diskussion mehr."[8] However, printed sources are available for all cited material, so that a connection with the realm of letters does exist, and access is possible for the researcher.

Some inherent dangers must be taken into account in the examination of such a diverse assortment of works of differing calibre. Are we not comparing 'apples with oranges'? Is this permissible? The answer is an unequivocal *yes*. Just as we may indeed compare apples and oranges if we restrict ourselves to relevant questions (such as: "What is their relative sugar content?"; or "Are they equally perishable?"), the external differences between the objects of our research, though of importance in other contexts, should not matter if we ask content-oriented questions about the significance of the Kaspar Hauser figure. Form, in each case, has a subsidiary function. As for the question of differences in aesthetic value — a contentious issue even if one were to stay within one single genre — it seems to be the consensus of modern researchers of *Stoffgeschichte* that minor works, too, can contribute to their findings. Perhaps Helmut Kreuzer expresses it most cogently: "Jedes literarische Produkt ist im Prinzip solange (und in dem Maße) legitimer potentieller Gegenstand der Wissenschaft, als seine Behandlung poetologisch oder historisch innovative, erkenntnisfördernde

---

[7] Herman Melville, "Billy Budd," *Typee and Billy Budd* (London: Dent, 1958; orig. publ., posthumously, 1924), see 285; Laurence Lerner, "Kaspar Hauser," in *The Man I Killed* (London: Secker & Warburg, 1980), 22; and, more obliquely, David Constantine, untitled poem ["Under the bag of soot ... "], in *The Poetry Book Society Anthology*, vol. 1 (London: Hutchinson, 1990), 70.

[8] Gerhard R. Kaiser, *Einführung in die vergleichende Literaturwissenschaft: Forschungsstand — Kritik — Aufgaben* (Darmstadt: Wissenschaftliche Buchgesellschaft, 1980), 52.

Resultate verspricht."[9] Besides, it is precisely the ubiquity of Kaspar Hauser's appeal which, in my opinion, allows us to draw broader conclusions.

With regard to the method of this study, I have taken a multiple approach (or what Hermand advocates as "synthetisches Interpretieren").[10] In view of the wide variety of works, stylistic and structural aspects serve as proof of particular thematic concerns rather than as objects of detailed analysis in their own right. Like any survey of how a literary topic finds its expression within a given time period, the examination of "Kaspar Hauser in twentieth-century German literature" manifestly has its roots in the tradition of *Stoff- und Motivgeschichte*, now happily rehabilitated with a changed approach thanks to the efforts of eloquent advocates such as Manfred Beller, Harry Levin, and Raymond Trousson.[11]

One controversy in this field of research which has not yet been resolved is the veritable chaos which reigns with regard to the meaning of relevant literary terms. To cite just two examples, the German word *Thema* is not the equivalent of the English term *theme* or the French word *thème*; the words *Motiv* and *motif* may be equivalent in a dictionary sense, but their interpretations are highly idiosyncratic. In the face of such disarray, precise formal distinctions will be avoided. In general, I see *Stoff* as the already existing pool of raw material from which the author draws his inspiration, and from which he selects the elements which suit his own purpose. It is usually referred to as *material*, and in the case of this study applies to the historical data about Kaspar Hauser, whether transmitted by way of documents or already existing literature. My use of the word *motif* agrees best with Frenzel's definition as "eine kleine stoffliche Einheit, die zwar noch nicht einen ganzen Plot, eine Fabel umfaßt, aber doch bereits ein inhaltliches, situationmäßiges Element darstellt."[12] In other words, it refers to content-oriented rather than structural elements of the Kaspar Hauser story, and will therefore not be divided into further sub-categories. It

---

[9] *Veränderungen des Literaturbegriffs* (Göttingen: Vandenhoeck & Ruprecht, 1975), 11–12.

[10] Jost Hermand, *Synthetisches Interpretieren: Zur Methode der Literaturwissenschaft* (Munich: Nymphenburger Verlagsbuchhandlung, 1968), see esp. 9–13.

[11] See e.g. Manfred Beller, "Von der Stoffgeschichte zur Thematologie: Ein Beitrag zur komparatistischen Methodenlehre," *Arcadia* 5 (1970): 1–38; Harry Levin, "Thematics and Criticism," in *Grounds for Comparison* (Cambridge, Mass.: Harvard University Press, 1972), 91–119; and Raymond Trousson, a) "Plaidoyer pour la Stoffgeschichte," *Revue de Littérature Comparée*, 38 (1964): 101–14, also b) "Les Études de Thèmes: Questions de Méthode," *Elemente der Literatur: Beiträge zur Stoff-, Motiv- und Themenforschung*, vol. 1, ed. Adam J. Bizanz and Raymond Trousson (Stuttgart: Alfred Kröner, 1980), 1–10.

[12] Elisabeth Frenzel, *Stoff-, Motiv- und Symbolforschung*, Sammlung Metzler, Realienbücher für Germanisten (Stuttgart: Metzler, 1963), 26.

will become evident in the course of our discussion that Kaspar Hauser's significance is multifaceted, and that therefore several motifs may overlap in a given work. Some of these may be of central importance for the author; others are used only in passing, but can nevertheless add to the overall picture of relevant concerns.

An overview of the secondary commentaries on the literary use of Kaspar Hauser certainly confirms the need for a more thorough and up-to-date investigation. The earliest survey is Olga Stern's "Kaspar Hauser in der Dichtung."[13] A large part of this short dissertation deals with the historical facts and speculations, and describes the plots of selected nineteenth-century examples. Stern hypothesizes on their likely sources both within and without the Kaspar Hauser material, and links them to the traditional themes of the genre of *Räuber- und Schauerromane* which had their heyday during the eighteenth century. She seems to recognize a change in literature at the turn of the century when she refers to Kaspar Hauser as now assuming a more central rather than peripheral role, and to previously absent psychological components. But she views this development from a purely aesthetic point of view, concluding "daß sich die Behandlung [des Kaspar Hauser Stoffes], vom ästhetischen Standpunkt betrachtet, in aufsteigender Linie bewegt, und zwar vom Schauerroman über das Rührstück zum psychologischen Roman."[14]

Otto Jungmann's thesis of 1935 takes a more scholarly approach. Working from the premise that Kaspar Hauser's story has become synonymous "für einen bestimmten Schicksalsablauf," he sets himself the task "darzulegen, welche Möglichkeiten literarischer Formungen der Hauserfabel innewohnen und welchen Wandlungen sie im Laufe ihrer literarischen Entwicklung unterliegt."[15] Although this formulation seems to resemble the quest of my own study, Jungmann's emphasis again is on aesthetic differentiations. Beginning his ascending scale with purely descriptive representations, he proceeds via "moralisch-lehrhafte Gestaltung" to "Psychologische Gestaltung und Thematische Erschöpfung," finally arriving at his apotheosis, "Neues Ethos," a category he reserves for his own time, the 1930s. While Jungmann's work contains valuable insights, it also exposes the danger of subjective ranking procedures, particularly when the proof rests with ethical, thematic components. Like Stern, Jungmann ignores Trakl and Arp, as well as the German *Nachdichtungen* of Verlaine's "Gaspard Hauser chante."

Apart from these two early dissertations, surprisingly few critics have so far tackled the subject directly. Paul A. MacKenzie's article, "Kaspar

---

[13] Ph.D. diss., University of Frankfurt a. M., 1920.

[14] Ibid., 81.

[15] *Kaspar Hauser: Stoff und Problem in ihrer literarischen Gestaltung* (Würzburg: Konrad Triltsch, 1935; Ph.D. diss., University of Frankfurt a. M., 1935).

Hauser in England: The First Hundred Years,"[16] concerns itself with the polemics of the case, arguing that Lord Stanhope's inexplicable siding with Hauser's enemies turned the foundling into an undesirable topic in England. Gottfried Stix uncovers many parallels between the imagery in Wassermann's and Trakl's works, most of which, however, are discounted by Reinhold Grimm, who prefers to stress Rimbaud's influence on Trakl.[17] Horst Martin convincingly proves some connections between Kaspar Hauser und Hugo von Hofmannsthal's Sigismund in *Der Turm*, a topic to which we will return in more detail below.[18]

Several articles take a more thematic approach, albeit with limited scope. Herbert Thiele, for example, examines "Das Bild des Menschen in den Kaspar-Hauser-Gedichten von Paul Verlaine und Georg Trakl" by means of textual comparisons.[19] A. F. Bance investigates the background of political and literary-philosophical currents to account for the tenacious survival of the Kaspar Hauser story in literature. His view that in the transformation of the original material "something is revealed of the life of ideas and the manner of their transmission"[20] agrees with the premise of this study, but only Gutzkow, Wassermann, Trakl and Handke are given brief (though insightful) analyses. An article by R. D. Theisz deals with Wassermann, Trakl, Arp and Handke in succession, focusing on aspects of the relationship between a special type of outsider and a conformist society.[21] In the same context, Hans Mayer contrasts the modern perception of chance with that of previous eras, based on the evidence of Peter Handke's *Kaspar*.[22]

In the wake of this latter play, linguistic angles have received special attention. Wolfgang Held probes the "Dialektik zwischen sprachloser Unmündigkeit und sprachmächtiger Manipulation" as expressed by Verlaine, Trakl, Wassermann, Hofmannsthal and Handke.[23] Hörisch,

---

[16] *German Life & Letters* 35, no. 2 (Jan. 1982): 118–37.

[17] Gottfried Stix, *Trakl und Wassermann* (Rome: Edizioni di Storia e Letteratura, 1968); Reinhold Grimm, "Die Sonne: Bemerkungen zu einem Motiv Georg Trakls," *Deutsche Vierteljahrsschrift für Literaturwissenschaft und Geistesgeschichte* 35 (1961): 223–46.

[18] "Kaspar Hauser und Sigismund: Über eine Quelle zu Hofmannsthals *Turm*," *Seminar* 12, no. 4 (Nov. 1976): 236–58.

[19] *Wirkendes Wort* 14 (1964): 351–56.

[20] "The Kaspar Hauser Legend and its Literary Survival," *German Life & Letters* 8 (1974/75): 209.

[21] "Kaspar Hauser im zwanzigsten Jahrhundert: Der Aussenseiter und die Gesellschaft," *German Quarterly* 69 (1976): 169–80.

[22] "Kaspar, der Fremde und der Zufall: Literarische Aspekte der Entfremdung," *Text und Kritik* 24 (1969): 30–42.

[23] "Kaspar Hauser und die Kritik der Sprache," *Beiträge zu den Sommerkursen 1969*, ed. Goethe-Institut (Munich: Goethe-Institut, 1969), 39.

following Derrida's concepts, unveils a semiotic *Paradigmenwechsel* in the historic social context, and Kaja Silverman interprets Kaspar Hauser's enforced integration as shown in Herzog's film in the light of Lacan's theory.[24] Most recently, Ulrich Struve makes a distinction between mythologizing works (Rilke, Wassermann, Trakl, and Klaus Mann), and authors who promote a critical view of reality (Arp, Handke, Erich Fried, and Dieter Forte).[25]

Aside from these motif-oriented approaches, the volume of secondary literature dealing with the individual works under consideration in different contexts is far too large to be outlined here. It is in the nature of the uneven background material that some works have received much more attention than others. Views expressed about short-lived works or very recent authors are understandably scarce. In contrast, for an internationally known poet such as Trakl or a 'notorious' author such as Handke, the range of available secondary material is so vast that a judicious selection was necessary.

Some of these commentaries deal specifically with works considered below, so for instance Metzner's and Marey's analyses of Trakl's "Kaspar Hauser Lied."[26] Most critics, however, look at the texts in question as part of a general evaluation of the author's oeuvre, and the significance of Kaspar Hauser consequently receives only fleeting attention, or none at all. With regard to the following discourse, only those works referred to in either text or notes, and those which played a role in shaping my opinions, will be listed in the bibliography.

As for the structure of this investigation, I am adopting a macroscopic or bird's-eye view of the subject. After a brief summary of the historical facts, and an overview of authors, influences, and general trends in the relevant literature, I shall concentrate on the most-encountered and dominant motifs which mark the literary preoccupation with Kaspar Hauser. The guiding objective here is to find common patterns in the figure's paradigmatic role, to determine which twentieth-century problems the employment of the figure addresses, and whether and how writers attempted to solve these problems.

---

[24] Jochen Hörisch, "Die Sprachlosigkeit des Kaspar Hauser," in *Ich möchte ein solcher werden wie ...*, ed. Jochen Hörisch (Frankfurt a. M.: Suhrkamp, 1979), 295; Kaja Silverman, "Kaspar Hauser's 'Terrible Fall' into Narrative," *New German Critique* 24/25 (1981/82): 75.

[25] "Mythenbildung und Aufklärung in der Kaspar-Hauser-Literatur des zwanzigsten Jahrhunderts," unpublished typescript (Marburg, 1988). The author is now working on an illustrated anthology of Kaspar Hauser literature, to be published in German by J. B. Metzler, Stuttgart, under the name of *Der Findling: Kaspar Hauser in der Literatur*.

[26] Ernst Erich Metzner, "Die dunkle Klage des Gerechten — Poésie Pure? Rationalität und Intentionalität in Georg Trakls Spätwerk, dargestellt am Beispiel 'Kaspar Hauser Lied'," *Germanisch-Romanische Monatsschrift* 24 (1974): 446–72; Suzanne Marey, "Georg Trakl et Kaspar Hauser," *Aspects de la Civilisation Germanique*, Travaux VII, 12 (1975): 189–203.

In the conclusion, an evaluation of the cumulative findings should reveal the prevalent patterns in the treatment of Kaspar Hauser in twentieth-century literature, and should yield some answers with regard to the foundling's metaphoric significance.

1

Who Was Kaspar Hauser?
The Historical Facts

THE FIVE YEARS OF the foundling's public life, first in Nuremberg (1828–1831) and then in nearby Ansbach (1831–1833), are extensively documented. In fact, the notoriety of the case, aided by the highly developed bureaucratic apparatus of the Metternich era, produced such a welter of material, much of it contradictory, that it is difficult to separate fact and fiction. The most extensive, and probably most reliable contemporary source of information is the account by Anselm von Feuerbach, president of the court of appeal for that region of Bavaria, who from the beginning took an active interest in Kaspar Hauser, and chronicled his life.[1] Although Feuerbach became convinced of the boy's birthright to the throne of Baden and therefore did his utmost to champion that claim, his legal training made him look at the case with a critical eye. Therefore, his writings give a balanced (though sympathetic) picture of the foundling's situation. Unfortunately Feuerbach died — allegedly poisoned by Hauser's foes — six months before his protégé was stabbed, and the slipshod investigation into the foundling's death no doubt reflects the absence of this great legal mind at the critical time. In the subsequent disagreements between the factions for and against Hauser, many of the original testimonies were taken out of context or distorted, even falsified. In this respect, the late Hermann Pies deserves much credit for making it his life's work to collect, sift, and corroborate the existing evidence as far as possible.[2] Thanks to his research, at least the major details of the story now seem beyond dispute.

Kaspar Hauser, as he came to be known, was found in Nuremberg on May 26, 1828. Estimated to be about fifteen or sixteen years old, he could not walk properly and was strangely dressed, striking witnesses as a comic, foolish figure. It turned out that he could scrawl the words 'Kaspar Hauser', which were henceforward taken to be his name. But his vocabulary consisted of only a few expressions, and was mainly limited

---

[1] See Feuerbach, *Verbrechen am Seelenleben*, 119–93.

[2] For the most up-to-date results of this research, see Hermann Pies, a) *Kaspar Hauser: Eine Dokumentation* (Ansbach: C. Brügel & Sohn, 1966); b) *Kaspar Hauser: Fälschungen, Falschmeldungen und Tendenzberichte* (Ansbach: Museumsverlag, 1973).

to the one request which, in one form or another, was to find its way into most of the Kaspar Hauser literature: I'd like to be a rider like my father used to be ("Ich möcht' ein solcher Reiter werden wie mein Vater einer war."). It was clear, however, that the youth did not understand the meaning of his words. Parrot-fashion, he would repeat whatever he heard last, a habit which initially led to some false assumptions about his background and comprehension. Similarly misleading were the two letters he carried. One declared him to be a no-longer-wanted foundling sent to join the light cavalry stationed in Nuremberg. The other, ostensibly from his mother, explained his initial abandonment. Both letters raised more questions than answers, and after repeated scrutiny of text, handwriting, and paper, they came to be regarded as fakes, purposely designed to mislead.

Locked up as a possibly retarded vagrant, the boy soon attracted intense attention due to his unusual traits and behavior. On the one hand, he seemed to be totally unfamiliar with even the simplest concepts or domestic implements, and could tolerate only bread and water, so that he was seen as a savage or "Tiermensch."[3] On the other hand, he is said to have been extremely peaceable and friendly, and he displayed some remarkable abilities. His hearing and sense of smell, for example, were hyper-acute, and he astonished his observers with the ability to see in the dark and to discern hidden objects. He also proved to be so adept at absorbing and memorizing new information that within a few weeks he could already express himself in a rudimentary fashion. Now he was able to report that he had been locked up, indeed tethered, in a low, dark room as long as he could remember. He had found bread and water whenever he awoke. Sometimes his water used to taste 'bad', and on those occasions he would wake up later to find that his hair and nails were short, and his clothes different.[4] During his captivity, his only means of diversion had been two wooden toy horses, known to him as *Roß*, a word that always retained a pleasant connotation for him. He claimed not to have known that other human beings existed until towards the end of his stay in his dungeon, when a man had appeared in order to teach him his few sentences, and to write his name. It was this man who had finally carried and pushed him to the place where he had been found.

Not surprisingly, people far and near flocked to view this strange creature. Feral children have always attracted great public attention, up

---

[3] Feuerbach, *Verbrechen am Seelenleben*, 139.

[4] One of the many experiments conducted with Kaspar indicated that the 'bad'-tasting water must have contained opium: he recognized the taste when given a minute sample of the drug, and reacted by sinking into a deep and prolonged sleep.

to our own time.[5] In Kaspar Hauser's era, the timeless desire for sensation mingled with scientific curiosity about the relationship between nature and nurture, as well as with a Romantic predilection for all things 'primitive'. This interest heightened even further when the rumor arose that Kaspar might be the rightful heir to the throne of Baden. The Duchy of Baden had recently passed to a morganatic branch of the ruling family when the male heirs of the ancestral line died in their infancy, reputedly under dubious circumstances. The older of the deceased princes would have been Kaspar Hauser's age, which left room for the hypothesis that he had been exchanged for a dying infant, was abducted to be held in captivity, and then released for as yet unknown reasons. If such a claim could be proven, Hauser would have been indirectly related to Napoleon (his purported mother, Stephanie Beauharnais, was Napoleon's adopted stepdaughter), and directly related to several royal houses of Europe. That possibility made the foundling's origin a matter of intense concern, not only for the present House of Baden or for those who might gain from such a political trump card, but also for the suppressed democratic factions of the bourgeoisie. In the contemporary revolutionary climate of Europe, many were eager for proof of corruption in the ruling circles.

In the light of this background, it is understandable that Kaspar Hauser became first and foremost an object of curiosity. He lived the uncomfortable life of a 'freak', and was handed on from one foster home to the next, a prize exhibit for his hosts, yet also a charity ward. In 1829, he barely survived being bludgeoned by a mysterious stranger, an attack which may or may not be linked to the fact that he was known to have begun writing his memoir.[6] Once again he was moved, this time from Nuremberg to the quieter district town of Ansbach, into the custody of a stern and narrow-minded schoolmaster whose demands made his life a misery. Some people evidently had his interests at heart, but others proved to be false friends. Notable among the latter was Lord Stanhope, an English adventurer and bon vivant (later shown to have some connections with the House of Baden), who befriended the youth and promised to adopt him, but then suddenly withdrew his favors for no apparent reason, and after Hauser's death was first among those who declared him a common swindler. As the foundling's achievements levelled off, and proof of his origin remained elusive, the public interest began to wane. But his sojourn among people was to end as dramatically as it had begun. On 14 December 1832, he was stabbed in the chest, and three days later died of his injuries. According to the

---

[5] For informative surveys of documented cases of feral children, see, e.g., J. A. L. Singh and Robert M. Zingg, *Wolf-Children and Feral Man* (Denver: Archon Books, 1942); Charles Maclean, *The Wolf Children* (New York: Hill & Wang, 1977); and Harlan Lane, *The Wild Boy of Aveyron* (Cambridge, Mass.: Harvard University Press, 1976).

[6] Variants of Kaspar Hauser's own recollections are reproduced in Hörisch, *Ich möchte ein solcher werden wie ...*, 87–113.

foundling, the perpetrator was unknown to him; he had lured him into the park with the promise of news from his mother. Kaspar's detractors suspected a self-inflicted wound as a means to regain publicity, although the evidence speaks against it. For others, these events gave renewed credence to the conjecture that he was of highborn descent, and that his existence endangered the present rulers of Baden.

While the whiff of scandal had fuelled much of the nineteenth century literature about Kaspar Hauser, the writers who were to adopt the foundling as a literary figure in the twentieth century showed little interest in this aspect of his life. Nor did they aim at a faithful reproduction of the 'truth'. The works under consideration range from a selective adherence to the chronological events to extensive departures from the historical details. Most focus on Kaspar Hauser as an individual, on his own experiences, perceptions, and reactions. Clearly, in our century the dominant attraction of the figure lies on a personal, subjective level rather than in the story itself.

Did the real Kaspar Hauser possess characteristics, attitudes, or abilities which can account for this literary appeal? The picture gleaned from historical testimonies reveals incongruities at almost every turn. Above all, it is striking how this apparently passive boy could provoke such vehement feelings for or against him. While some of his contemporaries were captivated by his innocence and gentle nature, or saw the hallmarks of a secret prince in almost everything he did, others persisted in their view of him as a crafty swindler, regardless of any evidence to the contrary. Some factions showered him with invitations and gifts, others watched him with envy, or avoided his company as a potential source of danger. Even neutral descriptions of his characteristics and physical traits show dual aspects. We are told that in spite of his presumed earlier deprivations he was of pleasing appearance and good build, with blond, curly hair and blue eyes, and a general expression of "Offenheit und kindlicher Unbefangenheit."[7] Yet he was often sick, and there are reports that when his mind became agitated, a nervous tic would distort his face. His eyes tended to become inflamed from exposure to strong light, and in spite of his apparent good health he remained as weak as a child, and never learned to walk with ease. As mentioned above, he initially absorbed new information at an astonishing rate, and showed a prodigious memory. Yet once he achieved a modicum of knowledge, his mental abilities dulled, and his fabled memory never helped him to unlock the secrets of his past.

While his continued preference for bread and water suggested innate simplicity, he was attracted to colorful and shiny objects, and showed a liking for fine clothes which in the eyes of some of his contemporaries bordered on vanity. Very eager to please and to conform to the demands

---

[7] Report by Dr. Osterhausen, 30 December 1830. Reproduced in Preu and others, *Kaspar Hauser: Arztberichte*, ed. Peter Tradowsky (Dornach: Rudolf Geering, 1985), 25.

of society, he nevertheless grew tired of his many lessons and the perpetual exposure to new situations, and often yearned for the tranquillity of his former prison. He said that there, where he had not yet known anything of this world, he had felt at peace, and had never suffered from the headaches which plagued him now. He enjoyed social outings and longed for close bonds and companionship, and yet often remained solitary and withdrawn, displaying a quiet melancholy ("eine stille Schwermut")[8] even when surrounded by people.

From the vantage point of our present-day insight into human psychological development, many of these seemingly opposing traits may not be so irreconcilable after all, but rather the logical consequences of Kaspar Hauser's peculiar circumstances and treatment. But it is equally easy to see how Kaspar's ambiguous disposition, which blurred the dividing line between appearance and reality, must have contributed to his reputation as "aenigma sui temporis," quite apart from the mystery of his origin.

As a point of departure for modern literature, these ambiguities are also significant. They furnish at least a partial, external explanation for the figure's literary versatility and longevity, since a multifaceted model can of course provide writers with more stimuli and greater leeway than a clear-cut, one-dimensional picture. On the thematic level, we shall see in the course of our discussion that for many twentieth-century writers, the ambiguities of the case, and the foundling's inner conflict, added to his appeal, since it reflected their own state of mind. But it is also worth noting at the very beginning that none of the writers under discussion sided with those who saw the foundling as a clever fraud; Kaspar Hauser as anti-hero, otherwise such a common figure in twentieth-century literature, simply does not exist, at least not so far.

---

[8] Anselm von Feuerbach, letter to Elise von der Recke, 20 September 1828; reproduced in Pies, *Dokumentation*, 37.

2

Authors and Influences

How did the modern preoccupation with the foundling of Nuremberg begin? Ironically, a major impetus came from a nineteenth-century French poem, Paul Verlaine's "Gaspard Hauser chante," a deceptively simple lay of melancholy tone, in which the motherless and friendless hero laments his hapless life. Verlaine wrote this poem in 1873, while serving his prison sentence for the assault on his former companion, the poet Rimbaud. It was a time when he himself felt lonely and dejected, and Kaspar Hauser's fate evidently provided a suitable metaphor for his unhappy state. How he came to know about the events which had happened in Germany forty-five years earlier is not on record. In the previous two decades, there are at least four different accounts of the story in French (one of them republished several times) which could have served as his model.[1] A second, later work inspired by the material, the unfinished fragment *Scénario pour ballet*, has more explicit parallels with details of Kaspar Hauser's life than the poem. But its hero (named 'Frédérique' rather than 'Gaspard'), though he also meets a tragic end, shows a boldness and vitality which stands in contrast to the world-weariness expressed in "Gaspard Hauser chante," perhaps a reflection of the author's own regained self-confidence.

While the *Scénario* remained almost unknown, the earlier poem captured the imagination of so many German writers that it was possible to describe it as "fast ein deutsches Gedicht."[2] Dehmel, George, Kalckreuth, Klabund, Klaus Mann, Schönhals, Wolfenstein, as well as several less-known writers produced their own versions of "Gaspard Hauser chante." Significantly, they declared these works to be *Nachdichtungen* rather than translations, which left them free to vary syntax and rhyme scheme, or to deviate slightly (or, in the case of Klaus Mann, to a considerable extent) from the nature, emphasis and sequence of Verlaine's motifs. Developments in the general theory of translations favored poetic infusions of this kind. Following Romantic theorists such as Schleiermacher, who had stressed that understanding due to an inner congeniality should be at the core of all literary interpretations, the emphasis had shifted from a demand for the utmost loyalty to the orig-

---

[1] See Hans Peitler and Hans Ley, *Kaspar Hauser: Über tausend bibliographische Nachweise* (Ansbach: C. Brügel & Sohn, 1927), nos. 216, 229, 237, 238, 240, 256.

[2] See Thiele, "Das Bild des Menschen," 351.

inal in form, style, and intent, towards capturing the deeper meaning behind the subject matter. Therefore, writers felt encouraged to leave their individual imprint on the borrowed poem's form, while staying faithful to its simplicity and melancholy mood. These came to be seen as the very essence of the foundling's nature, and in turn set the tone for other, future creations, although not all early works fall into this framework. Arp's "kaspar ist tot," for example, follows a very independent path. So does Rilke's poem "Der Knabe," if we accept that it, too, was inspired by the new fervor for Kaspar Hauser.[3]

Directly or indirectly, Verlaine's influence continued long beyond the first flurry of *Nachdichtungen*. Hofer, Klaus Mann, and Ebermayer all acknowledge his impact by including (transcribed) lines from "Gaspard Hauser chante" in their works. As recently as 1986, the Liedermacher Wolf Biermann wrote a free transcription of this poem as an appropriate contribution to a song festival in Nuremberg, the city of Kaspar Hauser's first appearance. In addition to these direct lines of influence, the introduction of the French poem had another, incidental effect. Since its cryptic brevity could not satisfy the renewed interest in the foundling, it stimulated independent research into his actual circumstances as a foundation for other, original works. Kurt Martens is a case in point. While his initial encounter with Kaspar Hauser admittedly came through Verlaine's work, he laid the groundwork for his own drama with laborious research in various libraries:

> Die biographische Literatur über Kaspar Hauser war umfangreich, lag aber verstaubt in den Bibliotheken begraben. Ich sammelte sie mir mühsam und war, je tiefer ich darin eindrang, um so mächtiger gepackt.[4]

Inevitably, those motivated to do their own research sooner or later came upon Feuerbach's account, which not only offered a wealth of details, but with its sympathetic evaluation of the figure reinforced the positive image derived from Verlaine. Feuerbach supplied much of the background information for Jakob Wassermann's lengthy novel, and together, these two works form a second strand of inspiration which can be traced throughout the century. Handke, for instance, credits Feuerbach with having shaped his views not only with regard to his play,

---

[3] The proof rests mainly on the resemblance between the poem's opening line ("Ich möchte einer werden so wie die ...") to Kaspar Hauser's initial sentence. However, Rilke had already used a similar optative statement as early as 1897 (i.e. prior to the literary renaissance of Kaspar Hauser), in an untitled poem beginning with the line: "Ich möchte werden wie die ganz Geheimen...." For a discussion of the connection, see Reiner Marx, "'Ich möchte einer werden so wie die ...': Zur Kaspar-Hauser-Allusion in Rilkes Gedicht 'Der Knabe,'" *Blätter der Rilke-Gesellschaft* 13 (1986): 117–18.

[4] *Schonungslose Lebenschronik* (Vienna: Rikola, 1921–24), 2:52.

Kaspar (1967-68), but to his own reality.[5] Most recently, references to Feuerbach and/or Wassermann — the distinction can sometimes be difficult — appear in Katja Lange-Müller's *Kaspar Mauser — Die Feigheit vorm Freund* (1988). Wassermann's initial interest in the story, however, dates back to his childhood in the town of Fürth near Nuremberg, to the tales of his grandfather, who could pride himself on having seen the foundling with his own eyes.

Personal interrelationships between some of the writers in question undoubtedly helped to disseminate the material. The publishing house of Samuel Fischer in Berlin played a facilitating role in this respect, since Hugo von Hofmannsthal, Wassermann, Richard Dehmel, and Otto Flake all published there, and would meet socially on occasion.[6] Dehmel in turn knew Kurt Martens, Flake was a friend of fellow Alsatian Hans Arp, and Ebermayer initiated a friendship with Klaus Mann after reading the latter's "Kaspar-Hauser-Legenden" in Mann's first publication, *Vor dem Leben*. In general, the young writers of that time saw themselves as part of an unofficial brotherhood of literary men; through visits and correspondence, they took an active interest in one another's work, so that we can take a certain amount of cross-fertilization for granted. The remarkable fact is that even in the presence of proven influences, the resulting literary products could take on entirely different directions. Klaus Mann, for instance, was familiar with Verlaine's and Trakl's work, and deeply moved by Wassermann's *Caspar Hauser*, yet he succeeded in finding his own way of converting the material into a vehicle of self-expression, adding some novel features in the process. Erich Ebermayer, despite his admiration for Klaus Mann's "Legenden," similarly proved with his drama *Kaspar Hauser* (1927) that inspiration need not necessarily lead to imitation.

In some cases, the figure exerted a strange and prolonged influence. The case of Hofmannsthal's prince Sigismund in *Der Turm* is a pertinent example. This figure had its origin in Calderón de la Barca's play, *La Vida es sueño,* which the author began to transform under the title *Das Leben ein Traum* (1910). But Calderón's work, still firmly anchored in an unquestioned Christian framework with a predetermined ending, could not serve Hofmannsthal as a testing ground for the contemporary problems which preoccupied him. What he looked for was a positive but time-related resolution for the physical and metaphysical obstacles with which he confronted his hero. It was in this situation that certain characteristics and hypothetical problems of the Nuremberg foundling began to infiltrate the conception of Sigismund, aborting Hofmannsthal's original project of *Das Leben ein Traum*, and adding immeasur-

---

[5] See Peter Handke, "Ich bin ein Bewohner des Elfenbeinturms" [1967], in *Ich bin ein Bewohner des Elfenbeinturms* (Frankfurt a. M.: Suhrkamp, 1972), 25.

[6] See Peter de Mendelsohn, *S. Fischer und sein Verlag* (Frankfurt a. M.: S. Fischer, 1970).

ably to the complexity and gestation period of *Der Turm*.[7] Many clear traces of Kaspar Hauser can be found not only in surface similarities, but above all in thematic changes, so that Sigismund finally became a hybrid figure, and should be accorded full attention in any evaluation of the Kaspar Hauser literature.[8] Although Hofmannsthal probably had already encountered Feuerbach's report during his law studies, witnessing the genesis of Wassermann's novel opened the door to Kaspar Hauser's literary influence. For almost twenty-three years, Hofmannsthal and Wassermann would spend the summer on adjacent properties in Altaussee, Austria, where they met almost daily to discuss their work or to read from their current manuscripts, including Wassermann's *Caspar Hauser; oder, Die Trägheit des Herzens*. Yet despite the affinities between Wassermann's and Hofmannsthal's heroes, the different genres, different contexts, and each author's different background and focus preserved their individuality.

Occasionally, Kaspar Hauser remained part of an author's imagination long after his role in a particular work came to an end. Thus he makes cameo appearances in Wassermann's later novels *Das Gänsemännchen*, *Christian Wahnschaffe*, *Bula Matari*, and *Der Fall Maurizius*. For Klaus Mann, the use of the figure mirrors his own development. First he tried his hand on the material as an exercise in *fin de siècle* decadence in his unpublished "Zwölf Lieder des Pierrot" (1921-22). He then used Kaspar Hauser as a catalyst for his rebellion against his famous father in the (also unpublished) fragment of a novella called *Vor dem Leben* (1924), in which a young prince named Kaspar, "sonderbarstes Kind eines strengen, zuchtvollen Monarchen,"[9] successfully plans his escape. Kaspar's odyssey through life in the "Legenden" in turn reflects the restless quest for a modus vivendi which occupied Mann at the time. Finally, incorporating aspects of Kaspar Hauser under the guise of other characters in *Anja und Esther* (1925) and *Der fromme Tanz* (1926), Mann demonstrates his growing social awareness. A similarly tenacious influence of the figure can also be observed in contemporary authors. When the young Peter Härtling wrote his "kasper" poems (1958), he needed a "Protestfigur gegen das regulierte Dasein der Erwachsenen" like his Yamin. Consequently, he invested his

---

[7] *Der Turm* (1925), *Dramen*, vol. 4 of *Gesammelte Werke in Einzelausgaben*, ed. Herbert Steiner (Frankfurt a. M.: S. Fischer, 1957), 339–425; *Der Turm* (1927), *Dramen*, vol. 4 of *Gesammelte Werke in Einzelausgaben*, ed. Herbert Steiner (Frankfurt a. M.: S. Fischer, 1958), 321–463. In the following, these different versions will be referred to as *Turm* I and *Turm* II.

[8] I have examined the relationship between Sigismund and Kaspar Hauser in my dissertation, "Kaspar Hauser in Twentieth Century German Literature" (Oxford University, 1989). See also Horst Martin, "Kaspar Hauser und Sigismund: Über eine Quelle zu Hofmannsthals 'Turm,'" *Seminar* 12 (Nov. 1976): 236–58.

[9] Klaus Mann, *Kind dieser Zeit* (Munich: Nymphenburger Verlagsbuchhandlung, 1965; first publ. 1932), 237.

hero with childlike wilfulness, traits partially borrowed from Arp's capricious protagonist.[10] The brief but cogent reference to Kaspar Hauser in his novel *Hubert; oder, Die Rückkehr nach Casablanca* (1978) reflects a more outward-looking personality, matured by the passage of time, with empathy for those caught up in the maelstrom of World War II. After a long hiatus, during which Härtling made several attempts to write about Kaspar Hauser, yet got diverted because he discovered "[Kaspar's] Verwandte ... im verstummenden Niembsch, im chiffrierenden Hölderlin,"[11] he finally returned to the foundling and his problems in their own context, in the poem "Kaspar Hauser" (1987).

Next to the evident formal adaptability of the material, it is this relevance to a wide range of time-related personal and general problems which helped the foundling survive through so many decades. He is equally at home in the symbolist *Nachdichtungen* of Verlaine as in Arp's Dada poem; as the protagonist of mimetic novels (such as Wassermann's or Röttger's) as in the postwar avant-garde and documentary theatre of Peter Handke and Dieter Forte. The material also refuted doubts about its appropriateness for the medium of film. In 1933, the prominent German film company UFA rejected a proposal for a film on Kaspar Hauser with the following argument:

> Uns haben im Laufe der Zeit eine grosse Anzahl Caspar-Hauser-Themen vorgelegen. Wir haben uns stets dazu negativ entscheiden müssen, da wir in der Titel-Figur keine ausgesprochene Tonfilm-Figur sehen, und wir ferner das gesamte Thema, abgesehen von seiner Unerquicklichkeit, als zu literarisch betrachten müssen.[12]

This judgment ignores the fact that at that time the material had already made its way onto the screen on at least three previous occasions.[13] In 1974, Herzog's *Jeder für sich und Gott gegen alle* gained wide professional acclaim as well as several prizes. And the protagonist, far from proving the figure's unsuitability for the cinema, has become one of the most memorable personifications of Kaspar Hauser in the twentieth century. With his entry into the field of contemporary German *Liedermacher* such as Reinhard Mey and Wolf Biermann, Kaspar Hauser confirms that he has indeed become a figure for all forms and 'for all seasons'.

---

[10] *Protokoll zur Person: Autoren über sich und ihr Werk*, ed. Ekkehart Rudolph (Munich: Paul List, 1971), 77.

[11] Peter Härtling, letter to author, 29 Feb. 1987.

[12] Letter of rejection, 8 July 1933, by Dramaturgische Abteilung, Universum-Film-Aktiengesellschaft (UFA). City Archives, Ansbach, Germany.

[13] See Peitler and Ley, *Über tausend bibliographische Nachweise*, nos. 627a (1916), 652 (1921), 726 (1924).

One marker in the diachronic picture is a noticeable hiatus during and immediately following World War II. Whether this should be attributed to a transient surfeit with the topic, or whether the political climate of that time and the preoccupation with practical, day-to-day survival kept the figure in abeyance at that time is a matter of speculation. We know that in principle historical topics were popular during the Nazi years, being not only safer from censorship, but also favored by a regime that prided itself on its revival of the German(ic) past. But neither the foundling's unheroic stance, nor his function as a catalyst for time-related concerns agreed with the official philosophy. The fact that Schäfer's drama *Richter Feuerbach* (1929) could be extolled as a harbinger of the 'new ethos' of the 1930s[14] — as Jungmann had done in 1935 — evidently rests on an ironic misunderstanding. Not only does Schäfer encourage resistance to uncongenial official modes of thinking, but he seems to expect the ethical renewal of the future to come from the East. In an epilogue to the past events, Feuerbach's son Ludwig tells his sister about his friend Bakunin:

> Er hat mir erzählt, dass es in Russland eine ganze Partei von jungen Menschen gibt, die einen Staat wollen, so wie ich ihn beschreibe. In diesem Staat hat jeder das gleiche Recht ... wenn also in Russland einmal die Menschen so leben werden, wie ich will, dann leben sie so, wie es der Vater gewollt hat.[15]

Other political considerations could also have a negative impact during that time. Klaus Mann and Ebermayer, for instance, collaborated on a script for a film entitled *Kaspar Hauser*, and in contrast to the case mentioned above, Ebermayer even succeeded in having the project accepted by UFA. But the film company hastily withdrew its approval when the co-authorship of Klaus Mann, by then persona non grata with the (Nazi) establishment, became known.[16]

In this age of feminist awareness it is perhaps germane to ask whether the survey of the Kaspar Hauser literature reveals any differences of approach between male and female authors. This does not seem to be the case. The fact that male writers dominate the array of relevant literature probably reflects general gender proportions in the métier rather than sex-based predilections. Those female authors who

---

[14] The reference relates to Otto Jungmann's evaluation in *Kaspar Hauser: Stoff und Problem.*

[15] Walter Erich Schäfer, *Richter Feuerbach: Schauspiel* (Berlin: Chronos, 1919), 67. Where appropriate, further references to this play will be given after quotations in the text.

[16] See Erich Ebermayer, *Denn heute gehört uns Deutschland ... : Persönliches und politisches Tagebuch. Von der Machtergreifung bis zum 31. Dezember 1935* (Hamburg: Paul Zsolnay, 1959), 41–42. My efforts to locate this film script were unsuccessful.

made use of the material (Hoechstetter, Hofer, Schaumann, Oppenheim, Lange-Müller, and most recently, Gielen) certainly exhibit no common 'feminine' denominators. What characteristic traits we find in their works can be attributed to individual stylistic preferences and talents, or to the literary ambiance of the particular decade. Certainly, shared traits in formal components cross the lines of gender. Otto Jungmann, for example, singled out Hofer's pronounced empathy for Kaspar Hauser as "typisch weiblich,"[17] yet comparably sentimental passages and comments are also legion in Karl Röttger's novel. Meret Oppenheim's wordplay in her poem "ohne mich ohnehin ohne Weg" has no feminine equivalent, but has much in common with Hans Arp's work. And not by coincidence: Arp was a friend, and both were fringe participants in the artistic circles in Paris which tried to make Surrealism the successor of the (by then defunct) Dada movement of Zurich.[18] Of the later works, Sibylle Gielen's almost wordless dramatization of scenes and symbols from Hauser's life, *Ein Mensch wie Kaspar Hauser* (1990), is comparable in its approach with works by male colleagues such as Carlos Trafic's *Kaspar Hauser* (1983), or Matthias Hoenig's mimed "theaterimprovisation" *kaspar hauser* (1985).

It is worth noting (though not as an example of a feminine approach), that it is one of the women writers, Sophie Hoechstetter, who contributes the closest to a touch of humor in the Kaspar Hauser literature. In her story *Die Damen von Irmelsleben* (1911), Kaspar Hauser is only an indirect presence. He is expected for a visit at a religious foundation, while passing through the neighborhood on a journey in search of his family roots. Before the noble spinsters in the convent — caricaturized with names such as "Gräfin Hackerode-Hockerode" or "von Katzenhüpfenhausen" — get a chance to meet the famous visitor, several of them make their way to the abbess, one by one, to confess that the foundling might be their own illegitimate son, abandoned at birth in order to preserve a facade of propriety. "Die Sommernacht, die Philomelen schluchzten, gräßlich — die arme Liebe," reads the confession of one of the ladies about her erstwhile faux pas.[19] However, the end of this story once again strikes a serious, even moralizing chord, undermining its unique feature.

Not only the knowledge of the tragic outcome of Kaspar Hauser's biography made it difficult to take a lighthearted approach: many authors identified with the foundling and his suffering on a very personal level, as they readily admit. Kurt Martens, who felt misunder-

---

[17] *Kaspar Hauser: Stoff und Problem*, 89.

[18] See Meret Oppenheim, *Husch, husch, der schönste Vokal entleert sich: Gedichte, Zeichnungen*, ed. Christiane Meyer-Thoss (Frankfurt a. M.: Suhrkamp, 1984), 83, 107.

[19] Sophie Hoechstetter, "Die Damen von Irmelsleben: Eine verschollene Kaspar-Hauser-Geschichte," *Das Herz: Arabesken um die Existenz des George Rosenkreutz* (Dresden: Carl Reißner, 1913), 15.

stood and lonely during his childhood and youth, remembers in this respect:

> Mir war, als hätte ich nach dieser einen Gestalt schon all mein Leben lang sehnsüchtig gefahndet, als hätte ich in ihr mein anderes Ich, mein ins Typische gehobene Spiegelbild entdeckt.[20]

Trakl's extreme inability to integrate with society also prompted a private identification with the foundling. In a period of despondence, he pronounced that he would always remain "ein armer Kaspar Hauser."[21] Klaus Mann, confessing how deeply Wassermann's novel had touched him when he first read it, reasoned about the inner bond he felt with the historical figure:

> Ich versuchte ... mir selbst zu erklären, warum dieses rätselhaften Knaben Schicksal und Geschichte so sehr, so fast persönlich mich berührte. Und bald erkannte ich das Gleichnishafte seines Lebens, und daß hier durch äußere Umstände nur betont, durch mancherlei Zufall mir deutlich gemacht war ein im Grunde inneres Los, das mir sehr nahe, das mir wohl allzu nahe bekannt und lange vertraut war.[22]

Even today authors regard Kaspar Hauser as reflections of their self. Guntram Vesper sees him as a 'secret stowaway', who has accompanied him since he first learned about the story from a book in his grandmother's treasure trove. For Vesper, he is a mirror of his own feelings of displacement, and of his continuing and unsuccessful search for identity.[23] Similarly, Härtling early on discovered in Kaspar Hauser "einen malträtierten Bruder," and Herzog reveals about the hero of his film: "Der fängt bei mir selber an.... Der Kaspar, der kommt mir vor wie meine eigene Existenz."[24]

Of course not all references to Kaspar Hauser spring from such heartfelt encounters. Some authors simply recognize that the public's growing familiarity with the figure permits them to use it, without much elaboration, as a prefabricated image for a pitiful fate. Walter Kempowski is one example. Unlike most authors, he does not remember when he

---

[20] *Schonungslose Lebenschronik*, 2:24.

[21] Georg Trakl, letter to Erhard Buschbeck, *Nachlaß und Biographie*, vol. 3 of *Gesammelte Werke*, ed. Wolfgang Schneditz (Salzburg: Otto Müller, 1949), 26–27.

[22] "Kaspar Hauser," *Die Weltbühne* 21, no. 1 (1925). Reprint (Königstein/Taunus, 1978), 511.

[23] "Und nie mehr hat mich dieses 'Kind von Europa' losgelassen," writes Vesper, "Einmal mehr, einmal weniger habe ich mich durch all die Jahre mit ihm beschäftigt." Letter to author, 11 Feb. 1986.

[24] Härtling, letter to author, 29 Feb. 1987; Herzog, cited by Wetzel Kraft, "Interview," in Ulrich Gregor and others, *Herzog — Kluge — Straub*, Reihe Film 9, ed. Peter W. Jansen and Wolfram Schütte (Munich: Hanser, 1976), 127.

first encountered the figure, nor where and how he used it in his works. And although he sees Kaspar's "große Heimatlosigkeit" as the most salient feature of the story, his interjections of the image in *Ein Kapitel für sich* (1978) and *Herzlich willkommen* (1984) do not link it to the concept of homelessness. Nor do they explore its evident potential relevance in the given contexts (in the former novel, the physical and spiritual isolation experienced by the narrator during his penal servitude in East Germany; in the second instance, the social bewilderment after his release to the West).[25] There is a danger that frequent usage of this kind may eventually lead to a degeneration of the figure into a one-dimensional literary cliché, causing serious writers to shy away from the topic. The evidence of the various recent works, however, suggests that this point has not yet been reached.

---

[25] Conversation with Walter Kempowski, London-Richmond, 30 May 1986. (For the relevant passages in the mentioned novels, see 276 and 199 respectively).

3

Alienation and Isolation: Kaspar Hauser as a Paradigm for the 'Outsider' in the Twentieth Century

I. The Negative Fairy Tale

ONE DOES NOT HAVE to be an expert on fairy tales to notice that the story of Kaspar Hauser contains several key ingredients of this genre. The prince held in a secret dungeon, the good-natured simpleton who turns out to have extraordinary abilities, the changeling or orphan in search of home and parents, or the social outcast who has to overcome his state of repudiation — these designations of the foundling are all familiar starting positions for the fairy tale hero which trigger expectations of a reversal of fortune. Fictional demonstrations that even immense odds can be overcome are not only timeless surrogate expressions of wishful thinking, but could also serve as socially useful exhortations. The idea that simple virtue and steadfastness will triumph in the end, and evildoers receive the punishment they deserve, found a particularly fertile ground in the nineteenth century: it concurred with the general mores of the bourgeoisie, and with its belief in upward mobility, which can account for the great success of the folk and fairy tales revived and disseminated by the Brothers Grimm.[1] It was reassuring to see it confirmed in writing that those who strive and are prepared to weather all trials will live happily ever after.

We know, of course, that in the real Kaspar Hauser's life the happy ending never occurred. His release from the dungeon led to further misery, the naive fool never gained the upper hand, and the potential kingdom remained out of reach. But literature need not be bound by cold facts. Indeed most of the writers under discussion made liberal use of their artistic freedom in the selection and presentation of their material. Why then did not at least some of these authors invent a happy ending or at least justice for the foundling, to satisfy the universal element of wishful thinking?

Nineteenth-century German treatments of the story still made allowances for the traditional expectation of a final balancing of the

---

[1] For a discourse on this topic, see e.g. Jack Zipes, *The Brothers Grimm: From Enchanted Forests to the Modern World* (New York: Routledge, 1988).

scales. While they exploit and embroider the suffering of the innocent for melodramatic effect, the culprits usually meet their deserved punishment. Even where this does not happen within the framework of the given story, authors divide their characters into good and evil, and defer to their readers' sense of righteousness. Thus in Friedrich Seybold's *Kaspar Hauser; oder, Der Findling* (1834), mysterious strangers and voices, or a fiery writing on a wall, bear witness to a supernatural system of justice, and forebode eventual retribution. Or, in Ludwig Scoper's *Kaspar Hauser; oder, Die eingemauerte Nonne* (1834), the ghost of a victim prevents the abbot from committing a further crime. In Gutzkow's more down-to-earth pedagogical treatise (*Die Söhne Pestalozzis*, 1870), the hero, after many trials, even reaches a modicum of happiness: his natural mother at last acknowledges him, and he gets married and embarks on what promises to be a contented, though unremarkable life.

When writers of the twentieth century take stock of the historical material to transform it into literature, they often show themselves aware of its fairy tale ingredients, and even make conscious use of them. Wassermann's tutor Daumer, for example, acknowledges Kaspar as a "märchenhafte[s] Geschöpf," whose appearance is like an ancient legend or myth ("wie eine uralte Legende ... ein Mythos"). On occasion, the novel even mimics formal elements of the genre, as in the rhythmic incantation with which Kaspar Hauser tries to summon his mother:

> Kenn ich dich, so nenn ich dich. Bist du die Mutter so höre mich. Ich geh' zu dir, ich muß zu dir. Einen Boten schick ich dir.[2]

Röttger's hero, in his dream of his journey to heaven, has to prove his fortitude in time-honored tradition by passing through three doors, each successive one holding greater terrors, while a voice admonishes him: "'Sieh nicht rechts und nicht links, geh hindurch!' Da ging er hindurch, und keins rührte ihn an."[3] Closest to fairy tale magic is Meret Oppenheim's symbolic tale, *Kaspar Hauser; oder, Die Goldene Freiheit*. Her protagonist undergoes several metamorphoses: he turns from child to lifeless statue and back again, becomes a caterpillar, slips into the carcass of an animal to hide, becomes a beautiful youth, even a golden table presenting nourishment for another.

None of these presentations, however, carries its hero to triumph. Wassermann's Kaspar never meets his mother; Röttger's wakens from his dream to find himself back on his deathbed; and Oppenheim's protagonist ends up where he began: under the golden mask — symbol of the

---

[2] *Caspar Hauser; oder, Die Trägheit des Herzens* (Zurich: Carl Posen, 1947; orig. publ. in serial form, 1907), 40, 384. Where appropriate, further references to this work will be given after quotations in the text.

[3] Karl Röttger, *Kaspar Hausers letzte Tage; oder, Das kurze Leben eines ganz Armen* (Berlin: Paul Zsolnay, 1938), 302. Where appropriate, further references to this work will be given after quotations in the text.

rumored princedom — which robs him of his freedom. Invariably, modern works on Kaspar Hauser emphasize, even seem to relish the negative turn of events. They do not gloss over the death of the innocent. On the contrary, it can become the writer's focal point, as titles like "kaspar ist tot" (Arp), *Die letzten Tage Kaspar Hausers* (Röttger), and *Kaspar Hausers Tod* (Forte) confirm.

Important tenets of the conventional fairy tale are that the hero is pure and good-hearted, and that his progress to victory is propelled by an active struggle against the encountered obstacles, or, alternatively, that he is lucky enough to find magic helpers to smoothen his path. While Kaspar Hauser measures up to the first requirement, he is woefully inadequate in the latter two. To be sure, there are works in which we find traces of promising self-reliance. It soon becomes obvious, however, that the writer incorporated these to demonstrate that in the foundling's case the odds are too great, and the struggle is of little avail. Kurt Martens, for example, gives his protagonist a (historically unfounded) stance of defiance that is unique in the Kaspar Hauser literature. But he also makes it clear that the hero's boldness merely hastens his downfall: it convinces the conspirators that this youth is far too dangerous to their plans to be left alive. Klaus Mann's "Legenden" also introduce an element of self-motivated activity congruent with the pattern of fairy tales. The child-hero wanders through forests and cities in search of a forgotten melody that could lead him home. His final smile even suggests that he may have found what he was looking for. But if this is so, we cannot ignore that the price for his success is death, which is not part of the classical fairy tale scenario.

Occasionally, authors invest their hero with extraordinary qualities which suggest that he does have the potential to overcome his obstacles. The capricious creatures of Arp's "kaspar ist tot," and of Härtling's early "kasper" poems come to mind. Their command of the forces of Nature (Arp: "auf dem meer verwirrte er die schiffe ... "; Härtling: "netzt wüsten sanft und schlitzt dann wolken auf")[4] could be construed as the magical arsenal of a fairy tale hero. But even in these cases the reader is not left with the satisfaction of a happy ending. These protagonists have disappeared under unexplained circumstances, and their departure is a cause of great regret. In the rare cases in which the historical figure's mysterious talents are presented, they also do not further the hero's cause. Wassermann, for example, describes the experiments performed to test Kaspar's strange ability to detect various substances at a distance. He uses this opportunity to show that even his benefactors abused their subject in this respect, indifferent to his welfare: "Man klatschte Beifall,

---

[4] Hans Arp, "kaspar ist tot," *Gedichte 1903–1939*, vol. 1 of *Gesammelte Gedichte* (Wiesbaden: Limes, 1963; orig. publ. Berlin, 1920), 26–27; Peter Härtling, "kasper," and "nachricht von kasper," in *Mein Gedicht ist mein Messer: Lyriker zu ihren Gedichten*, ed. Hans Bender (Munich: Paul List, 1961), 164–65.

man achtete nicht darauf, daß er blaß war und mit kühlem Schweiß bedeckt" (52).

If Kaspar Hauser is unable to prevail on his own against the superior strength of his opponents, what about the magical intervention by outside forces, which customarily presents itself to those fairy tale heroes powerless to help themselves? In the historical foundling's life, the sudden appearance of Lord Stanhope came close to filling that role for a while. This seemingly wealthy traveler promised not only adventure and riches, but above all the security and affection the foundling craved. His inexplicable betrayal of Kaspar's trust found its way into literature in various forms. Martens, Wassermann, Ebermayer, Röttger, and later Werner Herzog, all exemplify how the prospect of a miraculous turn for the better ended in bitter disappointment.

A more solid promise of help came from Anselm von Feuerbach, the patron and father figure who was willing to champion the foundling's claim to a throne at great personal risk. But in this case, too, writers float the balloon of hope only to puncture it. Wassermann and Schäfer, in whose works Feuerbach has the most prominent part, both convey that in spite of his courage, the judge was no match for Kaspar Hauser's opponents. They also both blame this figure for failing his ward on a personal level, portraying Kaspar as a mere matter of law and principle, an important case to be won. To the question whether his pursuit of justice warrants the suffering of the intended beneficiary, Wassermann's Feuerbach characteristically replies: "Ja! Auch dann, wenn er daran ver- bluten müßte!" (216). Schäfer's Judge Feuerbach, with similar single- mindedness, corrects the statement: "Es geht um das Recht eines Menschen," with: "Es geht um das Recht eines Menschen" (30; emphasis Schäfer's).

Nor can the poor foundling count on the liberating forces of love, an archetypal motif found already in, e.g., Hartmann von Aue's Der Arme Heinrich, in the story of Beauty and the Beast, or in Der Froschkönig.

Several authors do introduce the idea. Ignoring the historically attested fact that the artificial retardation of his development left Kaspar Hauser ignorant and disinterested in sexual matters,[5] Martens, Wasser- mann, Bihacht, Schaumann, and Lewandowski, each provide their hero with a love interest, as an incarnation of hope. Each then goes on to deflate the hero's (and the reader's) expectations, revealing the experience as yet another source of loss and pain. Bihacht's hero falls in love with a princess, who turns from him when he cannot prove his noble parentage. Martens' more robust protagonist falls in love with his landlord's daughter, even succeeds in persuading her to elope with him, but is rejected as soon as his prospects are endangered. A number of

---

[5] For a psychological evaluation of Kaspar Hauser's attitude towards the female sex in the historical context, see Holger Lakies and Gisela Lakies-Wild, Das Phänomen: Entwicklungspsychologisch bedeutsame Fakten des Hauser-Mysteriums (Ansbach: Ansbacher Verlagsgesellschaft, 1978), 159–65.

works elevate Kaspar Hauser's documented short-lived acquaintance with a married young woman, one of his visitors who took an interest in him and with whom he briefly corresponded, into a bond of deeper significance. As Wassermann presents it, Clara [alias Karoline] von Kannawurf reciprocates the foundling's affection, yet defers to social conventions and severs the relationship. Kaspar, unable to understand her reasons, sinks back into despair. Eight decades later, Härtling's poem "Kaspar Hauser" resurrects the notion of love as a panacea, once again alluding to the mentioned episode with Frau von Kannawurf (for whom the foundling had once drawn pictures as tokens of affection and gratitude):

> Damals, als sie ihn
> blindgemacht,
> ersann er Blumen,
> die's nicht gibt.
> Jetzt hat er sie
> für sie gemalt.[6]

However, the poem's use of the subjunctive ("eine Liebste / *möchte er* ...") exposes this idea as wishful thinking from the very beginning, on a par with the putative wish to become a rider. Härtling also introduces the fairy tale motif of physical transformation. Perhaps inspired by the historical foundling's reportedly androgynous traits — the almost feminine softness of his looks, and his preference for the bright colors and materials of women's clothing — he invests his hero with the desire for a different kind of union between male and female, one which can achieve a complete metamorphosis and serve as a means of refuge: "Wohn dich in mir ein / und ändre mich," Kaspar pleads with his imaginary lover, "Einer Prinzessin stellen sie nicht nach" (ll. 14–17). Again the possibility is a delusion, for at the end of the poem, the murderer steps out of the shadows, and there is no escape.

Lewandowski's *Tagebuch Kaspar Hausers* is the only work in which love bestows at least a brief interlude of happiness. Kaspar's poetic diary presents 'Frau von K.' as the fulfillment of all his needs. She is to him "mother, girl friend, sister, lover ... perhaps everything a woman can be."[7] But even this happiness is overshadowed by a presentiment of the futility of this interlude, and when it ends, the hero resigns himself to his approaching death.

Help from the animal kingdom is another favorite motif of myths and fairy tales. In this respect, it seems particularly promising to examine Kaspar Hauser's association with horses. The image of the horse

---

6 *Die Mörsinger Pappel* (Darmstadt: Luchterhand, 1987), 19, ll. 6–11. Further references to this poem will be given after quotations in the text.

7 "Mutter, Freundin, Schwester, Geliebte ... vielleicht alles, was eine Frau überhaupt sein kann." Herbert Lewandowski, *Das Tagebuch Kaspar Hausers: Eine Gabe für einsame Menschen* (Utrecht: Pfeil, 1928), 29.

pervades the relevant literature in many forms, and to a greater extent than its repeated mention in the historical records might warrant.[8] Several authors allude to the foundling's reputation as a 'born rider'. Wassermann's Kaspar Hauser has salvaged the wooden toy horse he had in his dungeon, and in times of crisis, he fetches it from its hiding place and talks to it. Before he sets out to meet the man who will become his assassin, he first takes leave of this secret talisman, and includes it in his hope for a brighter future: "O Rößlein, dachte er, hast mich manches Jahr begleitet, was wird nun aus dir? Ich will wiederkommen und dich holen, und einen silbernen Stall will ich dir bauen."[9] Schaumann, in the frame of her story of Kaspar's legacy, carries the idea of the bond between hero and horse into the supernatural realm by reuniting the two after death. When Kaspar is murdered, his (real) horse is said to reject other riders ("Ungern wurde es geritten, ungern trug es selbst die andern"),[10] and soon joins its dead master. Reminiscent of Storm's *Schimmelreiter*, Kaspar Hauser's ghost can from now on be encountered on horseback, galloping through the fields. Contemporary writers still allude to the secret alliance between horse and hero. In Herzog's *Jeder für sich und Gott gegen alle*, it may not be conspicuous to the casual viewer, but the script clearly shows the author's intention in this respect. On his first day in the city, Kaspar is temporarily housed with the horses in the cavalry captain's stable. He immediately feels more at ease in that environment, and is in turn accepted by the animals: "Ein Pferd beugt sich sachte über ihn und blickt ihn lange klug an."[11] Härtling's poem "Kaspar Hauser" also anthropomorphizes the horse: Kaspar imitates the song his toy horse had 'sung' for him in his dungeon ("Dann singt er / wie sein Holzpferd sang / in dem Verlies"; ll. 18–21), as if to conjure up his former source of comfort.

Yet in spite of these close bonds, in none of the mentioned examples can we compare the role of the horse with, say, that of the horse 'Fallada' in the fairy tale of *Das Gänseliesel*, who continued to talk and give sage advice to the heroine even after its head had been severed and nailed to a gate. For Kaspar Hauser, the animal companion cannot

---

[8] Besides its link with Hauser's famous request to 'become a rider', toy horses, as already mentioned, provided him with companionship during his time in the dungeon. Possibly because of this familiarity, he felt at ease when he was first lodged in the cavalry captain's stable. He was said to have maintained a particular liking for horses, and to have shown a talent for riding, though both these facts were exaggerated, and his preference for riding may have stemmed from the difficulty he continued to have in walking.

[9] *Caspar Hauser*, 422. In the non-German context, Suzanne Vega's "Caspar Hauser's Song," takes up the same motif, i.e. the animation of Kaspar's toy horse: "What was wood became alive." *Solitude Standing* (London: A & M Records, 1987).

[10] Ruth Schaumann, *Ansbacher Nänie* (Berlin: G. Grote, 1936), 6.

[11] Werner Herzog, *Drehbücher*, vol. 2 (Munich: Skellig, 1974), 120. Where appropriate, further references to this work will be given after quotations in the text.

change the tragic course of events. It is an impotent helper, whatever magic it may possess. Matthias Hönig's dramatization evidently relates this equine magic to the magic of childhood, which Kaspar is forced to relinquish, with great reluctance, in obedience to the taskmaster who will introduce him to the world of adults.[12] Of course the motif of the horse can serve other purposes as well, and we shall return to it later on.

By choosing a protagonist who so obviously combines many of the initial characteristics of the conventional fairy tale hero, and then drawing attention to the failure of the traditional and expected support system, authors can express their view that the established framework of beliefs has become questionable in their time, and that the victim can no longer count on outside help. Georg Büchner already used this approach as early as 1877, when in his *Woyzeck* he let the grandmother subvert the familiar tale of the *Sterntaler* into an image of existential disillusionment:

> ... und wie (das arme Kind) endlich zum Mond kam, war's ein Stück faul Holz. Und da is es zur Sonn gangen, und wie es zur Sonn kam, war's ein verwelkt Sonneblum. Und wie's zu den Sternen kam, waren's kleine goldne Mücken, die waren angesteckt wie der Neuntöter sie auf die Schlehen steckt. Und wie's wieder auf die Erde wollt, war die Erde ein umgestürzter Hafen. Und es war ganz allein. Und da hat sich's hingesetzt und geweint, und da sitzt es noch und is ganz allein.[13]

In the negative use of the fairy tale as in many other ways, Büchner was far ahead of his contemporaries. The twentieth-century authors had to rediscover his formula.

II. Kaspar Hauser as the Embodiment of the Poet's Alienation

There is a general consensus among literary historians that towards the end of the nineteenth century, German literature entered a time of crisis. As a corollary of the relentless drive for economic and technical progress, writers of that period perceived a cultural disintegration, and they began to see themselves as isolated and alienated from the mainstream of society.

Seen in objective terms, both the extent of the poet's social estrangement and the notion of the suddenness of this development may well

---

[12] See the comment by Klaus Witzeling on a performance of Hönig's *Kaspar Hauser-Versuch*, in *hamburger rundschau*, 17 Oct. 1985: "[Kaspar] trennt sich später, vor die Entscheidung zwischen kindischem Spiel und pflichtschuldigem Gehorsam gestellt, in stiller Verzweiflung von seinem Holzroß."

[13] *Werke und Briefe*, ed. Fritz Bergemann (Wiesbaden: Insel Verlag, 1953), 164.

appear somewhat exaggerated. For if we look at the most relevant period, the first decades of the twentieth century, the flourishing of new authors, literary journals, and important publishing houses such as Samuel Fischer, all seem to speak of continued esteem for the writer. Daring experiments in style and form vied for attention, and judging by the deportment of at least some authors, such as Stefan George or Gerhart Hauptmann, one had to conclude that artistic self-esteem was still very much alive. Conversely, one can also look back at other, previous periods to find literary testimonies for feelings of alienation, although these were not always explicitly tied to the figure of the artist. As Hans Mayer has pointed out, already Greek tragedy as well as comedy expressly devoted themselves to those individuals who did not fit the established framework of their society.[14] In a wider, Christian context, the concept of alienation has been traced back as far as the Genesis-account, "as one of the basic tenets of Western theology."[15] With particular reference to the history of German literature, pre-modern examples of heroes at odds with their time and place are also not difficult to find. The rebellious figures of the 'Storm and Stress' movement come to mind, as well as the many loners and wanderers of the Romantic era. Büchner's Lenz, and Kleist's disoriented protagonists come astonishingly close to the modern concept of estrangement from society.

Nor are theoretical reflections on man's state of alienation a recent phenomenon. Rippere, in investigating the justification of assertions that Friedrich Schiller ought to be seen as the 'father of alienation', arrives at the convincing conclusion that the concept was in fact already well-established, indeed quite conventional, by the time Schiller wrote his treatise *Über die ästhetische Erziehung des Menschen*.[16]

None of these points, however, invalidates the argument that by the twentieth century feelings of insecurity and estrangement from the world around them had pervaded the sensibility of most artists to a much greater extent than ever before. The disillusionment that accompanied World War I and its aftermath, and the disquieting events of the following decades soon turned this awareness into a widespread German *Lebensgefühl*, and spiritual loneliness and malaise became prominent and enduring themes of modern writing, indeed "one of the leading intellectual fashions of our century."[17] Well into the nineteenth century, it had still been possible to find ideas which could allay any

---

[14] Hans Mayer, *Aussenseiter* (Frankfurt a. M.: Suhrkamp, 1975), 14.

[15] See Karl E. Webb, "Trakl/ Schiele and the Rimbaud Connection: Psychological Alienation in Austria at the Turn of the Century," *Jahrbuch für Internationale Germanistik*, Reihe A: Kongressberichte, ed. Joseph P. Strelka (Bern: Peter Lang, 1984), 12.

[16] Vicky Rippere, *Schiller and 'Alienation'* (Bern: Peter Lang, 1981).

[17] Rippere, *Schiller and 'Alienation'*, 19.

feelings of estrangement that might arise. The Romantics had been able to compensate by embracing loneliness as the hallmark of genius, by cultivating their imagination, and by concentrating on the rare moments of exhilaration which brought them close to the fulfillment of their yearning. In the post-Romantic era, the conventional Christian faith was already endangered, but the existence of an absolute, higher order and plan was, on the whole, not seriously questioned. Only towards the end of the nineteenth century were these pillars of inner support critically undermined. And only now did man find himself on his own, "unbehaust" and "metaphysiklos,"[18] and the poet's role as mediator between earthbound man and the transcendental realm, so dear to Romantic thinking, became an anachronism. In the Wilhelminian era, writers, at least those who still wanted to uphold what was seen as 'tradition', reluctantly came to see themselves as "nutzlos[e] Glied[er] der Gesellschaft ... Schmarotzer," or "Luxusartikel der Bourgeoisie."[19] In short, as a generic group, artists no longer appeared to have a clearly defined or satisfying function.

Therefore, it is not surprising that many of them began to suffer from self-doubts and feelings of alienation. Judged in this light, the above-mentioned flowering of new directions in form and style can perhaps be seen not so much as a sign of healthy vitality, a heyday of German literature, but as part of a frantic search for a new course, and the elitist conceits of the proponents of 'art for art's sake' as a kind of 'whistling in the dark'. Walter Benjamin's early comment, "Das l'art pour l'art ist die letzte Schranke, die Kunst vor dem Philister schützt,"[20] supports such an evaluation. With specific reference to Kaspar Hauser, Klara Hofer, whose writing abilities were not suited to allow her to take shelter behind this 'last barrier', accordingly voices the characteristic pessimism about the poet's power. Although she throws the (admittedly modest) weight of her reputation as a writer behind Kaspar Hauser's cause, an introductory remark in her book reveals that she doubts the success of her effort from the start: "Nicht der Poet wird berufen sein, das letzte Wort in dieser Angelegenheit der Menschheit zu sprechen.... Der Philister behält recht, die platte Vernunft triumphiert."[21]

---

[18] Hans Egon Holthusen, *Der unbehauste Mensch: Motive und Probleme der modernen Literatur* (Munich: R. Piper, 1951), 20.

[19] Kurt Martens, *Literatur in Deutschland: Studien und Eindrücke* (Berlin: Egon Fleischel, 1910), 183; Frank Wedekind, cited in Hans Wilhelm Rosenhaupt, *Der deutsche Dichter um die Jahrhundertwende und seine Abgelöstheit von der Gesellschaft* (Bern: Paul Haupt, 1939), 14.

[20] Walter Benjamin, "Dialog über die Religiosität der Gegenwart," *Gesammelte Schriften*, vol. 2, *Frühe Arbeiten zur Bildungs- und Kultur-Kritik*, ed. Rolf Tiedemann and Hermann Schweppenhäuser (Frankfurt a. M.: Suhrkamp, 1977), 16.

[21] *Das Schicksal einer Seele: Die Geschichte von Kaspar Hauser* ((Nuremberg: J. L. Schrag, 1925), 208. Disapproving of some anonymous hostile comments on Kaspar Hauser's cause, Hofer states with pride: "Ich spreche nicht aus dem Versteck ...

In the early part of the century, the time was not yet ripe for writers to express the perceived defects of their society in a more militant and political manner. Marx's economic interpretation of man's estrangement from society as being solely rooted in the institution of private property did not yet play a significant role in the thinking of literary men. When it did begin to assert itself more overtly in the 1920s, its built-in trust in the possibility of solutions within the framework of determinism was to lead one stream of literature back to an active involvement with society, which continues to this day. But at the beginning of the century, the search for solutions was at best tentative and experimental.

It is in this general climate of deep-rooted insecurity in the field of literature that the figure of Kaspar Hauser could take root as a vehicle and catalyst for contemporary concerns. As we have seen above, the foundling entered the literary imagination of twentieth-century writers both as a spontaneous, home-grown rediscovery, and by means of various translations of Verlaine's "Gaspard Hauser chante." His role in the reputed webs of aristocratic intrigue, which had preoccupied so much of the nineteenth-century literature, seemed irrelevant in the present social climate, and therefore faded into the background. Where the possibly highborn descent and the attendant surmised plots to keep the youth from his inheritance still play a part — as for instance in Wassermann's *Caspar Hauser*, or in Schäfer's *Richter Feuerbach* — they are not introduced as the pretext for a particular plot, or to provide a titillating atmosphere of scandal in high places. Instead, they merely serve as a backdrop for a thematic development, or to explain the motivation of a dramatis persona, as for instance in Martens' and Wassermann's portrayal of Lord Stanhope as a weak, rather than evil, character.

In keeping with the introspective mood of the literary community, much of the attention now concentrated on Kaspar Hauser's psyche, and on his personal experience of his fate. Writers discovered that the most striking fact in the foundling's story is not what he might have been or become in the social and political situation of his era, but that he 'did not belong' to his place and time, from both society's and his own point of view. For his contemporaries, he remained an outsider throughout the five years he stayed in their community, regardless of how eagerly he tried to adapt, and of the astonishing progress he made in these efforts. At his initial appearance, it was his strange demeanor and lack of language which set him apart. When these first obstacles were overcome, public attention focused on Kaspar's uncommon ability to memorize by rote, and on the acuity of his senses of sight, hearing and smell. As these

sondern trete mit meiner Persönlichkeit und meiner literarischen Stellung für das, was ich verfechte, ein, und jeder Urteilsfähige vermag nachzuprüfen, ob meine bisher geleistete Arbeit mich zu meiner Aufgabe ... berufen erscheinen läßt oder nicht." Ibid., 1. Where appropriate, further references to this work will be given after quotations in the text.

faculties subsided and a superficial level of social integration was achieved, some remaining oddities, such as a lack of skills common in boys of his age, or his ignorance about social conventions, continued to set him apart, although from a modern, psychological point of view these differences are more than understandable, given his circumstances.

Nor did Kaspar Hauser himself ever really feel part of the world that tried to mold him. Not counting the minor and pathetic subterfuges to which his last tutor took such exception, he never rebelled, but did his best to fulfil the expectations of those around him, and to win their approval. Yet his prevailing disposition seems to have been one of puzzled melancholy. Feuerbach's astute account reports: "Der Grundton seiner Gemütsstimmung ist eine stille Schwermut, die er ... nicht selten in deutlichen Äußerungen zu erkennen gibt."[22] Like contemporary man, the foundling evidently experienced the present as a painful burden, and longed to be either back in the past, where his very ignorance of the outside world had protected him from unhappiness, or at some point in the future, where he might recover what he had lost.

It is not difficult to see how eminently suited Kaspar Hauser was for the conversion of the widespread awareness of estrangement described above into literary terms. For the alienated artist, this lonely and unhappy stranger with an aura of mystery could serve as a tailor-made emblem of his own plight, without entailing a loss of self-respect or dignity.

There are many instances in literature in which the poet's lot and loneliness are expressed in a direct manner. For example, Rilke's title "Der Dichter" for a poetic lament beginning with the lines,

> Ich habe keine Geliebte, kein Haus,
> keine Stelle auf der ich lebe,[23]

leaves no doubt about the nature of his concern. Where Kaspar Hauser serves as a symbol of the poet's predicament, the equation is usually not spelled out in such explicit terms. Of course, to be explicit is not necessarily a virtue in itself. Besides, whatever the foundling's special talents were, they did not lie in the artistic field, and therefore did not invite a direct analogy.[24] Nevertheless, there are several examples in literature which establish the link between Kaspar Hauser and art in other, subtle ways.

---

[22] Feuerbach, letter to Elise von der Recke, 20 Sept. 1828, cited in Pies, *Dokumentation*, 37.

[23] *Neue Gedichte*, vol. 1 of *Sämtliche Werke*, ed. Rilke Archives with the aid of Ruth Sieber-Rilke and Ernst Zinn (Wiesbaden: Insel Verlag, 1955), 511.

[24] Kaspar Hauser was taught how to draw, play the piano, and write verse as part of his general training in social accomplishments, but the results, though remarkable for someone of his background, were so conventional that they illustrate his gift to please and imitate rather than genuine creative talent.

One such possibility was the introduction of a sister art of poetry, music, reviving the Romantic notion that like the former it is the language of subconscious faculties. The designation *Lied* in Trakl's poem, or the use of the words *singen* or *Lied* in the titles of the various German *Nachdichtungen* of Verlaine's "Gaspard Hauser chante" fall into this category. Although on the surface Verlaine's poem itself portrays the protagonist not as an artist but as a simple and bewildered itinerant, he who 'sings' is a singer, and he who can offer his own, personal song surely represents art and creativity, however indirectly. The fact that this singer 'wanders' through the countryside is also significant. It not only recalls the conventional Romantic motif of the poet as a solitary wanderer, but can also evoke the even older idea of the poet-minstrel, thereby reinforcing the link between music and poetry still further. An even clearer indication of this connection, combined with a suggestion of the artist's present loss and unhappy state, can be found in Klaus Mann's "Kaspar-Hauser-Legenden." In this case Kaspar Hauser, like Verlaine's hero a naive and simple traveller, does not sing or own a song. Instead, he goes in search of a lost or forgotten melody, which he hopes will reinstate his previous happiness.

In this blending of the image of the wanderer with music one can discern, especially in Klaus Mann's presentation, vestiges of the Orphic myth with its promise of redemption through art, a happier life in the beyond, and the peculiar combination of special powers and vulnera- bility — in the story of Kaspar Hauser a constant motif, in the legend of Orpheus apparent in the hero's second, self-caused loss of Eurydice. But the idea of "Stirb und werde," that is to say the positive ingredient of the association, is left open to doubt. In the works of Verlaine and his translators, we do not know if the hero's final prayer for salvation will be answered. In Mann's "Legenden," this aspect is at least muted through the pervading sadness of the forlorn search. It is worth noting, as a metaphorical indicator, that the only person willing to proffer advice, an old woman Kaspar meets by the wayside, is blind, and there- fore unable to give him directions. However, it is precisely in this constellation, with its absence of certainty of a joyous conclusion, that the wanderer's quest for that almost forgotten but vital song can symbolize the plight of the modern *Dichter* and his yearning for a previous, happier state.

Later in the twentieth century, traces of the Orphic myth are still discernible in various allusions to Kaspar Hauser's love for music. In Röttger's novel, for instance, the author interjects the comment: "Vielleicht hört er die Musik tiefer und genauer als wir das tun, weil er … tiefer in der Sphäre lebt, aus der alle Musik geboren wird" (163). Vesper evokes the motif in his story "Kinder," which contrasts a 'wild child' (a composite of the 'wolf-boy of Hesse', the 'wild boy of Aveyron', and Kaspar Hauser) with a socialized, overeducated child, to the former's distinct advantage. He associates the feral child with music that is strange to 'civilized' ears: "Nachts gibt er bis jetzt noch einen unartikulierten wilden Gesang von sich."[25]

Herzog's *Jeder für sich und Gott gegen Alle* goes one step further, by explicitly linking the innate affinity with music to the vulnerable outsider. The author reintroduces the blind piano player from his earlier film *Lebenszeichen,* a figure reminiscent of the demented Hölderlin in his tower. Kaspar Hauser listens with rapt attention to the blind man's monotonous but haunting tune, and then asserts that this strange music touches him deep inside ("Die Musik fühlt mir stark in der Brust!").[26] His own idiosyncratic rendition of a well-known piece by Mozart may disconcert the cinema audience as much as his listeners within the film, but in one brief scene conveys his total absorption, his effort to make the tune his very own, and his being 'different' from those around him. A similar connection between Kaspar Hauser, art, and affliction or social estrangement infuses Herzog's presentation of an autistic child as the 'young Mozart', Kaspar's fellow exhibit in the travelling freak show. The exposure to the sober light of reason and conventional education ("er sagte, das weiße Papier [habe ihn] zu stark geblendet" [144]) have caused him to withdraw, to search out darkness and presumably listen to the music he carries within.

While associating music and poetry with the victimized and helpless expresses the new unease about the artist's status in society, endowing Kaspar Hauser with ennobling attributes could compensate for the hurt and salvage some of the former pride. The hero of Trakl's "Kaspar Hauser Lied," for instance, who can be seen as the author's "Medium der Selbstbegegnung"[27] both as a human being and as a poet, gains a special dignity through being singled out by God, be it for a mission or sacrifice, when the stay in his original, paradisiacal habitat comes to an end with the divine summons: "O Mensch." Even his subsequent loneliness in the inhospitable environment of the city acquires a nobler aspect if, as Casey suggests, the statement "Nachts blieb er mit seinem Stern allein" points to a special destiny.[28] The connotations of the adjective *silbern,* the gentleness of the verb *sinken,* and the use of the more majestic word *Haupt* rather than *Kopf* in the last line of the poem invest even the death of the hero with positive overtones. Evidently,

---

[25] Guntram Vesper, "Kinder," *Kriegerdenkmal ganz hinten* (Frankfurt a. M.: Fischer Taschenbuch Verlag, 1985), 38.

[26] Werner Herzog, *Jeder für sich und Gott gegen Alle* (1974); sound track.

[27] Walther Killy, *Über Georg Trakl,* 3rd, expanded ed. (Göttingen: Vandenhoeck & Ruprecht, 1967), 7.

[28] T. J. Casey argues, against Eduard Lachmann's interpretation (*Kreuz und Abend* [Salzburg: Otto Müller, 1954]) that in view of the preceding possessive adjective the word *Stern* must be understood as an "image of destiny." See *Manshape that Shone: An Interpretation of Trakl,* Modern Language Studies (Oxford: Basil Blackwell, 1964), 61.

Trakl still believed in the poet as a chosen instrument, however heavy his worldly afflictions might be, and regardless of the fact that his Kaspar Hauser is above all a cipher for the vulnerability of the poet. This dual vision also informs his tribute to Novalis, where, again combining the image of the stranger with that of someone chosen by God, he hails the admired writer and perceived kindred spirit as "der heilige Fremdling."[29]

Hofmannsthal as well had not relinquished the conviction that the poet had a special calling and status in society. "In ihm muß und will alles zusammenkommen," he said in a lecture entitled "Der Dichter und diese Zeit," for "er ist es, der in sich die Elemente der Zeit verknüpft. In ihm oder nirgends ist Gegenwart." The suffering which such an exposure entailed was in his opinion part of the poet's distinction. It could even be seen as a reward in itself: "[Der Dichter] leidet an allen Dingen, und indem er an ihnen leidet, genießt er sie. Dies Leidend-Genießen, dies ist der ganze Inhalt seines Lebens."[30] But self-awareness of this kind was difficult to reconcile with Hofmannsthal's growing conviction that men of letters should not stand aloof from the problems of their time, just as Trakl had felt, at least on one occasion, that he had "kein Recht, [s]ich der Hölle zu entziehen."[31] Writers, Hofmannsthal had come to conclude, ought to do more than reflect the present. They should, through their art, demonstrate positive solutions for the problems of their time, however distasteful they might find the involvement in mundane matters. Commenting on Freud's work, which he felt might provide a key to the dynamics not only of the individual but of society as a whole, he put his finger on the dilemma inherent in a lofty view of the writer's function. Poets, he said, had always possessed the key Freud just had discovered, but had so far been prevented by their very nature to use it in a practical way ("von ihm [dem Schlüssel] einen anderen Gebrauch zu machen als einen priesterlichen, durchaus verschleierten, esoterischen").[32] He tried to reverse this pattern by demonstrating, through his prince Sigismund alias Kaspar Hauser, how to break out of one's tower and survive in this world, without losing one's integrity. It was not an easy task.

Like his friend Hofmannsthal, and very likely under his influence, Wassermann also tried to integrate the belief in an elevated "dichterische

---

[29] "An Novalis," *Dichtungen und Briefe*, vol. 1, ed. Walther Killy and Hans Szklenar (Salzburg: Otto Müller, 1969), 324–26.

[30] *Prosa*, vol. 2 of *Gesammelte Werke in Einzelausgaben*, ed. Herbert Steiner (Frankfurt a. M.: S. Fischer, 1951), 282.

[31] Georg Trakl, quoted by Hans Limbach, "Begegnung mit Georg Trakl (1914)," *Georg Trakl: Die Dichtungen*, ed. Kurt Horwitz (Zurich: Arche, 1946), 211.

[32] "Briefe und Aufsätze für amerikanische Zeitschriften," *Gesammelte Werke in Einzelausgaben: Aufzeichnungen*, ed. Herbert Steiner (Frankfurt a. M.: S. Fischer, 1959), 289.

Sphäre," which cleansed experience "von den Schlacken der Wirklich-keit,"[33] with the conviction that the writer should not distance himself from the world, even if he despised it. None of the distinguishing attributes with which Wassermann invests the Kaspar Hauser of his novel are explicitly linked to the exaltation of the poetic spirit. However, Wassermann's introspective essays make it clear that he accorded the writer a special gift and status. However, he came to be persuaded that purely instinctive creation — or *naive Dichtung*, as Schiller understood it — which he had seen as his forte since his childhood days, was in fact an egoistic self-indulgence. It had to be overcome and replaced with a more conscious approach. Meticulous work and the honing of one's craft were from now on to be as much part of creative writing as the initial inspiration. The effort he spent in this endeavor convinced him that, even for a born writer, a dose of humility and a look beyond his own walls are appropriate. In an article written in 1909, Wassermann combines his belief in all three of the above–mentioned characteristics — the innate distinction of the creative artist, the need for humility, and a mandate for social commitment — in this succinct picture of what for him constituted the ideal artist:

> Der schöpferische Mensch ist von einer wunderbaren Bescheidenheit durchdrungen. Immer bleibt er gleichsam Bürger der Welt; er findet sich eingeordnet, nie bevorrechtet; gesteht man ihm höhere Rechte zu, so wird er schon an sich zu zweifeln beginnen. Er ist … sich selbst gehörig und der Welt und der Gottheit dienstbar, sein Künstlertum wahrend, keineswegs aber es als Schild benutzend oder gar als Postament.[34]

In his novel *Das Gänsemännchen*, Wassermann gives these insights artistic expression, making them one of his central themes. The hero Daniel Nothaft, a truly gifted musician, has to learn through painful experience that the artist should not feel himself to be above his fellowmen. The same point is made in *Christian Wahnschaffe*. Here, the dancer Eva Sorel, who personifies the beauty and perfection of art, also displays an overreaching pride, and therefore turns into an object of pity for the hero once his social conscience is aroused. In the turmoil of the Russian revolution, it becomes blatantly clear that Eva's exclusivity is an anachronism. Plagued by guilt feelings, she ends her life by throwing herself from a tower, a fitting metaphor.

Again Kaspar Hauser, by virtue of his ambivalence between the wish to 'belong' and a natural propensity for passive suffering, provided an ideal model for the symbolization of the conflict between inclination and duty. In this context, Hofmannsthal used the concept of royalty not

---

[33] "Selbstbetrachtungen: Skizzen zu einem Selbstbildnis," *Bekenntnisse und Begegnungen* (Bamberg: Bamberger Reiter, 1950), 45.

[34] *Lebensdienst* (Leipzig: Grethlein, 1928), 538.

merely as part of the external plot he adapted from Calderón's work, nor just to explore the demands and pitfalls of leadership, but also to express the idea that the poet — as personified by Sigismund — is inherently distinct from those around him. References to the hero as "eine fürstliche Kreatur,"[35] as someone who knows how to ride a horse (Pegasus?) without having to learn that skill, serve this purpose. The accolade, "Wie in lebendigem Flußwasser gebadet, so glänzt er von oben bis unten,"[36] recalls Trakl's use of the adjective *silbern* which gives his hero lustre even in death.[37] The conventional image of the poet's divine inspiration reverberates even more clearly in the physician's remark: "Es muß einmal ein Strahl in ihn gefallen sein, der das Tiefste geweckt hat."[38] But how precarious and dangerous this special gift can be, evolves in the further development of *Der Turm*.

It is interesting to note that even Arp, despite the irreverent attitude towards conventional art which he shared with all adherents of the Dada movement, retained the exaltation of qualities which set his protagonist, and by implication the poetic spirit, apart from ordinary people. Granted, what distinguishes the hero of "kaspar ist tot" has little to do with the sublimity of kings. Arp, after all, believed in a new breed of artists, able to combine serious intent with a sense of mischief. But he still saw the artist as mediator and healer, whose task it was to at least alleviate the harm being done to the individual in an increasingly mechanized world. "Wir suchten eine elementare Kunst," he explains in some of his theoretical writing, "die den Menschen vom Wahnsinn der Zeit heilen und eine neue Ordnung, die das Gleichgewicht zwischen Himmel und Hölle herstellen sollte."[39] His Kaspar, a very idiosyncratic and composite reconstruction of the Kaspar Hauser figure, had been able to control the elements and do the most capricious and astonishing things. Unpractical as these activities may appear, they had been an antidote to the constrictions and dullness of modern reality as conveyed through images like the entrapment in "der versteinerten tüte," or the meal "am einsamen barfüßigen tisch." Kaspar's antics — exemplifying the artist's approach to his work as it ought to be in Arp's view — had once been of use and help to mankind, for as the repetition of the doleful question "Wer ... nun [?]" implies, whatever the departed spirit did is now sorely missed. Given Arp's emphasis on the need for playfulness

---

[35] *Turm* I, 28; *Turm* II, 337.

[36] *Turm* I, 164; *Turm* II, 448.

[37] The metaphoric significance of Trakl's colors is admittedly controversial. In the case of *silbern*, however, most of the evidence in the poems supports a positive interpretation.

[38] *Turm* I, 27; *Turm* II, 336.

[39] "Dadaland," in *Unsern täglichen Traum: Erinnerungen, Dichtungen und Betrachtungen aus den Jahren 1914–54* (Zurich: Arche, 1955), 51.

and spontaneity, it is somewhat surprising to recognize in the reference to Kaspar's ability to explain the mysteries of the stars ("wer erklärt uns nun die monogramme in den sternen") the traditional assumption that the artist, here embodied in the figure of Kaspar, could act as a mediator, teacher, and guide. But Arp himself puts this view in perspective. By choosing the form of the elegy, he makes it clear that he is looking back at the past. The combination of two seemingly incongruous characteristics may be the ideal, but the poem shows that the realization of this ideal is definitely a thing of the past. New, more drastic approaches are now needed to deal with the present-day wrongs. It is a double-view of regret and realism, a modern dualism which fits in very well with the dichotomy of Kaspar Hauser's personality and life.

Arp's position and its literary presentation find an echo in two much later works, Härtling's poem "kasper" and its sequel, "nachricht von kasper." Like Arp's early figure, the hero of these poems is an imaginative *Spielgeist*, someone who thumbs his nose at reality ("... der Realität lange Nasen macht").[40] The resemblance to Arp is no coincidence. Härtling had commented on Arp's work on radio and in a published essay, and with regard to "nachricht von kasper," he acknowledges that this poem can be seen as "ein Zuruf an Arps Kaspar."[41] In "kasper," too, the apostrophized figure must be seen as a paradigm of art as it ought to be: lighthearted, and of childlike spontaneity. Significantly, the initial flash of recognition in line one, "du bist kasper," is in the very next line unmasked as an illusion, a mere glimpse of something that seemed familiar and desirable. Like Arp's hero, this figure is also someone who in reality is no longer with us: "deine augen / treiben längst am andern strand."[42] Even the reality of the present apparition becomes questionable, when we consider that it is no more than a fleeting impression behind glass walls:

> hinterm glashaus strampeln beine
> ·sind es deine.
>
> (ll. 5–6)

Whereas Arp's "kaspar ist tot" had been a wistful look back at a better past, Härtling's use of the subjunctive in the last stanza serves to construct a no less wistful evaluation of the present, expressing how joyful life could be if "kasper," alias 'Kaspar', were still with us today:

---

[40] Peter Härtling, *Spielgeist, Spiegelgeist: Gedichte* (Stuttgart: Henry Goverts, 1962); Interview, in *Protokoll zur Person*, ed. Ekkehart Rudolph (Munich: Paul List, 1971), 77, 163.

[41] "Auf der Linie im Kreis," in *Mein Gedicht ist mein Messer: Lyriker zu ihren Gedichten*, ed. Hans Bender (Munich: Paul List, 1961), 163.

[42] "kasper," in *Mein Gedicht ist mein Messer*, ed. Hans Bender (Munich: Paul List, 1961), 164–65 (ll. 1–3). Further references will be given after quotations in the text.

wärst du kasper
flögen plötzlich
helle vögel
durch die fäden
deiner freude.

(ll. 9-13)

In Härtling's resurrection of this figure in "nachricht von kasper," the display of fantastic antics once again hints at the hero's extraordinary powers. But as in the case of Arp's hero, these abilities are no comfort or defense against the present reality, for this 'kasper', too, is no longer with us: he is "fortgegangen" (l. 2). We are no longer able to witness the enchanting force of the poetic spirit firsthand, but — as the word "nachricht" of the title implies — hear about it only indirectly, and have to accept its continued existence elsewhere on faith. Furthermore, whatever new abode the hero may have chosen, the end of the poem indicates that even in that last refuge of the imagination, 'kasper', like the transitory state of childhood, could not endure: "am letzten sonntag ist ihm jäh sein kasperatem ausgegangen" (l. 22).

As if to prove that by 1961 writers had not entirely abandoned the belief in the poet's innate powers, and that the foundling could still serve as a relevant metaphor in this respect, Höllerer's poem "Gaspard" tempers the bleakness of a cityscape with another 'magical' figure, another antitype against the modern age. But once again, the awareness of endangerment intrudes. Explaining his conception of 'Gaspard', Höllerer describes Kaspar Hauser as the archetypal orphan or *Urwaise*. He equates and integrates the figure with other disadvantaged outsiders, such as the mythological black king of the nativity story, or the traditional *Kasper-Puppe*, who has to lash out "weil sie von Anfang an nicht mit anderen rechnen konnte."[43] These authorial explanations notwithstanding, Kaspar Hauser's presence in this encoded assemblage of visual fragments and reflections is not easy to detach. The most obvious indicators are the association with the name 'Gaspard' in the title and ending of the poem, and the allusion to Verlaine's famous poem in Höllerer's prefatory motto: "Priez pour le pauvre Gaspard!" Yet however indirect the foundling's presence may be, here, too, he personifies an elusive spirit which can give magic to life. We have to see him as the very essence of poetry, the inspiration of the moment. His ubiquitous presence in the poem's shifting bird's-eye view of Paris shows that he can be in any place he chooses, and can take on any perspective he likes. By allying himself to the historic relics of the city, he is even able to temporarily bridge and suspend time, and thus himself become timeless ("ohne Zeit"; l. 14). When Gaspard is involved, says Höllerer

---

[43] Walter Höllerer, "Fortgang," in *Mein Gedicht ist mein Messer: Lyriker zu ihren Gedichten*, ed. Hans Bender (Munich: Paul List, 1961), 96, l. 2. Further references will be given after quotations in the text.

elsewhere about this work, Paris can appear "als die Vereinigung der vielen jetzt möglichen Paris mit unserer Vergangenheit und unserer Zukunft" (98).

In spite of such magic properties, Höllerer's Gaspard, alias Kaspar Hauser, represents not so much a return to an unqualified celebration of the poetic spirit, as a metaphor for an inner resistance against the forces of the twentieth century. He can only safeguard a secret realm for a future, safer time, and supply rare moments of a wider vision. The invisible Gaspard is aware of shadows, and of places which are no longer reachable even to the imagination. In these cases, he can only bide his time and stand guard for the poet: "Ich halte Schildwacht für dich / Vor dem was du nicht erreicht" (ll. 40–41).

While Höllerer's companion spirit could at least still provide moments of poetic insights, in Vesper's novel *Nördlich der Liebe und südlich des Hasses* (1979), Kaspar Hauser, summoned to give guidance in the protagonist's search for his true self, can evidently no longer oblige in a constructive way. One underlying premise of Vesper's work is that we cannot divorce the present from the past. As he states in a prefatory quotation from Balzac, "das Heute ist nur der jüngere Bruder vom Gestern."[44] His loosely connected anecdotes give ample illustrations of this conviction. Former circumstances have a habit of repeating themselves, secret misdeeds will sooner or later come to light, and memories resurface. Stylistically, Vesper conveys this interweaving of past and present by intermingling times and tenses. The novel's framework is set in the present ("Es ist Sommer und vormittags elf Uhr," the author begins). But the narrator's recollections, and in turn the recollections of those he remembers, require changes to the past or present perfect tense. Then again, the narrator may identify so strongly with a historical episode that he reverts to the present tense, or he may interrupt the story to express wishful thinking in the subjunctive. In these mental excursions, the author's spiritual stowaway ("der blinde Passagier"), Kaspar Hauser, serves as a kind of leitmotif, " [er] steigt zu ... und hilft träumen." But the dreams provide no comfort. We may see a remnant of magic in Kaspar Hauser's ability to transcend the boundaries of time in step with the narrator's musings. Details of the life of this long-gone figure are told in the present tense, first in daydreams evoked by a visit to Hauser's burial-place, later in an effort to distract a sick relative with the story of a fate worse than hers. When the foundling actually intrudes into the protagonist's own, present life, the sequence of events becomes particularly blurred. Standing at the location of Hauser's erstwhile murder, for example, the narrator muses in the past tense as if he himself had witnessed the events of 1833:

---

[44] Guntram Vesper, "Preface," *Nördlich der Liebe und südlich des Hasses* (Frankfurt a. M.: Fischer Taschenbuch Verlag, 1981), 6. Further references to this work will be given after quotations in the text.

> Hier war's. Der Stein sah aus, als sei er am Vortag gesetzt worden. Im
> Erdreich die Spuren vieler Füße. Den Dolch fand ich auf der nahen
> Wiese, die Spitze in den Boden gestoßen. Hinter dem Stein lag auch der
> violette Stoffbeutel, und das Blut der kleinen Lache konnte ich ganz
> deutlich von den Schneewasserpfützen unterscheiden. (67–68)

A little further on we are back in the present:

> Ich gehe schnell zurück und setze mich ins Auto. An der ersten
> Straßenecke verfahre ich mich und muß lange suchen. Kaum habe ich
> das letzte Haus hinter mir, sehe ich ihn. Er steht am Straßenrand.
> Eigentlich hockt er. Die linke Hand hat er auf den Bauch gepreßt, mit
> der rechten macht er eine winkende Bewegung.

Yet the very next paragraph reverts to the past tense:

> Ich tat, als hätte ich ihn nicht gesehen, dann fuhr ich aber doch zurück.
> Sein Haar war naß, das Gesicht schlammbedeckt und blutverschmiert.
> Er zeigte auf das Blut. Hilfe. (68)

Such shifts of time on the formal, stylistic level corroborate the author's
thematic concern about the tenuous nature of reality and the reliability
of man's perception. Being kindred spirits, the narrator/author and the
foundling seem to expect aid and comfort from each other. But neither
can help the other. This Kaspar Hauser has no magical attributes at his
disposal which could make reality more bearable. He therefore cannot
assuage the feeling of displacement, and the fear of being a stranger in
one's own country. All the foundling is able to do is reconstruct his own,
sad story, as a mirror image of the protagonist's own search through
past and present to find out who he is, or should be.

   With Vesper's Kaspar Hauser figure, the long line of metaphoric
representations of the poet's inspiration appears to have reached its
lowest point. While in the examples discussed above the imagery chosen
to portray the poet's distinction shows, by virtue of its very connection
with the foundling, that the idea was becoming fragile, it could
nevertheless still serve to heal some of the artist's wounded pride, and
could be held up in defiance against the threat of the modern age. In
Vesper's case, however, the poet's alter ego no longer elevates him at all.
It is as helpless as the protagonist himself, leaving him to his own
devices on his path "eine düstere Allee hinunter und dem Ende zu" (61).

   Significantly, in subsequent works the figure is completely devoid of
secret auras or elevating characteristics. This indicates that by the later
twentieth century, the writer's belief in the artistic genius, or at least his
resentment at the diminution of his special status, had exhausted itself,
or was perceived as too elitist to be voiced in public.

   One last proof of how much the writer's belief in his own power had
suffered can be seen in the brief flowering of the German documentary
theatre. It replaces artistic invention with documented 'facts', which

presumably speak for themselves, and for which the author therefore does not have to feel responsible. Thomas and Bullivant see the whole phenomenon of documentary literature as a corollary of the "weakening of the identity, the demythologization of the writer, the denial of the claims of the work of literature to a special kind of insight and experience."[45] Dieter Forte's play *Kaspar Hausers Tod* (1979) is a remnant of this genre. In the literature under discussion, it is the only example of its kind, and next to Hochhuth's or Kipphardt's works (or, for that matter, Forte's own plays about Martin Luther and Thomas Münzer [1972], and Henri Dunant [1978]), not the most typical representative. But like earlier documentary works, Forte's script pays meticulous attention to the authenticity of even marginal historical details, names, dates, and quotations connected with Kaspar Hauser's life. Since the latter does not even appear on stage, and, as we shall see later on, merely provides a focal point for other concerns, it is difficult to see the need for such accuracy. In any case, the merits of such documentary buttressing, even where it serves a clearer purpose, have always been debatable. Already the process of selection of usable evidence from the pool of available data permits personal bias to interfere. While this may count as artistic privilege, it is incompatible with the pretension of objectivity which lies at the core of documentary theatre. Furthermore, the fact that a certain piece of evidence stems from a historical record does not guarantee its accuracy. As Blumer has pointed out, advocates of documentary literature tend to overlook "daß die Dokumente selbst keineswegs ein wahres Abbild der objektiven Wirklichkeit sind, sondern immer schon manipulierte ... Wiedergaben der objektiven Wirklichkeit."[46] Nowhere could this statement be more applicable than in the welter of documents about Kaspar Hauser.

While for many writers of the twentieth century the *Dichter's* special position was difficult to relinquish, it no longer allowed for a conscious self-aggrandizement. The tenor of a new and different time was generally acknowledged, albeit grudgingly. Where Kaspar Hauser is used to illustrate this particular state of affairs, his loneliness and isolation usually receive special attention, but not for the exclusive purpose of highlighting the artist's wounded ego and alienation.

---

[45] R. Hinton Thomas and Keith Bullivant, *Literature in Upheaval: West German Writers and the Challenge of the 1960s* (Manchester: University Press, 1974), 92.

[46] Arnold Blumer, *Das dokumentarische Theater der sechziger Jahre in der Bundesrepublik Deutschland*, Hochschulschriften: Literaturwissenschaft, no. 32 (Meisenheim a. G.: Anton Hain, 1977), 366.

III. The 'Human Condition': Kaspar Hauser as Everyman

It did not take long before the realization took hold that unhappiness
and social alienation were not just the prerogative of artistic circles.
While on the surface contemporary society continued to chart its
materialistic course and prospects with confidence, it offered a very
uncongenial atmosphere for most of its members. The quondam feelings
of optimism were giving way to a sense of great unease, for which
neither the Expressionists' search for a 'new man', nor the anticipated
catharsis provided by two world wars, proved to be a cure. Thus it
became another axiom and an enduring leitmotif of twentieth-century
literature that in modern, industrialized society the price for material
well-being is the loss of happiness and self-assurance, and that the speed
of progress and the corresponding breakdown of traditions render many
people lonely in both a physical and spiritual sense. Accordingly, even
authors who chose to deal with Kaspar Hauser without reference to the
artistic predicament often took up the motif of the social outsider and
his alienation, thus widening the emblematic function of the figure.

In some works it is difficult, if not impossible, to make neat distinctions between Kaspar Hauser as a symbol for the artist in distress, and
Kaspar Hauser as a paradigm for modern man in general. These notions
often merge and overlap. They even absorb reflections of purely
personal experiences, for as has already been mentioned above, several
of the writers in question identified with Kaspar Hauser's misery on a
very private level. In spite of this complexity, the author's intention to
give the figure universal meaning frequently manifests itself in stylistic
elements, or it transpires from the writer's secondary comments on his
work. Hofmannsthal and Wassermann are particularly eloquent in the
latter respect; their extensive theoretical musings leave no doubt that
they attributed a wider significance to their heroes. Even Trakl, usually
reticent in such matters, indicated on at least one occasion that he gave
high priority to the universal meaning of his poetry. Having revised one
of his works ("Klagelied"), he sent it to his agent with the comment:

> Anbei das umgearbeitete Gedicht. Es ist um so viel besser als das
> ursprüngliche, als es nun unpersönlich ist.... Ich bin überzeugt, daß es
> Dir in dieser universellen Form und Art mehr sagen und bedeuten wird,
> denn in der begrenzt persönlichen des ersten Entwurfes.[47]

In the "Kaspar Hauser Lied" itself, we can infer the universal significance
of the content from the abstract, generic use of the nouns: de[r] Hügel,
das Grün, der Baum, [der] Schwarzvogel, die Stadt. Other writers signal

---

[47] Letter to Buschbeck from Salzburg, n.d., *Nachlaß und Biographie*, vol. 3 of *Gesammelte Werke*, ed. Wolfgang Schneditz (Salzburg: Otto Müller, 1949), 25–26.

the general relevance of their statements by endowing Kaspar Hauser with contrasting characteristics, which make the description non-specific and therefore applicable to all mankind. Klabund's poem "Der arme Kaspar" forms the prelude in this respect, portraying the hero as "aussen und inn ... voll und leer ... ein All ... allein." Meret Oppenheim's poem ("Ohne mich ohnehin") gives a similarly antonymous description: "So rund war er etwas eckig zwar," and in Amann's play, Kaspar Hauser introduces himself as

von hohem und niedrigem Wuchs. Von ungewisser Statur. Hat halblanges, bald blondes, bald schwarzes Haar. Ein rundes, ovales Gesicht. Darin feine und buschige Augenbrauen. Lange und kurze Wimpern. Augen in den verschiedensten Farben. Eine spitze oder stumpfe, gerade oder gebogene Nase.[48]

A further sign that the figure's metaphorical use denotes the common man rather than just a select group is the diminishing emphasis on physical beauty or outstanding qualities. Already Schäfer's *Richter Feuerbach* describes Kaspar Hauser in deliberately prosaic terms. The hero is no more than "ein lieber Kerl," "ein mittelmässiger, gutmütiger und ziemlich einfältiger Mensch," and his good looks are not a mark of distinction but almost an object of derision: "ein Bursche wie vom Conditor. Locken, Bäckchen, eine Haut wie ein Weibsbild" (37, 8). Handke prescribes a bland mask to give his protagonist general validity, and when the enforced socialization process is completed, the hero is almost indistinguishable from the other 'Kaspars' who join him on stage.

The desire to strip the emblem of previous overtones of exclusivity is also transparent in Biermann's "Kaspar Hauser Lied," the latest revival of Verlaine's poem. To distance himself from any aura of aestheticism that might cling to Verlaine's work as a residue of the early wave of *Nachdichtungen*, Biermann adopts a deliberately casual tone and diction. He intersperses his stanzas with vernacular expressions like "ne Waise," "Mich fanden die nicht grade schön," or "der wollt ums Verrecken grad mich nicht." The feeling of isolation, and the perception of the world as a barren place are expressed in a vivid but prosaic, almost comical metaphor which would have been unthinkable at the turn of the century: "Auf diesem Kahlkopf steh ich als ein Haar."[49]

---

[48] Klabund [Alfred Henschke], "Der arme Kaspar," *Das heisse Herz: Balladen, Mythen, Gedichte* (Berlin: Erich Reiss, 1922), 7; Oppenheim, *Husch, husch, der schönste Vokal entleert sich*, 83; Jürg Amann, *Ach, diese Wege sind sehr dunkel* (Munich: R. Piper, 1985), 9. The title of Amann's play is taken from one of Hauser's deathbed pronouncements. Where appropriate, further references to this play will be given after quotations in the text.

[49] Wolf Biermann, "Kaspar Hauser singt" (nach Verlaine); typescript sent by Biermann to author, 27 May 1987; publ. in *Affenfels und Barrikade* (Cologne: Kiepenheuer & Witsch, 1986), 111.

Herzog's intention to portray Kaspar Hauser as an ordinary human being was aided by serendipity. In Bruno S., he found a performer whose background resembled that of Kaspar Hauser, and who therefore did not need to simulate the required tortured look and awkward bearing. Instead of trying to compensate for his actor's lack of physical beauty and (historically appropriate) youth, Herzog forces the audience to come to terms with these apparent defects, and to realize that they do not exclude great suffering and spiritual beauty — a point he had already made in his earlier work about a deaf and blind heroine, *Land des Schweigens und der Dunkelheit* (1971). Thus the film script insists on showing Kaspar Hauser in an unflattering light. It describes his flesh as flabby and pallid ("Kaspars Fleisch ist das eines Engerlings," 151), and the passage of time and various efforts to 'civilize' him do little to erase the outward contrast to the bourgeois neatness of his environment:

> Die Verwahrlosung ist an Kaspar noch immer zu sehen. Seine Bewegungen sind weiter bizarr und obwohl er nicht schlecht gepflegt ist, hat man den Eindruck, er sei schon lange nicht mehr gebadet worden. (151)

The foundling continues to be an abnormality, at odds with society. The definition of normalcy is of course a matter of opinion. Herzog is adamant that the seemingly eccentric protagonists of his works are "wirkliche Menschen" who in his eyes represent — or at least ought to represent — the quintessential norm.[50] Besides, while Kaspar Hauser's fate may be an extreme example of human isolation, the blind piano player and the freaks in the circus exhibition parallel his situation, indicating that his case is not unique. Even the common citizenry lead solitary lives; the cavalry officer takes cover behind a brusque demeanor and sartorial splendor, the clerk behind an air of zealous efficiency, and Lord Stanhope behind the mannerisms of high society. They all have little in common beyond the fact of an established status. Everyone for himself ("Jeder für sich," to follow Herzog's title) operates within a self-erected cocoon of protection against a seemingly hostile world.

Unlike the portrayal of the artist's isolation, which still tends to furnish the figure with remnants of former glory, the depiction of Kaspar Hauser as Everyman, as ordinary victim of his time and circumstances, does not offer any palliatives. Negative images prevail, and the foundling derives little dignity from having to carry his burden alone. The very name Kaspar Hauser bears significant connotations in this respect. Already in the nineteenth century, one commentator had interpreted the name 'Hauser' as the attribute of someone obscure and ignorant, "der

---

[50] Kraft, "Interview," 127. For Herzog's views on the difference between normality and eccentricity, see also Hans Günther Pflaum, "Interview," in Hans Günther Pflaum and others, *Werner Herzog*, Reihe Film 22, ed. Peter W. Jansen and Wolfram Schütte (Munich: Carl Hanser, 1979), 59–86.

nie aus dem Haus gekommen."[51] In modern German usage, the verb *hausen* implies living in unsuitable, insufficient quarters, an apt term not only for the foundling's stay in his dungeon, but also for his various temporary lodgings after he entered society. In a wider sense, it can also denote man's uncongenial abode in this century. The name 'Kaspar', too, has meaningful connotations. Arp's "kaspar ist tot," Härtling's early "kasper" poems, and (by the author's own avowal) Höllerer's "Gaspard," evoke the *Kasperle* of the puppet theatre, himself a non-conformist outsider in his never-ending battle against the odds. Höllerer's inclusion of the black King Kaspar of the Christmas story in the concept of his hybrid title figure 'Gaspard' further opens the epithet to connotations of racial prejudice:

> Gaspard ... der schwarze König abseits von den weißen. Denn selbstverständlich, und gegen alle Überlieferung, hieß der schwarze der drei Könige Caspar. Er stand immer etwas mehr beschwert als die anderen beiden, die glänzenden, vor der Krippe, so als müsse er sich für seine Schwärze entschuldigen, und er war es auch, der nicht Gold hatte, nicht Weihrauch: sondern Myrrhen. Gold lud zu Trinkgelagen ein und warb Soldaten; Weihrauch machte die Mengen stumm. Aber wozu Myrrhen? Ein Wort, so fremd wie der arme Gaspard.[52]

It is also important in this context to recall that due to the questionable evidence of the letter which the foundling had carried with him in 1828, the name 'Kaspar Hauser' was in effect a mere label rather than a signifier of the boy's true identity. This deficiency in itself invites metaphoric associations, since it can epitomize modern man's perception of having lost his traditions and selfhood. Guntram Vesper, whose own quest in *Nördlich der Liebe* is to discover his true self, finds modern relevance even in the speculations about the foundling's origin and death, which are of course closely related to the lack of a proper name, but as a literary topic in its own right had lost their attraction:

> Übrigens können auch diese Rätsel (Herkunft, Tod Kaspar Hausers) in einen modernen Kontext gesetzt werden. Denn wirken sie nicht wie Metaphern auf unsere Sicht des Mitmenschen? Denn was wissen wir von dem, was weiß er von uns? Der Fall Hausers ist wie eine Parabel.[53]

While the semantic richness of the foundling's name undoubtedly added to the literary appeal of the figure, only two writers exploit it directly in their works. Röttger refers to a "geheime, unterirdische Abneigung gegen den Namenlosen," and, with reference to the fictitious

---

[51] Georg Philipp Schmidt, *Über Kaspar Hauser* (1831), cited in Hörisch, ed., *Ich möchte ein solcher werden wie ...* , 230.

[52] Höllerer, "Fortgang," 96.

[53] Vesper, letter to author, 11 Feb. 1986.

name, to the common people's "Unwille darüber, daß dieser mit einem
verachteten bayrischen Ausdruck Benannte ('Hauser' bedeutete ein aus
Gnaden eingemieteter mittelloser Mensch), zwischen den Vornehmen
... einhergehen konnte, als gehörte er dazu" (175). On another
occasion, his hero himself elicits a negative interpretation of his name:
"Kaspar, das heißt der Spaßmacher, gelt, Herren?" he asks his tormentors. "Oder der Schwindelmeier" (182), is the sarcastic reply. Jürg
Amann's play *Ach, diese Wege sind sehr dunkel* devotes one scene to the
painful process of Kaspar Hauser's speech acquisition. It culminates in
the utterance of his own name, but not before the repetition of letters
and syllables has yielded a kind of anagram that equates this name with
his state of homelessness: "AUS HAUS HERAUS ER GESPERRT" (14).

Writers who wanted to illustrate this motif more explicitly could draw
on a wealth of incidents from the foundling's documented biography to
show how out of place he was and remained. The loss of one
foster-home after another alone was sufficient to exemplify the boy's
predicament. Wassermann is especially skilful in exploiting documented
events to support his main theme, and to structure the second part of
his novel around Kaspar's steadily worsening prospects and circumstances. To add — as especially Klara Hofer did to a large extent, and
Wassermann to a lesser one — direct comments on this plight seems like
gilding the lily, a quite unnecessary authorial intrusion.

More effective are various small liberties which some authors take
with their material, as when Wassermann invents an incident in which
the boy is physically evicted and his few possessions are thrown out into
the street, because the wife of his latest guardian takes a dislike to him.
Kaspar is pictured as sitting pathetically in the rain for several hours,
before the city fathers find him yet another temporary shelter. In similar
inventive fashion, several authors (Wassermann, Ebermayer, Schaumann,
and Röttger) resurrect the rumors about Kaspar's possibly incriminatory
secret diary, in order to demonstrate the ultimate state of dispossession.
No match for the meanness of some of his contemporaries, the
foundling is powerless to hold on to the record of his own thoughts, the
one object he could truly consider his very own. Even the defiant gesture of burning the journal — incorporated by both Wassermann and
Röttger — is shown to be of no avail; his opponents still get the better
of him by reconstructing the desired object from its charred fragments.

The depiction of Kaspar Hauser as a wanderer, already mentioned in
connection with the artist's predicament, can of course also serve as an
analogy for Everyman's rootlessness and loneliness. In the former, poetic
context, the image of the solitary wanderer still retains some positive
overtones by implying — as had been the case in many a Romantic
wandering poet or *Spielmann* — an indomitable spirit, or at least a free
choice of life-style, to offset feelings of melancholy. On the more down-
to-earth, purely social level of presentation, however, more uncongenial
inferences arise. The real Kaspar Hauser was under such close super-
vision that he never had the opportunity to be a 'wanderer' or 'vaga-

bond' in the literal sense of those words. Nevertheless, the image is in keeping with his unknown place of origin and his frequent, though in his case enforced, change of abode. Unobtrusively, it elicits the modern reader's knowledge that society views those without a steady home with great suspicion. They are on the lowest rung of the social ladder, and whatever kindness they may receive is regarded as a form of charity. This double connotation saves the image from striking the twentieth-century reader as a sentimental cliché. It certainly contributes to the impact of Verlaine's poem and its *Nachdichtungen*, and of Trakl's "Kaspar Hauser Lied," by enriching their deceptive simplicity. Klaus Mann's "Legenden" also explores the ambiguity of the image. His Kaspar Hauser may well be a secret prince, an incarnation of the poet, in search of his true home, but circumstances force him to mingle with the outcasts of society, indeed he is part of them.

In the more recent Kaspar Hauser literature, writers shy away from using the image of man as a wanderer in search of something special and elusive. Perhaps they are mindful of Walter Benjamin's sarcastic dictum that those who today still search for the *blaue Blume* must have overslept. Only Herzog recalls the motif in two of the sequences which show us Kaspar Hauser's dreams. Both these visions, however, conflate the image with other traditional symbolic representations of life per se, so that it applies to mankind as a whole rather than to man as an individual. In the first example, Kaspar dreams of a nomadic tribe wandering through the Sahara desert. Although their meanderings appear to have a purpose, it remains uncertain whether they ever reach their destination. In Kaspar's final dream, we see a long procession of people wandering up and down a desolate, fog-shrouded mountain. It is not clear if they, like Kaspar himself, are aware or come to realize that "oben auf dem Berg ist der Tod";[54] The screen images are deliberately hazy, and those ascending the mountain have the same resigned air as those descending.

Another technique, again more popular with earlier rather than more recent writers, is to symbolize social isolation by showing the hero on the outside of human habitations, unable to join those within. Like the image of the wanderer, this, too, is a revival of a conventional metaphor of the Romantic era. In particular Eichendorff's poetry provides a number of pertinent examples — the poems "Rückkehr" or "Weihnachten" come to mind — which show the hero wandering through dark streets, observing social activities in which he cannot take part. In Trakl's "Kaspar Hauser Lied," the line "Sein leiser Schritt / An den Zimmern Träumender hin"[55] belongs into this category. The poet

---

[54] *Jeder für sich*; sound track.

[55] *Die Dichtungen: Gesamtausgabe*, ed. Kurt Horwitz (Zurich: Arche, 1946), 109, ll. 15–16. Where appropriate, further references to this work will be given after quotations in the text.

contrasts the hero's solitary night-time roaming with the behavior of the rest of mankind, indifferently asleep in their beds. Wassermann also uses the metaphor to demonstrate the idea of social exclusion. His Kaspar sets out one night in search of human companionship, but then, remembering past disappointments, finds himself unable to enter the house he had wanted to visit:

> Aber als er angelangt war, als er am Gittertor stand und zu den erleuchteten Fenstern hinaufschaute, schwand ihm alle Lust und er fürchtete sich vor den hellen Zimmern. Sah er sich doch droben; hörte er doch schon die Worte, die ihm nichts waren und nichts galten; er kannte sie alle, er hätte sie auswendig an der Schwelle hersagen können. Ja, er kannte nun die Worte der Menschen, er erfuhr nichts Neues durch sie, sie fielen in das unermeßliche Meer seiner Traurigkeit wie kleine trübe Tropfen, deren Aufschall die Tiefe verschlang. Ein Schatten glitt an den Fenstern vorbei, ein andrer folgte. So weilten sie in ihren Wohnungen, still und emsig, zündeten ihre Lichter an und wußten nicht, wer draußen stand am Tor. (344)

Ebermayer's play incorporates the same motif, but it emphasizes the longing of the outsider rather than his disillusionment. Looking up at brightly lit windows which emit sounds of laughter and music, the hero ponders:

> Wer bei euch sein könnt' — im Warmen, Hellen! Nicht mittrinken, nicht mittanzen — nur in der Ecken [sic] stehen und zuschauen dürfen.... Im Lichten hat alles eher einen Sinn. (61–62)

Röttger in turn shows that even when the stranger is admitted he does not necessarily fit in. His protagonist does in fact take part in a festivity, but in spite of valiant efforts never really succeeds in being like everyone else. He tries to join the minuet, but disturbs the dancers' conventional, orderly pattern:

> Hauser stand allein. War es nun, daß er die Verabredung mißverstanden hatte ... sei es, daß er vergessen hatte, was jetzt geschehen solle: er hob wieder die Arme, diesmal nicht traumhaft, sondern in großem Schmerz, als reiße er aus dem Nichts die Partnerin, tanzte solo mit, einige Male um sich selber sich schwingend, als halte er ... Etwas (und sei es der Tod selbst), und fiel am Taburett nieder, lag reglos.... (72–73)

The reactions of his fellow dancers are revealingly petty and bourgeois: "Machen Sie kein Aufsehen," "Nur keinen Eklat," "Stehen Sie auf! Beherrschen Sie sich!" (173). Having fainted because of sensations he was unable to cope with, Kaspar Hauser eventually finds himself regaining consciousness sequestered alone in a small, dark room, away from all company. This symbolic repetition of his original situation in his cave or cellar suggests that his attempts at integration and his ostensible progress have in reality not advanced him at all. The fundamental indifference of even those who on the surface offer their hospitality is illustrated by the circumstance that Kaspar Hauser has in fact been totally forgotten by his hosts. A servant finally happens to find him long after the party is over, and comments: "Man hat den Herrn halt vergessen, seit man ihn da hereingelegt hat" (185).

The demonstration of such blatant indifference accords with the main theme of Wassermann's novel, namely that *Trägheit des Herzens* can be as pernicious as downright malice in causing the individual's misery. It is a motif which recurs in several subsequent works. Schäfer, for example, indicts this shortcoming in his drama when, in spite of painting Feuerbach's courage in glowing colors, he demonstrates that the judge neglects the human aspect of Kaspar Hauser's case. In his fight for abstract justice, the individual and his fate are only important in as far as they can advance his cause. "Dieser Hauser ist meine beste Propaganda," says Feuerbach, "über den Hauser werden die Frauen heulen, bis die Männer aufstehen und die Bastille stürmen" (43).

In Forte's play, Kaspar Hauser's individual worth becomes even less important. Preoccupied with their own, time-related worries, those gathered to commemorate and honor him quickly relegate his memory to the sidelines. Admittedly, in both Schäfer's and Forte's plays Kaspar Hauser had not been the main focus of the action to begin with. But the figure's very marginality matters, for it illustrates the distance between the lone individual and society, and the incompatibility of their concerns. It matters in particular to Forte, for whom the social outsider is of as great a concern as the fabric of society as a whole. "Aus persönlicher Betroffenheit versuche ich immer wieder," he says, "das Leben von Außenseitern darzustellen, die nur dadurch Außenseiter sind, weil die Gesellschaft sie dazu macht. Sie macht sich ein Bild von einem Menschen und verurteilt ihn damit zum Tode. Das kann man an Kaspar Hauser sehr schön zeigen."[56] In Handke's *Kaspar*, it is the anonymous, mechanical quality of the socializing agents which exemplifies the indifference of society towards its members. In his stage instructions, Handke expressly stipulates that the prompters' voices ought to be totally impersonal, "ohne Unter- und Übertöne," and that they do not operate "mit den üblichen Ausdrucksmitteln der Ironie, des Humors, der Hilfsbereitschaft, der menschlichen Wärme" (15).

In keeping with the possibilities of his medium, and as a matter of deliberate policy, Herzog often allows visual images alone to convey his message. Spatial relationships and body language underline Kaspar Hauser's social isolation in several scenes. Whether in the market square, on display in a carnival tent, at Stanhope's soirée, or, finally, on his deathbed: Kaspar Hauser is usually in the center of the screen, somewhat removed from those around him. On the one hand, this can signal his intrinsic worth and importance: It is *his* point of view which

---

[56] Letter to author, 18 Feb. 1989.

deserves attention and should set the standard. At the same time, the physical distance between him and his fellowmen also carries a negative connotation. Nobody touches him, and he himself does not reach out for help, but remains stiff and withdrawn. However, Herzog's most memorable device for demonstrating the heartlessness of society is the already mentioned (fictitious) episode of the freak show at a commercial fair, where Kaspar Hauser is exhibited, together with other hapless outcasts, to relieve the municipal coffers of the expense for his upkeep. The fact that this event takes place outside the city walls rather than in, for example, the market square, may have been no more than a matter of cinematic logistics. But intentionally or not, this physical distance from the heart of the community underlines the victim's social exclusion. From the viewpoint of the citizens of a sleepy Franconian town, these public exhibits are indeed exotic oddities which can disturb society's self-image and are therefore not to be tolerated in the midst of their normal transactions. Yet as presented in the film, sad and forlorn, their exotic quality dwindles in comparison with the obvious suffering of the excluded individual. Herzog, who from his various personal odysseys at home and abroad knows first-hand what it means to be outside established social boundaries, leaves no doubt that the viewer is meant to identify with the exhibits rather than with the onlookers. "Es ist eine tieftraurige Lustbarkeit," he comments in the script, "Der Raum ist von einer Trostlosigkeit erfüllt, die dadurch noch viel grauenhafter wird, weil sie die Besucher nicht bemerken und sich belustigen wollen" (141–42).

Several authors equate the outsider's extreme lack of power with the helplessness of a child. Consequently, several works emphasize Kaspar Hauser's childlike qualities. We shall see in the following chapter that this technique also serves a positive thematic purpose. But references to the foundling's naivety and to his yearning for his mother fuel the reader's awareness that Kaspar's lack of experience and parental protection make him particularly vulnerable. To be motherless — an 'orphan', as Verlaine calls it in his poem — means to be cut off from the source of life and well-being on which every human being once depended. Klaus Mann may have had this in mind when he devised his hero's search for his mother.

Occasionally, the depiction of childlike qualities is overdrawn, even downright sentimental. Röttger's constant references to Kaspar's longing for his mother, for instance, appeal to the reader's sympathy with an almost embarrassing insistence. Whenever the author mentions children in his novel, he uses the opportunity to remind us how much luckier they are than Kaspar Hauser. Watching a group of children play and then scatter, the "Niemandskind" (159) cannot help thinking: "Jetzt rennen sie zur Mutter" (38). On another occasion, Kaspar observes a mother and child in front of a window display at Christmas time:

Sah, wie das Kind sich an die Hand und in das Kleid der Mutter schmiegte, während es leise sprach. Es tat Hausern weh, das zu sehn; aber er fühlte keinen Neid, daß Mutter und Kind diese Vorfreude auf das Fest hatten. Es tat ihm nur weh, so allein zu stehn. Aber bewußt ward ihm dieser Grund nicht. (48)

We do not know to what extent the real Kaspar Hauser was consciously aware of his misery. His prevailing mood of melancholy and his frequently uttered wish to return to the dungeon, where he had not yet known that pain existed, indicate at least a subconscious comprehension of his plight.

Where literary works show Kaspar Hauser's state of mind to reflect the mood of twentieth-century man, self-awareness and melancholy also predominate. Whether its expression is subtle or obvious depends on the nature of the work, and on the skill of the author. Hofmannsthal's Sigismund is probably the most articulate among the literary Kaspar Hauser figures to voice the confusion of those condemned to live in an inhospitable and uncongenial environment. Like Kaspar Hauser — and like his creator — he vacillates in his reaction, now trying to adapt, now withdrawing from the fray. Trakl's poem conveys the sadness associated with Kaspar's entry into the city by contrasting the brightness and "Freude des Grüns" of his initial habitat with the negative imagery of darkness ("dunkle Klage," "Dämmergarten," "dunklen Zimmern," "nachts," "dämmernden Hausflur," "Schatten des Mörders") and the cold barrenness of winter ("Schnee," "kahles Gezweig") that later surrounds him. Handke's stylized parable does not easily lend itself to the expression of emotions, especially after his hero begins to adopt the demeanor of his insensate trainers ("Seine Stimme wird der der Einsager ähnlich" [80]). Nevertheless, as Kaspar gains insight into the futility of his quest, his disillusionment transcends the mechanical chatter. The threefold repetition of the sentence: "Jeder Satz ist für die Katz" (92) must count as a genuine expression of disappointment, and the question: "Warum fliegen da lauter so schwarze Würmer herum?", an allusion to the last words of Ödön von Horvath's dying heroine in *Glaube, Liebe, Hoffnung*,[57] indicates the darkening of Kaspar's mood as much as the disintegration of his intellect.

In longer, less abstract works, expressions of self-awareness are, as a rule, much more overt. Wassermann even takes care to let his hero's perceptions about himself keep pace with his increasing sophistication. In the initial stage of his socialization, Kaspar's views on the distance between him and society are still vague and confused. Throwing his hopes on Stanhope as a possible savior, he lets his thoughts ramble without a clear focus:

---

[57] Handke himself drew attention to the parallel with Horváth's sentence. See "Horváth und Brecht," [1968] in *Ich bin ein Bewohner des Elfenbeinturms* (Frankfurt a. M.: Suhrkamp, 1972), 64.

Der aus der Ferne kam im silbernen Kleid vielleicht und mit vielen Rossen, der brauchte nicht zu fragen, er wußte alles von selbst, die andern aber, alle die Nahen, die immer da waren, immer hereingingen und immer wieder fort, sie sahen niemals aus, als ob sie von schäumenden Rossen gestiegen wären, ihr Atem war dumpf wie Kellerluft, ihre Hand müde wie keines Reiters Hand; ihr Antlitz war vermummt, nicht schwarz vermummt wie das Gesicht dessen, der ihn geschlagen und der ihm so nah gewesen wie keiner sonst, sondern undeutlich vermummt; darum redeten sie mit unreiner Stimme und in verstellten Tönen, und darum war es auch, daß Caspar sich jetzt verstellen mußte und nicht mehr imstande war, ihnen fest ins Auge zu sehen und alles zu sagen, was er hätte sagen können. Er fand es heimlicher und trauriger zu schweigen als zu reden, besonders wenn sie darauf warteten, daß er reden solle; ja, er liebte es, ein wenig traurig zu sein, viele Träume und Gedanken zu verbergen und sie zu dem Glauben zu bringen, daß sie ihm doch nicht nahkommen könnten. (117)

Later, he has learned to reason more clearly about his fate:

Allmählich wurde es ihm klar, daß er unter lauter fremden Menschen herumging und von der Mitleidsschüssel speiste. Einer nahm ihn und nährte ihn, da kam ein Wagen, und er wurde geholt. Ein andres Haus; eines Tages wirft man sein Zeug auf die Gasse; wieder woandershin. (150–51)

Röttger, who like Wassermann strives for a psychologically realistic picture, did not have to worry about showing a gradual dawning of insight, since his work deals only with the final days of Kaspar Hauser's life. In this case, the hero's acute perception transcends his naive diction:

I hab alleweil so viel bitten müssen, daß i da bin, um Entschuldigung bitten müssen; nimmer hab' ich's recht machen können für die Menschen. (43)

Or, on another occasion:

[Die Menschen] haben's doch gewußt, wie einem ist, der aus dem Dunkel kommt und find't nicht zurecht. Die Stuben is kalt, und das ganze Haus kalt, und dadraus kommt die innere Hitzen, die mich nun plagt an die zwei Jahr'. (58)

Herzog's more recent hero, less aware of his predicament, nevertheless describes his move from physical captivity to spiritual isolation amongst men as "ein harter Sturz." "Die Menschen sind mir wie die Wölfe," is his verdict.[58] In addition, he indirectly advances the interesting notion that the expression of unhappiness is not an innate form

---

[58] Statements based on *Jeder für sich*; sound track.

of behavior, but a skill to be learned. We witness how the 'uncivilized' Kaspar does not comprehend the cruelty of his tormenters. When in his ignorance he burns his hand by reaching into the flame of a candle, he does not know how to show his pain. Once he has acquired the means to express himself, he writes in his diary about the tears he shed when uncaring people destroyed what he had sown in his garden. We might compare this with the paradoxical situation of Handke's hero, who can express his distaste for language only by learning it.

Given this literary catalogue of existential malaise, it is somewhat surprising that the option of suicide as an easy way out or, nobler, as a last bastion of free choice has scarcely been raised in the literature under discussion. Seminally, the historical material contains that possibility, i.e. could have served as a model, since one faction contended that Kaspar Hauser's fatal wound was in fact self-inflicted. It is true that those who knew the foundling personally were almost unanimous in dismissing that theory. Even its advocates thought less of deliberate suicide than of an attention-seeking gesture inadvertently gone awry. But even without a model, such a measure would be compatible with the general literary stance, as an ultimate example of how the individual might react if driven too far. Only one minor, one-act play, Victor Curt Bihacht's *Kaspar Hauser* (1911), includes the idea of suicide in its dramatic climax. Indirectly, the motif is embedded in the apparent death wish of Klaus Mann's protagonist, and in Kalckreuth's transcription of Verlaine's more neutral question: "Qu'est-ce que je fais en ce monde?" as the more explicit lament: "Was soll mir, ach, des Lebens Dauer?"[59] — possibly a foreshadowing of the poet's own impending suicide. One can also argue that Hofmannsthal's Sigismund provokes his own death. In *Turm* I, the hero, aware that the meeting with the gypsy from the enemy camp may endanger his life, dismisses his concerned entourage and thus deliberately exposes himself to the fatal act of treachery. In *Turm* II, it is also possible that the prince, who has after all talked of retreating to a place where he can no longer be reached by those he despises, intentionally courts death. Despite his companions' warnings, he goes to the window to show himself to the crowd, thus presenting himself as a target for the fatal bullets of his enemies. However, the evidence is not conclusive in either of these plays; Sigismund's death can also be construed as a consequence of his Kaspar-Hauser-like trusting nature, or as proof for the arbitrary workings of chance.

If even those authors who were so affected by the darkness of their century that they eventually were to take their own lives, that is to say Trakl, Kalckreuth, Klaus Mann, and Tucholsky, did not make explicit use of the suicide-motif when using the foundling's lot as a mirror of modern man's fate, we must assume that at the time of their writing they

[59] Kalckreuth, Wolf Graf von, "Caspar Hauser singt," *Gedichte und Übertragungen*, ed. by Hellmut Kruse (Heidelberg: Lambert Schneider, 1962), 109.

were still considering other ways to end or escape the dilemma. A first step in that direction is to accept the situation as perceived, even to embrace and take pride in the condition of the outsider. A few authors attempted to do just that, through their proxy, Kaspar Hauser. One passage in Wassermann's novel implies that not being part of the mainstream can have its compensations. Discovered as an eavesdropper at a festive gathering to which he had not been invited, Kaspar defiantly looks at those who have cornered him, and "hätte jauchzen mögen, denn er erschien sich fremd und zugleich von allen angebetet; sie senkten das Haupt, sie erkannten den Herrn in ihm; ja er ahnte, was er war und von wo er kam, ... ein geisterhaftes Lächeln umspielte seine Lippen" (159). But this fleeting moment of self-confidence and triumph is linked to a temporary upswing of Kaspar's prospects; it is not characteristic of the overall tenor of the novel.

Handke's *Kaspar* represents another possible exception in the catalogue of regrets about man's alienation from society. When the hero's initial wish to overcome his isolation succeeds only too well, he comes to realize that he has fallen into a trap, and that being like everyone else does not bring happiness: "Schon mit meinem ersten Satz bin ich in die Falle gegangen" (98). Social integration does not necessarily equal social harmony, as the cacophony of the hero's new community of fellow Kaspars conveys in onomatopoeic fashion. By letting Kaspar's quest end in a cul-de-sac, Handke indicates that the attempt had been a mistake to begin with, and that solitude might be the preferable option, at least in a reprehensible society.

More recently, Katja Lange-Müller's work, *Kaspar Mauser — Die Feigheit vorm Freund* (1988), makes the same point more forcefully. Due to his illegitimacy and racially mixed origin, the title figure and Kaspar Hauser surrogate is a misfit in German society from the very beginning. His name, 'Amica', the feminine version of 'friend' in Latin and Italian, corresponds to his androgynous qualities, but also contributes to his disorientation. Even further confused and isolated after his move from (what was then) East Germany to West Berlin, the hero feels cornered. He categorically renounces society, both socialist and capitalist, by withdrawing into non-conformance, solitude, and silence:

> Von nun an wort-, ja sprachlos, wie weiland — erst mal — Caspar Hauser, würde er darauf bestehen, die Unperson, die jeder ist — in *solcher* Lage — auch gänzlich zu sein *und* zu *bleiben*: Nicht Bürger des einen, nicht Bürger des anderen (Deutsch)-Landes, gar kein Bürger, nicht einmal staatenlos [emphasis Lange-Müller's].[60]

A simple affirmation of the outsider status is of course no permanent solution to the problem of modern man, neither from the individual's,

---

[60] (Cologne: Kiepenheuer & Witsch, 1988), 63.

nor from society's point of view. Such gestures of defiance could at best alleviate the non-conformists' present pain.

4

The Attempt to Go Back:
The Rousseau Syndrome

I. Kaspar Hauser as 'Noble Savage'

As IMPORTANT AS SELF-EVALUATIONS can be, it would be a
sorry reflection on the authors in question if all they did was bemoan
the lot of the poet or the present state of man in general. To be sure,
one could argue that writers who see Kaspar Hauser mainly as a victim
and outsider form a preselected group. Since those who were drawn to
the topic often identified with the foundling's suffering on a very
personal level, they might be predisposed to generalize their own
experience and to sense the spiritual desolation of their age with
exceptional intensity. It is also conspicuous that very few of these
authors participated in the more belligerent strands of literature which
actively sought to change social and political reality. The satirist
Tucholsky is one of the exceptions. But although he published 199
articles of *Zeitkritik* under the pen name 'Kaspar Hauser', the latter's
gentle passivity was alien to his combative temperament, and not always
suitable for his purpose. When the resolution of a copyright dispute
allowed him to return to one of his (temporarily suspended) more
acerbic pseudonyms, he typically showed relief:

> Ich darf nun wieder Theo Tiger heißen. Die Maske fällt: kein nürenber-
> ger Kind bin ich — laßt mich die Menschen beißen, die gut genug für
> meine Füttrung sind.[1]

Klaus Mann's antifascist stance developed only later, under the pressure
of fascist persecution. Of the present-day writers, Dieter Forte gained his
reputation for political activism mainly through his play *Martin Luther
& Thomas Münzer; oder, Die Einführung der Buchhaltung*, in which he
dared to impugn the motives of a traditional cult figure, Martin Luther.
The social and political commitment of the songwriter Wolf Biermann
is of course undisputed; but his involvement with Kaspar Hauser is
correspondingly very peripheral.

---

[1] *Die Weltbühne* 1 (1920): 408.

If one were to characterize the overall tone of the mainstream of the Kaspar Hauser literature, the word *sadness* would probably come most readily to mind. But this impression may well be deceptive. Sadness about existing conditions does not necessarily equal total resignation. It does not rule out the desire for change, nor the search for a way out of the perceived dilemma. If we look a little closer at how Kaspar Hauser is presented, and in what contexts, we discover that his functions go far beyond the expression of grief. Through him, writers explore not only the roots of the current state of affairs, but also various possibilities of dealing with the predicament of the modern age without surrendering deep-seated ideals.

One noticeable feature in the Kaspar Hauser literature is a persistent undercurrent of what seem to be Romantic or, more specifically, Rousseauistic ideas. If all these writers had been content to retell the nineteenth-century mystery, one would not be surprised to find a Romantic slant to fit the tale. But in virtually all cases, writers use the historical elements with discrimination, in order to express other, superordinate ideas. So the question arises whether these Romantic or Rousseauistic ingredients are merely anachronistic embellishments, vestigial remains of the original ambiance of the story which have hardened into conventions or even clichés, or whether they are in fact integral parts of the authors' statement, signalling a desire to revive tenets of Romanticism as an antidote to the sterility of our technical age. Several critics have seen a conspicuous relationship between the mistrust of the putative forces of progress in the Age of Romanticism and the *Zivilisationspessimismus* of the twentieth century, which would point to the latter possibility.[2] It is significant that Wassermann, a leading proponent of Kaspar Hauser's relevance to our century, also saw signs of a revival of Romanticism in his time: "Es will mir scheinen, als ob eine neue Romantik heraufdämmerte ... eine Renaissance des Herzens, eine Neugeburt der lebensgestaltenden Phantasie."[3]

Before we go on to extract samples of Romantic or Rousseauistic thinking from the literature under discussion, we have to clarify the use of these terms in our context. In particular the words *Romantic* and *Romanticism* have become such vague and controversial concepts that some critics dismiss them as useless for literary analysis, unless and until a consensus about their meaning can be reached. By concentrating on the legacy of Rousseau, whose place at the core of Romantic thinking is

---

[2] See, e.g., Paul Kluckhohn, *Das Ideengut der deutschen Romantik*, 2nd ed. (Halle/Saale: Max Niemeyer, 1942), 180; also Theodore Ziolkowski, "Das Nachleben der Romantik in der modernen deutschen Literatur," in *Das Nachleben der Romantik in der deutschen Literatur*, ed. Wolfgang Paulsen (Heidelberg: Lothar Stiehm, 1969), 15–31.

[3] Jakob Wassermann, "Habt Mut zu euren Träumen," *Tagebuch aus dem Winkel* (Amsterdam: Querido, 1935), 128.

undisputed, we can at least narrow the field, and so sidestep some of the problems of the long-standing debate.

Of course Rousseau's wide range of interests and his dogmatic but not always consistent approach have brought about controversies of their own. Furthermore, it has been shown that his ideas were neither as unique nor as new in the Age of Reason as they appeared to be at the time.[4] Be that as it may, there is no doubt that it was Rousseau who gave some of these ideas such a cogent expression that they caught the public imagination throughout Europe, and have been associated with his name ever since.

The notion which particularly concerns us here is Rousseau's concept of the 'noble savage' who lives in harmony with Nature. It arises from the philosopher's following basic and familiar premises:

a) Nature, as God's creation, is inherently good, incorporating order, harmony and proportion.

b) In contrast, civilization has become unnatural through its pursuit of rational and superficial goals, and especially life in the cities exerts a corrupting influence. These tenets are summed up in the first sentence of *Émile*: "Tout est bien, sortant des mains de l'auteur des choses: tout dégénère entre les mains de l'homme."[5]

c) It follows that only those who are not yet contaminated by this corruption, that is to say children, primitive tribes, and those still living in rustic simplicity, are pure and noble.

In keeping with these views, Rousseau naturally regarded the past as more wholesome than the present. But he was astute enough to realize that a physical 'return to Nature' was unrealistic in his time, and that man could not simply revert to the primitive ways of his ancestors to recreate a golden age. "Cet état primitif ne peut plus subsister," he acknowledged, and he believed that the present unsatisfactory situation could only be dealt with by leaving nostalgia aside and proceeding "en prenant les hommes tels qu'ils sont."[6] Compromise solutions had to be found to retrieve a more natural way of life. It was towards this end that he devised his *Contrat Social* as a blueprint for a new and better society, and his novel *Émile* as a detailed scheme for the education of a more natural man.

These qualifications, however, were largely ignored when Rousseau's postulates first attached themselves to the public image of Kaspar Hauser. At the time of the boy's appearance in 1828, simplified versions

---

[4] In this regard, see esp. Irving Babbitt's somewhat polemic *Rousseau and Romanticism* (Austin, Texas: University of Texas Press, 1977; first publ. 1919), 297; also J. Huizinga, *Jean-Jacques Rousseau: The Making of a Saint* (London: Hamish Hamilton, 1976), 21, 55.

[5] *Émile; ou, De l'Éducation*, vol. 1 of *Oeuvres Complètes de Jean-Jacques Rousseau* (Paris: Imprimerie de Décourchant, 1831; orig. publ. 1761), 11.

[6] Jean-Jacques Rousseau, *Du Contrat Social*, ed. Ronald Grimsley (Oxford: Clarendon Press, 1972; orig. publ. 1762), 114, 103.

of Rousseau's ideals had seeped down to the general population, and had become acceptable, even fashionable for the average citizen, little as they affected his everyday life. It is perhaps of interest that the 'wild boy of Aveyron', who had stirred such great public interest in the true nature of man at the beginning of the century, was still alive at this time, although admittedly no longer in the public eye.[7] So it is not surprising that the idea of a new, German 'noble savage' immediately captured the public imagination. Already the earliest assessments of the foundling invest him with the hallmarks of Rousseau's ideal, ungainly and incoherent as he seems to have been in external aspects. Above all else, witnesses extolled his innocence. His first guard saw in his behavior "ein[en] rein[en] Spiegel kindlicher Unschuld." The mayor of Nuremberg praised in him "die höchste Unschuld der Natur," and Freiherr von Tucher "das unschuldige Kind von dem reinsten, fleckenlosen Gemüte." Even Feuerbach, who as president of the Bavarian High Court of Appeal took pride in being an astute observer of mankind, rhapsodized: "In sittlicher Beziehung ist Kaspar Hauser eine lebendige Widerlegung des Lehrsatzes von der Erbsünde."[8]

The nineteenth-century literature about Kaspar Hauser, which began already during his lifetime, made surprisingly little use of Rousseauistic motifs, concentrating mainly on the possible scandal surrounding the boy's lineage. Of course the German Romantic movement, which had absorbed much of Rousseau's idealization of Nature and childlike simplicity, had by this time long passed its literary zenith. Only Gutzkow's *Söhne Pestalozzis* takes up Rousseau's postulation of man's inherent goodness, albeit with certain reservations. The central character of this work, whose circumstances incorporate many factual details of Kaspar Hauser's life, is named Theodor Waldner, 'Theodor' meaning 'the God-given', and 'Waldner' a reference to the forest where he was found. Rousseau's novel *Émile* is referred to by name and in various allusions, as when Waldner's tutor rejoices at his task:

> Dieser Knabe ist mein! Das ist der Urmensch — die Tafel, die noch des Lebens verworrene Runenschrift nicht bekritzelt hat mit den Vorurtheilen von Jahrtausenden! Das ist der Mensch, der neugeborne.[9]

It is noteworthy, however, that Gutzkow tempers this enthusiasm for the innocent primitive by showing that idealism is not enough to guide such an ingenue in a fruitful direction. The hero's education almost founders,

---

[7] For a detailed account of the progress of this earlier foundling in France, see Harlan Lane, *The Wild Boy of Aveyron* (Cambridge, Mass.: Harvard University Press, 1976). François Truffaut gives an idealized version of this story in his film *L'Enfant Sauvage* (1970).

[8] Pies, *Dokumentation*, a) 19, 28, and 35 respectively. b) 36.

[9] Gutzkow, *Söhne Pestalozzis*, 3:277.

and its final product is not a 'new man', but merely another well-adapted though unremarkable citizen.

In the twentieth century, the idea of Kaspar Hauser as a paradigm for the innate goodness of man gained a much wider foothold in literature, as if its evocation could fill a perceived void. It plays a particularly vital part in the works written in the early part of the century, in tune with the 'O Mensch'–posture of the Expressionists. Count Myshkin, the widely admired hero of Dostoevski's recently translated novel *Der Idiot*, had already shown that the archetypal idea of the wise fool or innocent in a corrupt world could fall on very fertile ground at the turn of the century. Both Trakl and Wassermann greatly admired Dostoevski, and may have melded aspects of Myshkin with Kaspar Hauser.[10] At least remnants of the motif can be found throughout our century, even in the latest works.

But the reassertion of the Rousseauistic dictum was not an automatic and uniform process, and shows some intriguing inconsistencies. This should probably not surprise us, given the disintegration of previous metaphysical certitudes, and indicates the tentative nature of the search for solutions in the given climate. One reason for hesitancy is surely the fact that by now the nature of goodness was no longer an unproblematic notion. On the one hand, the concept of man's innate purity obviously contradicts the Christian doctrine of original sin. On the other hand, the stress on Kaspar Hauser's particular kind of virtue, that is to say his gentleness, lack of malice, and empathy with all his fellow creatures, clearly bears a Christian stamp. It also runs counter to the Darwinian and Nietzschean philosophy, which had an important influence on twentieth-century literature, but in which 'goodness' of the type Kaspar Hauser displayed was an irrelevant, or even a detrimental attribute.

The absence of clear-cut, dogmatic beliefs is particularly striking where the exposition of Kaspar Hauser's innocence introduces the concept of pre-existence. It carries the negation of the present to the extreme, inferring that man's corruption begins at birth. Kunze sees the merit of this particular linkage in the fact that it extends our thoughts beyond the narrow limits of man's life-span in both directions, thereby throwing light on "die volle Unsterblichkeit des Menschen," which he feels had been neglected in previous literature.[11] One might also argue that to surround Kaspar Hauser's life on earth with a 'before' and 'after' gives poignancy to the brevity of his — and by implication our own — existence. But at least with regard to Trakl's and Hofmannsthal's works the real questions behind the allusion to the hero's pre-existence seem

---

[10] Many external and thematic parallels can be drawn between Count Myshkin and Kaspar Hauser. With regard to this relationship in Wassermann's novel, see Ruth Richter, *Der Einfluss F. M. Dostojevskijs* [sic] *auf die Werke Jakob Wassermanns* (Ph.D. diss., University of Bonn, 1951).

[11] Wilhelm Kunze, *Mythos, Gestalt und Schicksal von Kaspar Hauser* (Nuremberg: September Verlag, 1931), 11.

to be as follows: Is pure goodness possible in a corrupt world? If so, can it be maintained, or, if not, can it perhaps be regained?

In Trakl's poem the first stanza, with its suggestion of a 'tree of life' and imagery of brightness, patently refers to a paradisiacal era in which man was both innocent and happy. Once the hero is released from this realm, however, his status becomes somewhat ambiguous. Trakl's epithet "der Ungeborne" for the hero at the end of his pilgrimage through life suggests that at least for some human beings, the entry into this world need not mean a loss of purity, and that their previous state somehow continues. On the other hand, the hero's awareness of unfulfilled desires ("Ich will ein Reiter werden"), and the consciousness of loneliness and pain which call forth his "dunkle Klage," seem to indicate that he, like Adam, has eaten from the tree of knowledge. Seen in this way, Kaspar's innocence is not absolute. It only exists because he is singled out by God's favor (the distinction of the poet?), and in contrast to the corruption of those who inhabit the city. But the gentle transfiguration suggested by the last line of the poem, "Silbern sank des Ungebornen Haupt hin," implies that it is possible to regain the innocence and happiness of paradise.

The concept of pre-existence also plays an important part in Hofmannsthal's thinking. For him, it is not so much a synonym for the purity of a biblical paradise, but a term for the state of unconscious grace experienced in childhood and youth, which is not yet inhibited by the sober insights and responsibilities of adult existence. But the bliss of this pre-existence is not entirely unmarred. "Der Anfang ist pure Magie: Praeexistenz" [sic], he wrote in his private notes. But he also saw it as state coupled with danger ("glorreicher aber gefährlicher Zustand"), and talked of the ambivalent feelings ("Bangen und Sehnsucht") which accompanied the decision to leave this condition behind.[12] In his own life, Hofmannsthal, and consequently his critics, have associated this period of dreamlike pre-existence with his early days as a neo-Romantic poet, during which he had been able to draw on his creativity with almost somnambulic confidence, but which he had felt compelled to cast off in favor of what he saw as more serious, world-related pursuits.

It is easy to see how in this frame of mind Kaspar Hauser's cellar and Sigismund's tower could merge for Hofmannsthal into a fitting metaphor for the sheltered environment in which contentment is possible despite deprivations, and innocence could be fostered and preserved. "Anzuknüpfen: jener Begriff der Praeexistenz," Hofmannsthal wrote in his plans for *Der Turm*. But the artifice of such confinement by necessity bodes future unhappiness, so that in Sigismund's eyes "Seele und Qual ohne Ende" assume equal weight.[13]

---

[12] Hugo von Hofmannsthal, "Ad me ipsum," *Aufzeichnungen*, ed. Herbert Steiner (Frankfurt a. M.: S. Fischer, 1959), 238, 213, 214.

[13] Ibid., 242; *Turm* I, 27; *Turm* II, 336.

Once the Kaspar-Hauser-like Sigismund leaves his sphere of pre-existence, the play turns to the question of whether and how man himself can safeguard his innocence in a corrupt world, the very problem which had prompted Rousseau to devise his *Contrat Social* and the educational guidelines of *Émile*. Hofmannsthal's symbolic exploration of the issue does not arrive at such categorical solutions. In *Turm* I, the hero attempts to maintain his innate Kaspar-Hauser-like peaceableness, but demonstrates through his involvement in his country's brutal civil war that adulthood is easily tainted by its necessary tasks. He comforts himself with the thought that the end will justify the means ("Es ist noch die Zeit nicht, daß ihr mein sanftes Gesicht sehet, sondern das kommt später"),[14] but does not live to see that end. By letting his hero die an ignominious death by poison (a telling metaphor for his involuntary corruption), and having him succeeded by the utopian figure of the unarmed *Kinderkönig*, Hofmannsthal manages to uphold the principle of virtue. In *Turm* II, the author tries out a different scenario. Here, the hero appears to succeed much better in preserving his inner nobility in the face of power plays and violence, but only at the price of failing his people, whose entreaties for leadership he answers in only a halfhearted manner. What he wants and achieves is to erect another kind of tower, an inner sanctum into which he can withdraw from elements which are alien to him, and to rejuvenate his innocence. In both versions of the play, Sigismund's peaceful, in the case of *Turm* I even radiant departure from life[15] suggests that in spite of his contamination through knowledge — the equivalent of the biblical Fall — he is, like Trakl's hero, able to recapture the state of grace through death. We know that Hofmannsthal admired Kleist's reflections on the relationship between grace and innocence in *Über das Marionettentheater*, since he included this story in his *Deutsches Lesebuch*.[16] His Sigismund illustrates the idea that letting go of one's concerns might open a back door to paradise even for those who have eaten from the 'tree of knowledge'.

While the notion of pre-existence does not recur elsewhere in explicit terms, several other authors toy with the idea that only complete separation from society, as represented by Kaspar Hauser's incarceration, can safeguard man's inherent goodness and even provide a measure of contentment absent in everyday life. In this vein, Wasser-

---

[14] *Turm* I, 199.

[15] See the words of the *Kinderkönig* at Sigismund's deathbed: "Dein Gesicht! Wer ist dieses Göttliche, das jetzt auf die Schwelle tritt?", *Turm* I, 207. In *Turm* II, 462, the dying prince rejects the hope that his life might be saved, and readily accepts his death: "Mir ist viel zu wohl zum Hoffen."

[16] Heinrich von Kleist, "Über das Marionettentheater," *Werke in einem Band*, ed. Helmut Sembdner (Munich: Hanser, 1966; orig. publ. 1810), 802–7. For Hofmannsthal's reprint, see his *Deutsches Lesebuch*, vol. 1 (Munich: Bremer Presse, 1922), 192–202.

mann, while not glossing over the external misery of Kaspar's imprisonment, also highlights the inner peace experienced there: "Er wünschte nicht, daß etwas anders sein solle, als es war, es schreckte ihn kein Ungefähr, nichts Künftiges lockte ihn, nichts Vergangenes hatte Worte" (22). Ebermayer similarly stresses that the prison walls represent a shelter as much as a deprivation. "Dort im Käfig war alles gut und still," says his hero, "Dunkel und Einsamkeit und viel Frieden ... Nichts hat mir gefehlt" (60). And Hofmannsthal's Sigismund: "Mir ist gut. Hab zu trinken und Brot. Nicht zu warm, nicht zu kalt."[17]

Even some more recent works celebrate the idea of preconsciousness as a state preferable to conscious reality. When Handke's Kaspar is finally able to construct a proper sentence, it is the nostalgic reflection: "Damals, als ich noch weg war, habe ich niemals so viele Schmerzen im Kopf gehabt, und man hat mich nicht so gequält wie jetzt, seit ich hier bin," and he adds a little later: "Ich sah weder etwas noch hörte ich etwas, und es ging mir gut" (29). Herzog's hero shocks his tutor with the observation that for him, his entry into the world of men was a hard fall ("ein harter Sturz").[18] And Härtling's recent poem, "Kaspar Hauser" implies that life in the dungeon had had its compensations, for despite loneliness and darkness, imagination had been able to take flight: "Damals ... / ersann er Blumen / die's nicht gibt" (ll. 6, 7–8).

Evaluated on their own, these equations of happiness with no more than the absence of pain and human contact have a disturbingly modest and pessimistic ring. But we can also regard them as an active rejection of current conditions, and as the indication of a Rousseauistic desire to go back to the very beginning and start afresh. The conviction that man is initially good and innocent — and therefore potentially worth saving — also transpires from the conspicuous emphasis on Kaspar Hauser's childlike qualities. There was of course a realistic basis to this particular focus. After all, Feuerbach had described the foundling as "ein kaum zwei- bis dreijähriges Kind in einem Jünglingskörper,"[19] and although the boy's socialization made significant progress, he continued to be noted for his childlike behavior. But more important is the abstract notion that the child, being still close to its origin, was as yet uncorrupted and could therefore be seen as the ideal of mankind, or, in the terms of Romanticism: "Das Kind ist die schöne Menschheit selbst."[20]

Closely related to this motif, and no doubt a reinforcing factor, is the secret nostalgia most adults tend to harbor for the innocent and carefree

---

[17] *Turm* I, 146; omitted in *Turm* II.

[18] *Jeder für sich*, sound track.

[19] *Verbrechen am Seelenleben*, 123.

[20] Wilhelm Heinrich Wackenroder and Ludwig Tieck, *Phantasien über die Kunst* (reprint, Stuttgart: Reclam, 1973; orig. publ. as *Phantasien über die Kunst für Freunde der Kunst*; Hamburg: Friedrich Perthes, 1799), 44.

days of their childhood.[21] Schaukal, another of Verlaine's *Nachdichter*, once summed up these feelings as follows:

> Es gibt einen einzigen Gegensatz im Leben, der wirklich durch keinen Gedanken, keinen noch so starken Willen zu vernichten ist: den zwischen Kind-sein und nicht-mehr-Kind-sein. Was helfen mir alle Erinnerungen: ich bin nicht mehr Kind. Ich bin nicht mehr das Kind, das ich gewesen bin, ich bin nicht mehr ich. Denn bin das ich, der ich da hinüberträume, ins verlorene Paradies? Nein, das ist ein völlig anderer, ein Vertriebener, Verstoßener, Enterbter. Ich habe vom Baum der Erkenntnis genossen und bin nach außen sehend geworden, also nach innen erblindet.[22]

The futility of such yearning dominates Schaukal's thoughts. But Kaspar Hauser's example demonstrates that the purity of childhood can in fact be maintained even against overwhelming odds. Perhaps through him there was a lesson to be learned, or at least comfort to be gained?

Any or all of these factors may have prompted writers to turn to the Kaspar Hauser material, for much of the literature under discussion endeavors to portray Kaspar Hauser as the quintessential child, that is to say childlike beyond what verisimilitude or the desire to engage the reader's sympathy might require. Writers like Wassermann or Röttger could stress these qualities by accumulating incidents in the foundling's life which demonstrate the boy's simplicity of heart, such as the conviction that his toy horses could feel hunger and pain. Works of narrower scope rely on the telling detail, such as Kaspar's trusting eyes mentioned already by Verlaine and most of his *Nachdichter*, or the suggestion of playfulness in Arp's and Härtling's poems. Klaus Mann, less subtle, uses a simile: his hero is "strahlend rein, wie Kinder sind, und lächelnd."[23] Handke underlines the childlike effect of his figure by way of explicit make-up instructions: "Das Maskengesicht ist rund, weil auf runden und breiten Gesichtern der Ausdruck der Verwunderung theatralischer ist. Kaspar muß nicht groß sein.... Er ist die verkörperte Verwunderung" (12).

Handke's directions notwithstanding, the emphasis on Kaspar Hauser's childlike features seems to diminish in the more recent literature, together with the earlier mentioned accentuation of his physical beauty. One explanation for this development may of course be that to a large extent authors can by now take the public's familiarity

---

[21] A. F. Bance makes some pertinent remarks in this regard, linking the "longing for pre-conceptional life" to the modern psychological concept of "childhood amnesia"; see "The Kaspar Hauser Legend and its Literary Survival," 204.

[22] Richard von Schaukal, *Frühling eines Lebens* (Vienna: Herold, 1949), 42–43.

[23] Klaus Mann "Kaspar-Hauser-Legenden," *Vor dem Leben* (Hamburg: Enoch, 1925), 193. Where appropriate, further references to this work will be given after quotations in the text.

with the figure for granted, so that some of the connotations need no longer be expressly evoked. It is noteworthy, however, that even writers who deliberately depart from the conventional positive picture of Kaspar's looks — such as Werner Herzog — invest their hero with a natural dignity and sagacity which make it clear that the belief in the noble savage has in itself not been abandoned.

Several authors even manifest an incipient hope for the future by crediting Kaspar Hauser's childlike innocence with a positive, cleansing effect on those around him. "Du wirst mich reinmachen von meinem elenden Leben, denn du bist rein wie kein anderer auf dieser Erde" (45), says Ebermayer's villain, Stanhope. In Wassermann's novel, Kaspar's obvious virtue calls forth such remorse in the profligate lord that he ends his misspent life by suicide. Martens and Röttger do not go as far, but they, too, show through Stanhope's hesitation to carry out his plans that Kaspar's innocence burdens his conscience. Kaspar Hauser's trusting look alone can inspire mortification, as in Wassermann's scene where 'Frau Behold', one of the hero's tormentors, falsely accuses the boy of lying: "'Ei du Tropf! ... schau mich einmal aufrichtig an!' Er schaute sie an. Da mußte sie die Augen senken" (137). Klaus Mann uses a similar idea in his hero's encounter with the prostitute: "... sie lachte frech, so daß ihr Gesicht wie eine bunte verzerrte Maske wurde. Er sah zu ihr auf, und da ihre Augen sich trafen, wurde auch ihr Blick ernst" (169–70). The further development of these works shows that nothing of lasting value results from these encounters. Yet in the eyes of the authors, the potential for individual improvement evidently exists, and could come to better fruition under different circumstances.

Apart from the portrayal of Kaspar Hauser himself as a paradigm of man's as yet unsullied nature, the spectrum of his social encounters can also reveal the Rousseauistic tenet that man's corruption is proportional to the degree of his sophistication. At one end of this scale, Wassermann's and Röttger's novels illustrate through Kaspar's interaction with the world around him that women, who may still possess primordial instincts ("untergründiges Weibswissen," in Röttger's words [242]), and servants, who presumably have not had a chance to become spoiled and *verbildet*, are more attuned to the boy's problems than those who consider themselves to be pillars of society. Where the author allows the hero to find a true friend, as in the case of Wassermann's young batman Schildknecht and Ebermayer's Peter, it is worth noting that these figures' simplicity of heart matches the simplicity of their background and learning. Sigismund's loyal keeper Anton in *Der Turm*, and the child-narrator of Reinhard Mey's ballad who has befriended Kaspar Hauser despite adult prejudices, also belong into this category. In Hofmannsthal's drama, we see that Sigismund feels a special affinity with the lowliest of his subjects, who appear before him in symbolic nakedness.

"Das sind unverzierte Menschen," he says, "Wir wollen im Freien miteinander wohnen, die in Häusern wohnen gefallen mir nicht."[24]

Almost in passing, Herzog's film introduces a particularly apt symbol of the endangered noble savage. One of Kaspar's fellow exhibits at the circus is Hombrecito, the very last of a primitive tribe and himself at great risk "vom bösen Atem der Menschen." In spite of his own trials, he continues to play his flute in the belief that this might avert the doom of mankind. Gradations in the proclivity towards simplicity are also clearly apparent in this work. The children who first take the unmannered boy under their wing intuitively grasp his problems. The jailer and his wife, very simple people, still show a natural patience and charity. But already Kaspar's guardian, altruistic as he may be, has expectations his protégé cannot fulfil, and cannot hide his disappointment. His most telling phrase is: "Kaspar, das versteh' ich nicht!". The inverse scale continues with the men of learning, who feel compelled to display their artificial superiority, and culminates in the caricature of the English lord.

It is interesting that of all people Herzog chose this last figure, the very antithesis to the 'noble savage', to seemingly mock the traditional Rousseauistic view. At an elegant soirée, the foppish lord exhibits Kaspar with the words: "Quite the noble savage!" Then, having tired of his protégé, he tells his enraptured listeners about the charms of mingling with the "einfache Landbevölkerung" in Greece (the ideal country of Romanticism), where, in peasant garb, he had ridden a donkey. Considering the tainted source of such comments, these need of course not devaluate a genuine admiration for simplicity. But the episode nevertheless reveals that in our time Rousseau's ideas could no longer be simply resurrected without reflection and qualifications. The modern reservation against a too naive Rousseauistic stance is also evident in another scene which Herzog had originally planned to include in his film. It was to show tutor Daumer and the pastor, Fuhrmann, rhapsodizing about the beauty of God's countryside, while the farmhand they address speaks only of his hard work, and tries "sich seine Anstrengung von seiner Rückenlast nicht anmerken zu lassen" (180).

Despite the plethora of evidence for a basic agreement with the Rousseauistic outlook, it would be a misconception to regard this as a whole-hearted neo-Romantic regression. One can discern a general awareness that the mere approval of the 'noble savage' is no solution for the problems of the modern age. But at least the example of Kaspar Hauser's continued good nature in the face of the most trying circumstances gave reason for hope that there might be after all some way of preventing or even reversing the process of corruption.

[24] *Turm* II, 450.

II. The Role of Nature

For the correlative to the Rousseauistic ideal of the 'noble savage', the latter's intimate bond with Nature, the historical material offered scantier justification. It is true that some of Kaspar Hauser's contemporaries were initially all too ready to make that connection. Only four days after the boy's appearance, when he was still quite unable to verbalize his experiences, the examining physician jumped to the conclusion: "Er ist wie ein halbwilder Mensch in Wäldern erzogen worden." The mayor of Nuremberg rhapsodized about "die höchste Unschuld der Natur."[25] Acute sensory abilities, an apparent liking for animals and horseback riding, and a delight in celestial phenomena all seemed to speak for an organic connection with Nature. But of course prolonged confinement in a dark cell is a singularly unsuitable way of establishing any rapport with the natural world. Therefore, the above judgments have to be balanced by other, contrary reports that Kaspar actually felt uneasy out of doors, and that he hated the color green and the smell of flowers, which excluded much of what Nature had to offer. Although much was made of the boy's compassion for captive creatures, and of his solicitude for even the smallest insect, in reality he could at first not even distinguish between major animal species, and expected them all to behave like human beings.

These reservations notwithstanding, much of the twentieth-century Kaspar Hauser literature found in the material what it wanted to find. Directly or indirectly, many works reflect the conviction, or at least the hope, that Nature represents a sane and wholesome counterpole to the subversive forces of the technological age. Accordingly, they tend to align the hero with this 'better' world, and elaborate on the relationship.

The private stance of several of the writers under discussion makes it clear that in the dichotomy between Nature and the so-called forces of progress they stood firmly on the side of the former. Wassermann expressed his own preference by retreating from the city to an isolated farm in the countryside, and, according to Sell, he delineated the merit of his fictional characters "durch ihre Einstellung zur Natur."[26] Trakl, whose private love of Nature has been substantiated by Reinhold Grimm,[27] was at one point so disenchanted with civilization that he contemplated moving to the jungles of Borneo. Lacking Wassermann's kind of resources for a country refuge, he had to content himself with

---

[25] Cited in Pies, *Dokumentation*, 24, 28.

[26] Anneliese Sell, *Das metaphysisch-realistische Weltbild Jakob Wassermanns* (Bern: Paul Haupt, 1932), 60.

[27] See "Die Sonne: Bemerkungen zu einem Motiv Georg Trakls," *Deutsche Vierteljahrsschrift für Literaturwissenschaft und Geistesgeschichte* 35 (1961): 235.

invectives against the cities he knew: Salzburg became for him a
"verfluchte" and "vermorschte Stadt," Vienna "diese Dreckstadt,"
Innsbruck, he felt sure, would always repel him.[28] Arp was more
specific in his contempt: "Die Neuzeit mit ihrer Wissenschaft, ihrer
Technik hat den Menschen größenwahnsinnig gemacht," he wrote, "Die
schauerliche Verwirrung unserer Zeit ist die Folge dieser Überschätzung
der Vernunft."[29] He tried to react in a constructive way by adopting
spontaneity, a quality he regarded as Nature's main creative principle,
as his own artistic guideline, in his poetry as well as in his painting and
plastic art.

The personal views of contemporary authors are as yet less well
documented, but various signposts indicate that they, too, are firmly on
Nature's side, and seek solutions in its realm. Handke's essays contain
some revealing comments in that regard. For example, he defends the
use of Nature in the literature of the Third Reich, which is commonly
denounced as cheap escapism, as a necessary coping device: "Und daß
so oft die Natur beschworen wird ... in der allein man noch aufatmen
kann, ist damals lebensnotwendig gewesen. (Wie dummdreist die
Attitüde, Naturschilderungen pauschal als vergangene literarische
Methode abzutun!)"[30] His play *Über die Dörfer* (1981) adopts a
decidedly Rousseauistic stance, by glorifying Nature and, in its final
scene, paying tribute to a child-savior reminiscent of Hofmannsthal's
Kinderkönig. Vesper demonstrates his preference by choosing a small
Hessian village as his domicile, and Herzog through his by now
notorious penchant for confronting Nature in the untamed regions of
Africa, South America, and Australia.

Given their partiality, many of the authors who saw in Kaspar Hauser
a symbol for the original goodness of mankind tried to resurrect the
myth of the foundling as a 'child of Nature', or at least tested the idea to
see whether it could still pass muster. Inevitably, the concretization of
the motif took a variety of forms.

At the simplest level, the hero is directly equated with the animal
world. In some cases, the connotations are entirely positive. Klara
Hofer's reference to Kaspar Hauser as "Taube sonder Gallen" (5), for
example, and the repeated appearance of a white swan in Herzog's film,
make use of traditional symbols of purity to evoke the idea of Kaspar's
natural innocence.

On occasion, the author's preference for Nature can take on rather
quaint forms. Wassermann, for instance, at one point compares Kaspar

---

[28] Citations in order of reference: a) *Nachlaß und Biographie*, vol. 3 of *Gesammelte
Werke*, ed. Wolfgang Schneditz (Salzburg: Otto Müller, 1949), 18; and *Die Dichtungen*
1:503; b) *Nachlaß* 3:48; c) Ibid., 27–28.

[29] *Unsern täglichen Traum*, 80.

[30] Peter Handke, "Jemand anderer: Hermann Lenz," *Als das Wünschen noch geholfen
hat* (Frankfurt a. M.: Suhrkamp, 1974), 95.

to an animal "das sich nur mit ein paar schüchternen Sprüngen ans Licht getraut, und, während es über den Acker hüpft, possierlich mit Schwanz und Ohren wackelt, um seine Feinde zu ergötzen, dabei aber ängstlich nach allen Seiten spitzt, um bald wieder ins erste beste Loch zu kriechen" (146). With similar whimsicality, Hofer likens the foundling to a "Hündchen, das bald den einen, bald den anderen durch freundliches Bitten und seine armen kleinen Künste anfleht, sich seiner zu erbarmen" (5). Röttger visualizes Kaspar as a trapped mouse, and his hero recalls his former self as "so a sonderbars Viecherl" (35, 64).

In contrast to the despondency suggested by these timid creatures, Hofmannsthal's many animal metaphors show his Sigismund as a wild animal, or even a predator, implying that the victim is potentially still able to defend himself. "Mein Haar ist kurz und sträubt sich. Ich zeige meine Tatzen," the hero asserts, or he threatens that he will deal with his enemies "wie der Sperber im Hühnerhof."[31] Klaus Mann aligns his hero with the animal world in a more neutral manner: "[Sein] Haar [war] unberührt wie eines Tieres Mähne," we hear of Kaspar, or: "Wenn er einen Menschen ansah, war dem, als würde er von einem seltsamen Körper berührt, vom weichen Felle vielleicht eines fremdländischen Tieres" (169, 170).

One particularly popular way of investing the link between man and Nature with positive overtones was to build on Feuerbach's report that the foundling had been deeply touched by the sight of a starry sky. Wassermann's novel forms the prelude in this respect, devoting considerable space to this episode. Kaspar's instinctive reaction to the stars is "leidenschaftliche[s] Entzücken" and "ein unbeschreiblich seliges Lächeln," which give way to "langes, nicht zu stillendes Weinen" (50), thus demonstrating not only the hero's capacity for childlike wonder, but also his extraordinary receptiveness to the grandeur of Nature. Hofmannsthal uses the episode in a very similar vein. Still in his primitive state, Sigismund has the insight: "Licht ist gut. Geht herein, macht's Blut rein. Sterne sind ein solches Licht. In mir drin ist ein Stern. Meine Seele ist heilig."[32] Later, after he has entered the world, he draws courage from his early experience of the stars, and from what Julian had taught him about their purifying power:

Fasse ganz, was du selber in mich gelegt hast, wenn du mich hinauftrugest an deiner Brust unter die Sterne, die aufziehen überm Turm — denn so hast du mich erhöht, um meine Seele heil zu erhalten vor der Starrnis der Verzweiflung. Da ich gewaltiger Mensch eins bin mit den Sternen, so lehrtest du mich, darum warten sie wissend auf mein Tun.[33]

---

[31] a) *Turm* I, 124; *Turm* II, 405. b) *Turm* I, 125–26, *Turm* II, 407.

[32] *Turm* I, 27; *Turm* II, 336.

[33] Ibid., *Turm* I, 139; omitted in *Turm* II.

Röttger expands the motif to encompass Kaspar Hauser's later disillusionment. Remembering how his tutor had first shown him the stars, and how he had marvelled at their beauty, Kaspar writes in his diary:

> Jetzt frag' ich mich, was den Menschen die Sterne angehn, weil ich sie allesamt nicht hinaufschaun seh. Was gehn mich die Sterne an? Mir wird so einsam ums Herz, wenn ich hinschau, und ich fang' an zu weinen. (64)

The encounter with the star-studded sky has even made its way into some of the more recent literature. Herzog's film script shows that he had meant to include an episode, entitled "Freies Feld, Nacht," which is in close agreement with Feuerbach's account.[34] Dieter Forte's play resurrects the historical incident second-hand, by letting the mourners regale each other with what they remember about the deceased.

In other instances, the picture of Kaspar's relationship with the stars transcends the original model. Trakl's hero has his personal star for companionship and comfort ("Nachts blieb er mit seinem Stern allein;" l. 17). Arp's figure could decipher "die monogramme in den sternen" (l. 26), and has possibly turned into a star himself ("warum bist du ein stern geworden"; l. 13). Similarly, the first version of Hofmannsthal's *Turm* places Sigismund's significance on a higher plane, "außer [der Zeit], wie ein Sternbild" (208). Kunze, in his radio play, reverses that direction when he lets his Kaspar Hauser sing of his origin: "Von den Sternen stieg ich nieder, / in den Sternen wohnt das Glück."[35]

The modern reader may well find this surfeit of stars dangerously close to the romantic platitudes we meet with in countless popular songs. But however well-worn this particular motif has become, it is appropriate to bear in mind to what great extent twentieth-century science has demystified the stars. Stubborn insistence upon their mysterious power and their interrelationship with man therefore surely constitutes a sign of resistance to the prevalent forces of our time.

But Kaspar Hauser can also illustrate the brotherhood between the unspoiled individual and Nature on a more down-to-earth level. Wassermann gives an especially vivid example in the following idyllic scene, in which the tutor encounters his young ward in the garden:

> Es gab eine Stunde, wo Daumer eines paradiesischen Bildes gewahr wurde: ... Schwalben ziehen ihre Zickzackkreise um ihn, Tauben picken vor seinen Füßen, ein Schmetterling ruht auf seiner Schulter, die Hauskatze schnurrt an seinem Arm. In ihm ist die Menschheit frei von Sünde, sagte sich Daumer.... (55)

---

[34] *Drehbücher*, II, 185.

[35] Wilhelm Kunze, "Das Kaspar Hauser Hörspiel," (unpubl. manuscript [1930s], City Archives, Ansbach, Germany), 6.

At a later point in the novel, Nature's affection for the foundling is reciprocated. In a rare moment of happiness, Kaspar feels the urge "sich ins Gras zu werfen und die Arme in die Erde zu wühlen, für die er plötzlich Dankbarkeit empfand" (387).

Many other examples illustrate through the foundling's example that the union between man and Nature is possible and beneficial. Arp's hero frolics with wind, water, and fire; Ebermayer's dreams of a homecoming "unter schweren Bäumen" where "alles duftet und blinkt im Tau" (30),[36] and Klaus Mann's wandering child finds comfort in the shadows of the forest. In a congenial relationship with Nature, even the raindrops on the window panes communicate: "Wann die Regentropfen ans Fenster klopfen, das ist schön.... Das ist eine Sprache, die i versteh" (64), says Röttger's hero. The mere experience of the seasons can give consolation. Trakl hints at this in his line: "Frühling und Sommer und schön der Herbst / Des Gerechten" (ll. 14-15). In more recent times, Reinhard Mey's ballad grants his Kaspar a similar peaceful interlude before his violent death:

> Kaspar und ich wir pflügten zu zweit
> bald war alles bestellt.
> Wir hegten und pflegten jeden Keim,
> brachten im Herbst die Ernte ein.[37]

Demonstrations of Kaspar Hauser's ability to attract or control animals also express the desire for harmony with Nature. So does the literary perpetuation of the rumor of Kaspar's extraordinary horsemanship, although in this case we have seen above that it has important additional functions. We further remember that Trakl's hero is followed by "Busch und Tier" (l. 11), that Wassermann's hero pacifies a rabid dog, and that Arp's Kaspar had been able to lure the deer and calm the horses.

In the same context, Wassermann and, in his wake, Hofmannsthal, convert the historical figure's physiological inability to tolerate meat into a trait denoting an innate empathy with all of Nature's creatures. Wassermann's protagonist witnesses "wie der Metzgerbursche das rohe und noch blutige Fleisch aus dem Korb nahm und auf die Anrichte legte. Eine unendliche Wehmut malte sich in Caspars Zügen, er wich zurück, zitterte und war keines Lautes fähig, dann floh er mit bedrängten Schritten" (135). The foundling's continued preference for bread and water logically fits into this picture. Hofmannsthal's Sigismund, once he has shed the characteristics of Calderón's prototype (in which state he used to kill the vermin around him to pass the time) and assumed those of Kaspar Hauser, is equally revolted by the idea of eating the flesh of his

---

[36] *Kaspar Hauser*, 30.

[37] "Kaspar," in *Ankomme Freitag, den 13.*, LP recording (Leinfelden: Intercord, 1968).

fellow creatures. He remembers with anguish how he once had to watch the slaughtering of a pig: "Weißt du noch das Schwein, das der Vater geschlachtet hat, und es schrie so stark und ich schrie mit — und wie ich dann kein Fleisch hab anrühren können, und hättet ihr mir mit Gewalt die Zähn aufgebrochen."[38] Some of the more recent authors also refer to Kaspar Hauser's empathy with the animal world. Forte lets his tutor Daumer recall Kaspar's "Abneigung gegen alles, was einem Menschen oder Tier nur den leisesten Schmerz verursachen könnte."[39] Herzog introduces the idea visually. On several occasions, his hero tries to befriend the birds he encounters, and stares sadly at a caged bear.

As the above selection of examples shows, the desire to anchor Kaspar Hauser in a harmonious relationship with Nature manifests itself throughout the twentieth century. Of course some works set themselves specific thematic tasks which leave little room for the inclusion of Rousseauistic motifs. Handke's *Kaspar* is a case in point. Yet even in this parable of linguistic indoctrination it is possible to introduce Nature as an indirect motif. According to a review by Botho Strauß, Günther Bloch, the producer of the première in Oberhausen, succeeded in inserting a hint of Kaspar's original concordance with Nature: Kaspar is initially presented as "ein vertierter Waldmensch," and his bucolic origin is suggested by the sound of twittering birds in the unseen region behind the curtain from which he appears.[40] Even where Kaspar Hauser's function in a particular work is too marginal to allow any elaboration on Rousseauistic tenets, the motif may well appear in another guise. In Härtling's novel *Hubert; oder, Die Rückkehr nach Casablanca*, for instance, the hero's move to a garden house in an allotment is a very realistic ingredient, given the novel's postwar background with its attendant housing shortage. But the move may also symbolize the wish to retreat into Nature, as a counterpart to the novel's more dominant motif of escape into the fictitious realm of film.

Yet all is not well in the twentieth-century garden of Eden. There are various indications that although authors use Kaspar Hauser to conjure up the ideal of Nature as a haven for the alienated outsider, they find the wholehearted belief in this ideal increasingly difficult. Thus negative elements may creep in to undermine what at first glance seems to be an unreserved celebration of the natural universe. For instance, Lewandowski, who derives most of his imagery from Nature, occasionally exposes the latter's vulnerability, as when his Kaspar Hauser describes himself as "ein südlicher Vogel, den ein unverständiger Grönländer am

---

[38] *Turm* I, 87; *Turm* II, shortened version, 375.

[39] Dieter Forte, *Kaspar Hausers Tod: Ein Theaterstück* (Frankfurt a. M.: S. Fischer, 1979), 8. Where appropriate, further references to this play will be given after quotations in the text.

[40] Botho Strauß, "Anläßlich Kaspar," *Theater heute*, Sonderheft (1968): 68.

Nordpol gefangen hält," or "ein Spinngewebe, von einer kranken Spinne im tosenden Wasserfall ausgespannt."[41]

Hofmannsthal's Sigismund demonstrates, like Kaspar Hauser, that inborn nobility can co-exist with an animal-like existence, but at the same time he gives another, more sinister perspective of Nature and foreshadows his own capacity for cruelty when he asserts: "Grausig ist das Tier. Es frißt die eigenen Jungen, noch feucht aus dem Mutterleib.... Und doch ist es unschuldig."[42]

The evidence of such ambiguity is even stronger in the more recent literature. Härtling's poems "kasper" and "nachricht von kasper," for example, still suggest that the childlike spirit has power over the forces of Nature. But as discussed above, the element of joyful mischievousness, which had still imbued Arp's nature sprite if only as a memory and inspiration, is notably muted in Härtling's works, since in the first poem Kaspar is seen as captive, and, in the second, as irretrievably departed. In the domain of Höllerer's 'Gaspard', Nature has obviously suffered defeat, despite the poetic spirit's sentry duty. The stream is restrained by concrete and stone: ("Fische erfallen im / Eckigen Strom"), the water rears against the bridge pier with its statues ("Wo das Pferdchen starr / Den Strom aufbäumt"), and insects flutter "laternengefangen."[43]

The dichotomy between wish and reality is probably most palpable in Herzog's *Jeder für sich und Gott gegen Alle*, as the medium of film can make it visible in the true sense of the word. Herzog had previously dealt with the contrast and collision between Nature and civilization, most notably in *Fata Morgana* (1971), *Land des Schweigens und der Dunkelheit* (1971), and *Aguirre, der Zorn Gottes* (1972). Therefore, when in the opening scene of *Jeder für sich* the camera lingers on views of a calm lake and greenery, we may see these as symbols for the wholesomeness of Nature. But there are people intruding into this bucolic scene: a woman is doing her laundry in the lake, and a boat traverses the water. And the green vistas in the following pictures are not wild meadows, but cultivated fields. Clearly, man is exploiting Nature, beautiful as it may appear. A superimposed caption also warns us that tranquil appearances may be deceptive. We read: "Hören Sie denn nicht das entsetzliche Schreien ringsum, das man gewöhnlich Stille nennt?", an allusion to Georg Büchner's Lenz, another lonely wanderer who could not cope with the misery of creation.[44] A dual perspective

---

[41] Herbert Lewandowski, *Das Tagebuch Kaspar Hausers* (Utrecht: Pfeil, 1928), 81.

[42] *Turm* I, 93; omitted in *Turm* II.

[43] Walter Höllerer, "Gaspard," in *Mein Gedicht ist mein Messer: Lyriker zu ihren Gedichten*, ed. Hans Bender (Munich: Paul List, 1961), 100–101, ll. 18–19; 7–8; 35.

[44] Büchner's original wording reads: "Hören Sie denn nichts, hören Sie denn nicht die entsetzliche Stimme, die um den ganzen Horizont schreit und die man gewöhnlich Stille heißt?", *Werke und Briefe*, ed. Fritz Bergemann (Wiesbaden: Insel Verlag, 1953), 107.

also pervades the scene in which Kaspar and his warder, on their way to the city, stop for a rest on a mountaintop. Again, we see a sweeping view of the countryside, the sky is blue, and birds sing in the background. But the foundling is not only excluded from human company — here visualized by the turned back of his sinister guard — but also has no part in the natural beauty around him: he lies face-down on the ground, with contorted features.

When Kaspar arrives in the city, and stands alone in the market place, the viewer's attention is drawn to a tethered animal in the background, running in circles and getting itself into an increasing entanglement, a visual metaphor for the foundling's predicament. The caged bird, the captive bear, and the circus camel forced to walk on its knees also illustrate the subjugation of Nature's creatures. In Herzog's script (though not in the film itself), Kaspar puts the perception that all is not well with Nature into words. "Da war der Wald kranck [sic]" (144), he remembers an impression from his journey to the city; and, looking at the caged circus bear, he comments: "Der Bär ist krank" (146). In a later episode in the teacher's garden, Kaspar is not surrounded by friendly animals, as Wassermann had portrayed him. Instead, he complains that the watercress with which he had sown his name, a symbolic representation of the desired union with Nature, has been trampled by people. Meanwhile, in the background of this scene, a stork is devouring a live frog. It seems that neither man nor Nature can be trusted; in both, the stronger will have their way.

Vesper's novel *Nördlich der Liebe* also makes the endangerment of Nature a dominant motif. There are repeated descriptions of how highways and cities encroach upon the countryside, and of the disintegration of village life. A better past is implied in nostalgic laments, such as: "Die Störche sind weggeblieben, und wann siehst du noch Reiher, die früher beinahe auf jeder Eiche saßen.... Der Wald abgeholzt, die Feldwege unter Teer verschwunden, die Obstbäume verkommen oder umgemacht, das Land zersiedelt, besprüht, gespritzt, überdüngt, vergiftet" (81). Sinister incidents reveal that even what seems to remain of the peace of Arcady is just an illusion. A farmer, ploughing his field, comes across a human foot. The delight of finding a nest of baby hedgehogs is marred by the realization that they are in fact dead.

But perhaps the most telling indications that the trust in Nature's benevolence is on shaky ground are episodes which show how Kaspar Hauser seeks protection from Nature, but learns that it is a futile hope. Evidence of this motif can already be found in Wassermann's work. After depicting a particular unpleasant encounter between Kaspar and his tormentor, teacher Quandt, Wassermann writes:

Er wünschte sich das Angesicht einer Blume, um keinen Blick eines Menschenauges erwidern zu müssen. Oder er wünschte wenigstens sich im Schoß einer Blume bergen zu können. (319)

The immediate continuation of the conflict reveals the fruitlessness of this desire. That the beleaguered boy's prayers to the oak-tree and the sun also go unanswered,[45] lies of course in the nature of the historical model, which Wassermann followed at least in the overall development of his novel. However, it is significant that not even temporary happiness is granted.

Hofmannsthal's Sigismund as well expects to find salvation in Nature. "Ich spüre ein weites offenes Land," he says, "Es riecht nach Erde und Salz. Dort werde ich hingehen."[46] He does not know at this point that the events which will lead to his defeat are just about to begin. The end of *Turm* I transfers all hope for the future from Sigismund to the *Kinderkönig* and his young companions. With their bare feet and dowsing-rods, they still maintain an atavistic contact with Nature. "Wir sind Heilkräuter selber. Wir sind im Gebirge groß geworden," they promise.[47] But we have to keep in mind that the author lost faith in this answer to the problems of his time. With the ending of *Turm* II, he opted for a more modest, self-centered solution.

As to the more recent works, Herzog once again translates the idea of Nature's inability to give sanctuary into visual terms. When Kaspar and his fellow sufferers attempt to flee from the circus, across the meadow and into the orchard, the trees cannot hide them, and they are easily retrieved by their pursuers. A related image occurs in Vesper's novel, in one of the stories from bygone days meant to illustrate the similarities between past and present. We hear of a young teacher who moves to the country, filled with Rousseauistic ideals, and hoping to share them with the village children. Soon disillusioned in this endeavor, he retreats into the forests, that is to say into an even more 'natural' environment. But society flushes him out wherever he goes. He turns into a pitiful vagabond and, when finally cornered, into an axe-murderer, thus gaining a drastic though futile revenge.

If a very recent work by Wolfgang Wenger is a valid indication, the disillusionment about what Nature can do for man has begun to affect the foundling's behavior. In the sketch "magie der sprache," Wenger's Kaspar Hauser reacts with indifference, or even hostility. He squashes the beetle that runs up his leg, is scared at the sight of a frog, aimlessly tears up fern, and hides his face from the sun.[48]

On the whole, however, we can infer from this representative selection of motifs that Rousseau's antithesis between Nature and civilization is still very much alive, and plays an important part in the

---

[45] See *Caspar Hauser*, 255, 273.

[46] *Turm* I, 166; *Turm* II, 449.

[47] *Turm* I, 204.

[48] See Wolfgang Wenger, "magie der sprache," *weit weg in den filmen* (Salzburg, Vienna: Residenz Verlag, 1990), 99.

Kaspar Hauser literature of our century. But it would appear that while in principle most writers are in accord with Rousseau's thinking, they often distance themselves from a simplistic revival of nineteenth-century ideas. Again and again, attempts are made to establish Nature as a potential ally of modern man, as symbolized by the figure of Kaspar Hauser. But these efforts are only partially successful, and are usually undermined by ambiguities and skepticism. Increasingly, the idea of Nature as a refuge is recognized as wishful thinking, a possibility wistfully considered and then dismissed.

5

The Attempt to Go 'Beyond':
Aspects of Religion

I. Kaspar Hauser as Redeemer Figure

THE DELIBERATE REGRESSION OBSERVED in the attempted revival of Rousseauistic tenets often went hand in hand with a search for
solutions in the irrational sphere, mainly in the sphere of religion. For
like the common nostalgia for a vanished simplicity and its concomitant
desire for refuge in Nature, the idea of a supernatural level of existence
can constitute a rejection of pragmatic materialism, and had been a
notable component of the Romantic stance in the previous century. Now
this potential expedient to escape the perceived predicament of modern
man assumed a renewed appeal. But just as the feasibility of the simple
life and of man's closeness to Nature was by now viewed with some
doubt and pessimism, the resurrection of spiritual values was also no
longer an easy or straightforward task. Since by the twentieth century
traditional religious values had been greatly eroded and dissipated,
indeed more often than not openly repudiated as an outmoded obstacle
to social and material progress, it was now almost as much of an
innovation to return to conventional forms of religion as to invent a new
mythology. So it is not surprising that the search for the way beyond is,
on the whole, also very tentative, and takes on a variety of forms, with
different degrees of emphasis and conviction.

The fact that writers came from a variety of denominational back-
grounds no doubt accentuated this situation. Wassermann, for instance,
had renounced his Jewish faith because he found its strictures too
oppressive. Judging by the overall tenor of his fiction and especially his
essayistic writing, his subsequent belief cannot be pinned down to any
particular confession. It is perhaps best summarized by the self-descrip-
tion he attributes to the mayor of Nuremberg, Herr Binder, in his novel
about Kaspar Hauser: "Wenn ich selbst auch nicht kirchlich-fromm
gesinnt bin, ... so ist mir doch die modische Freigeisterei von Herzen
zuwider," since it could only lead to "ein ehrfurchtsloses Weltwesen"
(77). Trakl came from a mixed, i.e. Catholic-Protestant parentage and
education, which according to some critics may explain the ambivalence

and tension he exhibited in religious matters.[1] For Hofmannsthal, his Catholicism was not a prominent topic of discussion, neither in his extensive correspondence nor, it would appear, in his conversations with friends. Fiechtner accounts for this paucity of private evidence with the social conventions of that time: "Über sein Verhältnis zur Religion hat Hofmannsthal mit keinem seiner Freunde gesprochen. Das war damals, im Unterschied zu heute, kein Konversationsthema."[2] A more likely reason for the author's reticence is that in this very private domain he suffered from uncertainties which he preferred to test in the literary domain rather than in public pronouncements. Certainly, religious imagery permeates his work, and the protagonist of his Chandos-letter — usually seen as Hofmannsthal's alter ego — early on served as the mouthpiece for the author's own ambivalence, combining the confession of a personal loss of faith with an undeniable desire to regain what had been lost:

> Mir haben sich die Geheimnisse des Glaubens zu einer erhabenen Allegorie verdichtet, die über den Feldern meines Lebens steht wie ein leuchtender Regenbogen, in einer stetigen Ferne, immer bereit, zurückzuweichen, wenn ich mir einfallen ließe, hinzueilen und mich in den Saum seines Mantels zu hüllen.[3]

This desire to touch the elusive rainbow of faith remained with Hofmannsthal; it is still clearly discernible in the final versions of *Der Turm*.

Klaus Mann represents yet another variant in the kaleidoscope of creeds. At the tender age of twelve, he was a precocious atheist. But just prior to writing his "Legenden," under the influence of works by Angelus Silesius, Jakob Böhme, and Novalis, he began to long for their kind of spontaneous, personal belief, a religion without dogma.

As for postwar generations of writers, their faith was obviously even more sorely tested by historical events than that of their predecessors. Most show an even greater reluctance to discuss their private faith in public than Hofmannsthal once did, so that it is difficult to ascertain where they stand in religious matters. In their works, too, overt avowals of God or Christ are rare, in any case much rarer than they used to be in the literature of the earlier part of the century. Nevertheless, even ostensibly secular works sometimes contain Christian allusions, or at

---

[1] See e.g. Helga Cierpka, "Interpretationstypen der Trakl-Literatur: Eine kritische Betrachtung der wissenschaftlichen Arbeiten über das Werk Georg Trakls" (Ph.D. diss., Freie Universität Berlin, 1963), 52; also Hans Szklenar, "Georg Trakl: Ein biographischer Abriß," *Text und Kritik* 4/4a (1973): 43.

[2] Helmut A. Fiechtner, "Nachwort," in *Hugo von Hofmannsthal: Die Gestalt des Dichters im Spiegel der Freunde*, ed. Helmut A. Fiechtner (Vienna: Humboldt, 1949), 369.

[3] Hugo von Hofmannsthal, "Ein Brief," *Prosa*, vol. 2 of *Gesammelte Werke in Einzelbänden*, ed. Herbert Steiner (Frankfurt a. M.: S. Fischer, 1951), 12.

least passages which speak of the dissatisfaction with mundane reality, and indirectly suggest a renewed search for a higher plane of existence. It is perhaps well to remember at this point that one of the earliest stimuli for the twentieth-century Kaspar Hauser literature, Verlaine's "Gaspard Hauser chante," already incorporated a distinctly religious element. The cryptic supplication: "Priez pour le pauvre Gaspard," is particularly memorable by virtue of being the final statement of the poem. It could not but leave its imprint on those writers inspired by this work, prompting not only the formal inclusion of this ingredient in all of the German *Nachdichtungen* of Verlaine's poem, but also further reflections on the religious implications of Kaspar Hauser's situation.

Those authors who took the trouble to research the original material on Kaspar Hauser could, of course, find an abundance of references to religion, since an intensive theological indoctrination formed an important part of the contemporary efforts to integrate the foundling into society. But like most other aspects of his story, the reaction of the historical Kaspar Hauser to this process of edification shows a dichotomy which, in the context of religion, allows for both orthodox and un-orthodox literary possibilities. Initially, the religious conventions which those around him could take for granted were totally alien to the foundling. Having brought with him from his confinement, as Feuerbach puts it, "keine Idee, keine Ahnung von Gott, keinen Schatten eines Glaubens an irgend ein höheres, unsichtbares Dasein,"[4] the youth at first responded with skepticism to what he was being taught about God. He doubted that one single creator could be responsible for all the miracles of Nature. When he got used to that idea, and began to understand his environment better, he had trouble reconciling God's reputed goodness and wisdom with the evident evil and suffering in this world, an attitude with obvious appeal to the disillusionment of twentieth-century thinking. No doubt a lack of empathy on the part of overzealous educators contributed to the foundling's doubts and objections. His first tutor, Daumer, somewhat more sympathetic and imaginative at least in matters of abstract concepts, remarked in that respect:

> Er quälte sich damals in Folge des ihm ertheilten Religionsunterrichtes, bei welchem man ihn so ganz seiner Natur zuwider, auf bloßes Glauben verwies und über das Dunkle darin nicht zu forschen und zu grübeln ermahnte, gleichwohl gar sehr für sich selber ab, um das Verhältniß Gottes zur Menschheit insbesondere zu dem Bösen im Menschen und dem Ursprung des Bösen zu fassen.[5]

---

[4] *Verbrechen am Seelenleben*, 175.

[5] G. F. Daumer, *Enthüllungen über Kaspar Hauser* (Frankfurt a. M.: Meidinger, Sohn & Co., 1859), 96.

Towards the end of his five years in society, however, the reluctant
initiate finally appears to have conformed to the expectations of his
mentors. Reports of his deathbed demeanor attest to his "christlich
liebevolle ... Gesinnung." He joined in prayers for his soul, and despite
much physical pain faced death with piety and composure, declaring:
"Ich habe ja alle Leute, die ich kenne, um Verzeihung gebeten, warum
sollte ich da nicht ruhig sein?". He in turn absolved his fellowmen from
guilt by detaching himself from all wrongs committed against him, even
from the attack that would now cost him his life. "Warum sollte ich Zorn
oder Haß oder Groll auf die Menschen haben," he asked, "es hat mir ja
niemand etwas getan."[6]

With regard to religion, therefore, both positive and negative components are already present in the original Kaspar Hauser material, and
writers could choose between two contrary options without in fact
violating the actual sources. In agreement with Hauser's early, unbiased
appraisal of the inconsistencies of the Christian dogma, they could bring
the negative aspects of the latter to the fore, and in the process
experiment with some more unconventional — though not necessarily
new — views of religion. Alternatively, they could reassert the traditional
tenets of Christianity, in keeping with the foundling's later stance. The
relevant literature shows that both these possibilities were explored.

It is noteworthy that where writers chose the critical path, the
negative judgment does not concern religion itself so much as its
narrow-minded interpreters. It is *Kirchenfeindlichkeit*, rather than a
categorical denial or rejection of God. This, too, is in itself not a new, i.e.
twentieth-century attitude. Already one of the very first examples of
Kaspar-Hauser-literature, Ludwig Scoper's novel of 1834 (*Kaspar
Hauser, oder; Die eingemauerte Nonne*), served as a vehicle for open
criticism of the clergy by casting an abbot in the role of chief villain. But
rather than a blanket rejection of institutionalized religion, the novel
was part of a denominational quarrel, reserving its disdain for Catholic
monasticism and its unscrupulous representatives.

Twentieth-century literature is more evenhanded in its criticism, not
singling out or sparing any particular denomination. For instance,
Wassermann and Röttger elaborate on the absurdity of Kaspar Hauser's
religious instruction. They also both treat schoolmaster Meyer's spouting
of Christian precepts with irony, thereby making the foundling's
reluctance to conform understandable. "Gott hat den Meyer nicht
geschaffen" (274), is Kaspar's conclusion in Röttger's novel. Even the
good-natured pastor Fuhrmann, his religious mentor in Ansbach, cannot
quite overcome the foundling's distrust: "Er zweifelte nicht an Fuhr-
manns gutem Herzen, wenn auch etwas Trennendes war: eben, daß Herr
Fuhrmann Pastor war" (131). This critical view of the clergy still suffuses
some of the latest Kaspar Hauser works. In Herzog's film, Kaspar's

---

[6] For these quotations and relevant descriptions of Kaspar's demeanor in his final
days, see Pies, *Dokumentation*, 133–60.

examination by the two bigoted 'men of the cloth' is one of the most memorable scenes. Originally, the author had planned to confront his hero with "einer Übermacht von vier Pastoren." His description of pastor Fuhrmann as a person "mit dick verquollenem Gesicht, Moos auf den Zähnen und immer etwas Eidotter vom Frühstück auf dem Rockkragen" (156) confirms his averse opinion of the clergy. In Forte's play, the description of Fuhrmann also has negative overtones. Although he is basically well-disposed to Kaspar Hauser, statements like:

> Wir sollten uns nicht so leidenschaftlich um menschliche Einrichtungen kümmern. Jede Regierungsform ist ein Joch, und es ist das Geschick des Menschen, ein Sklave zu sein, und deshalb muß er lernen, seine Ketten ohne Klage zu tragen. (60)

clearly relegate him to the reactionary faction of the author's dramatic constellation. He typifies the prevailing Biedermeier atmosphere of resigned stagnation which Forte denounces in his play as a parallel to the conditions of political repression in his own time.

The most obvious way of overcoming the present spiritual desolation was, of course, a simple reaffirmation of traditional Christian values. Towards this end, the life of Kaspar Hauser readily offered comparisons with several familiar biblical motifs, and these were indeed employed in various forms. One might argue that the inclusion of such motifs could have a merely poetic value. But the fact that a number of writers made pointed use of the mythological explanations and parables of Christianity, and in some cases even made them central to their work, indicates a more profound significance, namely a deliberate attempt to return to former sources of comfort which had been out of favor for some time.

One example of the revival of biblical motifs has already been discussed above, in connection with the resurrection of Rousseauistic concepts: it is the clear or veiled allusion to the Christian interpretation of man's origin. We have seen that Kaspar Hauser's disposition and demeanor are repeatedly compared to the innocence of Adam in paradise, and the state of the world around him to the Fall from Grace through the gain of knowledge. Much as the foundling's curious case galvanized the public interest, selfishness and indifference characterized the actions of at least some of his contemporaries. Where these failings are seized and enlarged upon, and contrasted with the helplessness of the victim, the parable of the good Samaritan in St. Luke's gospel readily comes to mind, as a silent reproof. Hofer and Röttger in particular openly appeal to the Christian charity of their readers. In the latter's novel, Judge Feuerbach sets the tone and moral standard in this respect, when he declares with conviction:

> Es ist nicht um das Prinzentum des jungen Mannes, der doch ein Kind ist, es ist um die Entscheidung, die man, Auge in Auge mit der Gottheit,

geben muß: sieh, da ist ein Namenloser, ein Fremder, dir fremder als
jeder andere Mensch. Hältst du nun ihm die Treue, den du kaum
kennst? so fragt die Stimme, und ich muß antworten: Ja! (23)

The thematic underpinning of Wassermann's novel, the indictment
of mankind's *Trägheit des Herzens* falls into the same category, even
though in view of the author's Jewish upbringing and his own earlier
exposure to a heartless world, it was probably firsthand experience
rather than a particular section from the New Testament which provided
the inspiration.

The converse concept, that suffering, bravely endured, somehow
ennobles the soul and is therefore pleasing to God, in fact a kind of
prerequisite for redemption, also readily suggests itself. It infuses those
passages in which Kaspar Hauser's inner nobility takes on almost saintly
aspects, yet is directly linked to the hardships he undergoes. This
blending of suffering and purity revives the notion of life on earth as a
mere testing ground and preparation for the life to come, a solace which
again represents a return to Christian tenets which are at odds with the
pragmatism of the twentieth century. Wassermann alludes to a more
congenial sphere after death, colored to his own liking, in his description of Kaspar Hauser's deathbed delirium. In "krankhafte[n] Ent-
zückungen," the foundling catches a glimpse of the cosmic tree of life in
a region where he does not feel his pain, and all is one:

Und inmitten des Weltalls stand ein Baum mit weitem Gipfel und
unzähligen Verästelungen; rote Beeren wuchsen aus den Zweigen, und
auf der Krone oben bildeten die Beeren die Form eines Herzens. (440)

Trakl's hero is compensated for his ordeal by his transfiguration in
death, and in Röttger's novel, a dream foreshadows how an angel will
guide Kaspar from a barren world to paradise. The unhappy wanderer
in Klaus Mann's "Legenden" is not taken home until he has experienced
the degradations of life. Hofmannsthal's hero also experiences life as a
testing ground. He, too, struggles to preserve his integrity in the face of
extreme tribulations, until he is finally removed — or removes himself
— to a higher realm. His dying smile, and the words: "Mir ist viel zu
wohl zum Hoffen," imply that he has reached sanctuary. That at the
same time he did not pass his earth-bound test is another matter.

Yet another rather obvious motif in the traditional Christian context
relates to the pitiful briefness of the foundling's public existence. It is
the admonition of *memento mori*, the reminder that our time on earth
may be shorter than we think, and that we had better use it well. This
thought is the leitmotif of Hoechstetter's story, "Das Totenhemdlein des
Kaspar Hauser," in which an unexpected encounter with the dead
foundling's clothing many years after the tragic events causes the
narrator to ruminate about the futility of this life ("das Nichts des
Erdenwallens"). In this case, however, some comfort is gained from the

fact that the memory of Kaspar Hauser has survived and continues to make an impression, short as his life had been:

> Warum sollten wir nicht glauben dürfen, daß auch unser Herz noch [jemand] berühren kann über Zeit und Fremde hinweg? Glauben, daß durch Nacht und Finsternis und selbst Vergessen die Spur nicht erlischt, die von unserem Herzen hinaus will — in die Unendlichkeit?[7]

Less explicitly, in some cases possibly even unintentionally, the *memento mori* motif also infuses all those passages which draw attention to the untimeliness of Kaspar Hauser's death. The reader senses it as an undercurrent wherever a writer puts extra stress on Kaspar Hauser's childlike qualities, since such emphasis indirectly brings home the incongruity of his premature end.

While the appearance of these religious components in an age which generally subscribed to the dictum that 'God is dead' indicates a search for a way out through the way back, the outlined motifs per se are fairly conventional in literature. Much more interesting is the fact that authors frequently turn Kaspar Hauser himself into a Christlike figure, either through choice of imagery or through direct biblical allusions. The slight savor of heresy which adheres to such exaltations of what is, after all, a very human figure (and a pitiful one at that), sets this motif apart from tradition-bound routine, and makes it distinctly modern. It also raises the germane question whether Kaspar Hauser, when depicted as the 'man of sorrows', simultaneously holds the promise of being a redeemer of mankind.

Our initial examination of Kaspar Hauser as the quintessential outsider has already focused on the various literary portrayals of his suffering. We have argued that this suffering stood for the suffering of modern man in general, and for that of the poet or artist in particular, who felt isolated from society and therefore closely identified with the foundling's experience. Looked at from a more objective point of view, the suffering of a pure and blameless victim, misunderstood and mistreated by most, can of course also evoke the 'ecce homo' motif of the New Testament. Within our occidental culture, this interpretation would not even require any particular piety on the part of the reader, or explicit reminders on the part of the author. Wassermann's Kaspar Hauser is a case in point. Although the author's carefully crafted realistic touches turned him into a lifelike, psychologically rounded figure, he is also the epitome of the innocent victim. As his story unfolds, it assumes the aspects of a passion-play. There are well-meaning adherents withdrawing their support, cowards, a prominent traitor, and a fickle populace. A relentless progression from trial to trial, stoically endured, culminates in a seemingly pre-ordained death. The end of Wassermann's

---

[7] Sophie Hoechstetter, "Das Totenhemdlein des Kaspar Hauser," *Mein Freund Rosenkreutz* (Dachau: Einhorn, n.d. [1917]), 324, 326.

novel confirms the validity of a biblical comparison. Here, a bystander prompts the dying Kaspar Hauser to pray: "Vater, nicht mein — ," and the latter readily completes the words of Jesus on the cross: "sondern dein Wille geschehe" (441). And, in accord with the celestial phenomenon which supposedly accompanied Christ's death, we are told that when Kaspar Hauser died, "sei zu der Stunde Mond und Sonne gleicher Zeit [sic] am Firmament gestanden, jener im Osten, diese im Westen, und beide Gestirne hätten im selben fahlen Glanz geleuchtet" (442). Klaus Mann, probably inspired by Wassermann, uses similar imagery to mark the significance of Kaspar Hauser's death: "[Der Himmel] stand durchsichtig und in einem gläsernen Grün, so daß es Tag nicht war und nicht Nacht, und man ward gewahr, daß Mond und Sonne zugleich am Himmel standen" (193).

Such unequivocal allusions to the 'man of sorrows' occur in many other works. They are particularly obvious in Röttger's novel, a noteworthy fact in view of the year of its publication, 1938. Röttger's Christian stance had already manifested itself in the *Christuslegenden* he published in 1914, at the beginning of World War One. With the creation of his Kaspar Hauser figure at a time of similar martial hysteria, he evidently wanted to reaffirm his belief that what was needed in troubled times was a renewal of faith. Parallels between Kaspar Hauser and Christ are clearly spelled out in this narrative. For example, when pressed at one point to reveal his true identity, the hero replies: "Eines Menschen Sohn bin ich" (179). As if to assure that the reference is understood, Kaspar Hauser's audience reacts to this answer with dismay, calling it "biblisch," or "horrend und fast blasphemisch" (179). In another instance, the foundling is referred to as "der kaum erstandene Hauser" (174), and his smile is described as "das des Gegeißelten" (179). Commenting on the murder of the foundling, someone utters the insight: "Wir sind alle — schuldig am Tod des Gerechten" (317), a counterpart to the self-incrimination at the end of Wassermann's novel: "Schuldig sind alle, die wir da wandeln" (446).

Ebermayer's play alludes to Christ's suffering on the cross with visual rather than verbal images. His Kaspar, on his way to the city, is teased and jeered by the uncouth followers of a wedding procession. He is lifted high above the crowd, and we get the following description, suggestive of the traditional picture of the dying Christ with his crown of thorns: "Sein Gesicht ist schmerzverzerrt, sein Haupt, geschmückt mit Blumen und Bändern, tief nach rückwärts gesunken" (15).

Hofmannsthal, too, makes extensive use of religious imagery in *Der Turm*, so that the portrayal of his hero as someone select also assumes Christlike dimensions. Repeatedly, he associates Sigismund's physical degradation with an emanation of sacredness. Even "bis an die Knöchel im Unrat," the hero appears "erlaucht und zum Größten auserlesen....

Die Knie wollten sich beugen."[8] Julian and Anton, who know the prince at his most debased, nevertheless feel compelled to address him as "Genossen der Engel," and "heiliger verklärter Marterer" [sic].[9] Appellations like "das Lamm mit gebundenen Füßen," or "Lamm Gottes" evoke the image of Christ more directly.[10] Later, his subjects need for a savior is also expressed in terms with religious overtones, especially in *Turm* II. "Die Herde hat keinen Hirten," they plead with Sigismund. Anxious to surround him with the trappings of divinity, they offer him the cloth from an altar as a suitable garment, and a carriage with bells so that he can ride along "als [wäre er] eine Kirche auf Rädern."[11]

Sigismund himself initially distances himself from such comparisons. In his earlier stage of degradation, he shows a Kaspar-Hauser-like rejection of the teachings of the New Testament, and a similar childlike logic. Urged to be patient in view of Christ's much greater martyrdom, he replies that compared to himself, Jesus had had an enviable life: "Hat frei herumgehen dürfen! auf einem Schiff fahren! Hochzeit mitessen! Burg einreiten aufm Palmesel und alle gejubelt um ihn!"[12] But as he becomes more aware of his mission to save his people, he also resorts to expressions which recall the Son of God. When he first expects to be put to death, he calls out: "Vater — in deine Hände...." Evidently, Hofmannsthal shied away from completing the biblical quote, and in the second version of his play, he altered the line, without, however, abandoning the allusion: "'Auserlesen!' er wirft die Hände nach oben, 'Vater — jetzt komme ich — '."[13]

The tenacious historical rumor that Lord Stanhope had been paid to facilitate Kaspar Hauser's murder conveniently suggested a comparison with Judas Iscariot, to complement the scenario of a passion-play. In Wassermann's work, the — historically incorrect — fact that Stanhope hangs himself, like Judas, brings up this parallel. Ebermayer and Röttger achieve a similar effect by highlighting the promise of a pay-off for Stanhope's betrayal. In Hofmannsthal's *Turm*, it is the manipulative Julian who assumes the role of the biblical traitor, in this case Peter rather than Judas. "Verratet ihn nicht!" the physician pleads with Julian on Sigismund's behalf, "Lasset diese Trompeter nicht sein wie das

---

[8] *Turm* I, 33; *Turm* II, 340 (second part of quotation omitted).

[9] Ibid., *Turm* I, 93, 97; In *Turm* II, the first quotation is replaced by: "Lichtgeist, vor dem die Engel knien," 379; second quotation: 381.

[10] *Turm* I, 46; *Turm* II, 449.

[11] *Turm* II, 450, 449.

[12] *Turm* I, 89; omitted in *Turm* II.

[13] *Turm* I, 99; *Turm* II, 382.

dreimalige Krähen des Hahnes. Verratet nicht um der Heiden willen den, der in Eure Hand gegeben ist."[14]

In Klaus Mann's work, the already mentioned allusion to Golgotha is augmented by the veiled resemblance of the hero's journey through life with the life of Jesus. Like the latter, it shows a sympathetic contact with the outcasts of society. There is an encounter with a fallen woman ("Kaspar Hauser und die Hure"), a demented person ("Kaspar Hauser und das irre kleine Mädchen"), and even a "Lazarus," albeit one who is not resurrected in body but in spirit ("Kaspar Hausers toter Freund"). The use of the term *Legenden*, of course, also implies a religious significance, as does the pronouncedly pious transcription of Verlaine's Kaspar Hauser poem which precedes Mann's "Legenden," with the narrator's sevenfold request to pray for him.

Whether the protagonist of the much earlier "Kaspar Hauser Lied" by Trakl can also be linked to Christ is open to debate. The indirect reference to paradisiacal origin, and God's appellation "O Mensch," point to Adam rather than God's son. But this is a multivalent figure. We have already referred to its significance as a mirror of man in general, of the alienated poet, and of the author's self. In view of the poem's explicit mention of God, and its less explicit reference to paradise, yet another, Christlike dimension is in principle quite conceivable, just as it is for Hofmannsthal's hero. The word "wahrlich" of the first line ("Er wahrlich liebte die Sonne") has a biblical ring, and the final image of the sinking "Haupt" as well as the apparent transfiguration in death are all compatible with the conventional image of the dying Christ.

It may seem inappropriate to talk of religious overtones in Arp's "kaspar ist tot," for although there can be no doubt about the seriousness of the author's concerns behind his art, the hero of this poem lacks the requisite dignity. But as Last has recognized, religious inferences are fitting in this case as well. "The passing of Kaspar," Last comments, "is as great a disaster as the death of Christ ('Why have you forsaken us' is a deliberate borrowing from the last words). But He died and rose again, whereas Kaspar's death is irrevocable."[15] At the risk of stretching the analogy too far, one can draw further parallels between the miracles wrought in each case, and between the icons that are kept in memory of the departed: Kaspar's "büste wird die kamine aller edlen menschen zieren," like Christ's portrait or crucifix the homes of the devout. Thus notwithstanding the incongruity between Christ's Passion and Kaspar's antics, certain similarities do exist. Arp's deliberately spontaneous approach to his work very likely rules out a carefully planned transcription of Christian ideas and symbols. But he was certainly irreverent enough

---

[14] *Turm* I, 50; omitted in *Turm* II.

[15] Rex W. Last, *Hans Arp, the Poet of Dadaism*, Modern German Authors: Texts and Contexts, no. 1 (London: Oswald Wolff, 1969), 39.

about conventions, and serious enough about art and life, to make such comparisons in order to express the spiritual dearth of modern life.

In the recent, post-war literature, allusions to religion or to Kaspar Hauser's Christlike nature tend to be not only less frequent, but also rather oblique or offhand, and to link them with an active search for spiritual values is a hazardous undertaking. Handke's *Kaspar*, which forms the prelude to the more recent Kaspar Hauser works, is a good example. Most of the play's vocabulary and imagery is confined to mundane objects. Nevertheless, amidst the welter of commonplace homilies which serve to enforce Kaspar's adaption, we do find some quasi-biblical precepts which can be interpreted in a Christian context. "Jedes Leiden ist natürlich," the prompters announce, as well as: "Du bist nicht zum Vergnügen auf der Welt," and: "Niemand hat das Recht, den anderen auszubeuten" (36, 41, 49). Each of these sayings takes up a motif already encountered in previous Kaspar Hauser literature. The question is whether we can still infer the same meaning. It is less important in this respect that the impact of these maxims is diminished by the barrage of other, either sinister or nonsensical advice; this in itself need not exclude the validity of each adage. But while, for instance, in Wassermann's and Röttger's works the admonitions clearly came from a high moral vantage point, in Handke's play they are part of a negative and detrimental process. Their very source makes these sentences suspect. Therefore even if we assume that Handke himself would endorse at least the maxim that no one has the right to exploit his neighbor, we cannot confidently interpret these proclamations as literary evidence of a desire for the traditional Christian way of life.

One other group of statements in Handke's play needs to be considered, since it also evokes the idea of a higher plane of existence. Kaspar is told: "Das Blut schreit zum Himmel. / Das Unrecht schreit zum Himmel." This is followed by the adjunct: "Ohne das Blut könnte das Unrecht nicht zum Himmel schreien" (50). Focusing on the latter statement alone, two interpretations are possible in the religious context. The more farfetched one is that Handke alludes to the saving blood of Christ. More plausibly, these words can signal a belief in the existence of heaven as a resort of appeal. The adjunct then appears to relay the conviction that by drawing attention to injustices, our suffering does indeed serve a higher purpose. But here, too, some qualifications must be made. The vivid metaphor "zum Himmel schreien" has by now degenerated to a common cliché. It may draw our attention as something potentially meaningful, but is not really out of place in the prompters' recital of platitudes, and need not necessarily convey a serious intent. Furthermore, the general context in which these words are presented detracts from their inherent significance to a larger extent than in the previous examples. For in this case, the conclusion "ohne ... könnte ... nicht" is part of a particular syntax pattern, designed to accustom the hero to more complicated thought processes. This drill also contains quite illogical variations of the pattern, such as: "Der

Ballon schwillt an. Der Jubel schwillt an. Ohne den Ballon könnte der Jubel nicht schwellen" (50). We cannot divorce separate statements from the overall purpose of the play, which is to show that our way of acculturation allows for the infiltration of any kind of message. Handke's target is the whole system of man's education, in which good, bad or nonsensical pieces of information can be transmitted with equal ease. Therefore, if we look for proof that Handke wished to return to former spiritual values, the inclusion of the above statements may perhaps be a subliminal signal; it was not, at this stage in the author's work, a conscious concern triggered by the figure of Kaspar Hauser.

In Forte's *Kaspar Hausers Tod*, the religious component is equally unobtrusive. The guests at the foundling's post-funeral assembly repeatedly eulogize the foundling's goodness and purity. Retrospectively, they turn the departed into a saintly, Christlike figure, and we have to ask ourselves what purpose this serves. At one level, the laudatory comments merely provide the play with verisimilitude, since most are based on documentary sources. But it also looks as if Kaspar Hauser represents an elusive ideal, a yardstick for the behavior of others which, as the play goes on to show, will expose their own shortcomings and selfish behavior. Ironically, the characters themselves remain unaware of this. Their remembrance of the deceased soon degenerates into small talk and gossip. For all their high-minded praise, the foundling has not changed anyone's outlook.

We can see another, possibly unintended reminder of the last days of Christ in the stage tableau which dominates almost the entire play. Excluding what we might call the impartial observers — the journalist and the physician in charge of Kaspar Hauser's post-mortem — we have twelve people gathered around a large table, sharing a meal in honor of the extraordinary person who is the link between them. None of them can be singled out as Judas the traitor, few will prove to be true disciples, and of course the Christ-figure is no longer in their midst. Nevertheless, this constellation is strongly reminiscent of the Last Supper. There, too, the central figure had been mysterious and misunderstood, and the guests mainly concerned with their own future well-being.

A similarly veiled, and possibly unintended reference to Christ occurs in Vesper's novel, where at one point, when the hero is especially desolate, Kaspar Hauser mysteriously appears to him by the wayside, as Jesus did to the two disciples on their way to Emmaus. But the comfort gained from this fleeting encounter is markedly smaller.

As for Herzog's film, *Jeder für sich und Gott gegen alle*, the title alone articulates this work's basic stance of disenchantment. While it still postulates the existence of God, it precludes any association with the promise of redemption through Christ, that is to say with the core of orthodox Christian teaching. Throughout the film, the hero's attitude is in keeping with this negative view of God. When, after the first attempt on Kaspar's life, the minister explains to him that "auch jener Mordversuch ... nicht ohne Gottes Willen vorgefallen [sei]," Kaspar concurs. "Das leuchte ihm ein," he says, "Gott müsse, so, wie es um die Menschen bestellt sei, etwas gegen diese haben" (179). The implication that man himself bears some responsibility for his despair may represent a ray of hope for the future. For if God still exists, and is merely 'angry' with mankind for taking a wrong direction, one can assume that it lies within man's reach to placate him and undo the damage.

The film itself does not explore that possibility any further. Allusions to Christ occur only in connection with the suffering He had to undergo. For instance, during the first stage of Kaspar's painful adjustment to society, the camera lingers repeatedly on a crucifix in the jailer's house, with greater emphasis than this otherwise quite realistic requisite would warrant. The viewer cannot but interpret the image of the crucifix as a parallel to Kaspar Hauser's inner torture. According to Corrigan, a less obvious reference to Christ's Passion occurs in an earlier scene — already mentioned earlier for its semiotic significance with regard to Kaspar Hauser's state of exclusion from Nature — in which the foundling and his initial keeper, on their way from the dungeon to the city, rest on top of a mountain:

> Just behind Kaspar and vertically perpendicular to his body sits the mysterious, black-cloaked stranger, his back to the camera. As usual, the camera does not budge, and the cross-like figure that Kaspar and the dark guardian form contrasts sharply with the brilliant landscape of the background and so creates a stunning icon of tragedy and death.[16]

Herzog never ameliorates these images of Christlike suffering, and the negative tenor of his title remains valid throughout the film. Yet as Kaspar's dreams of the desert caravan and of the pilgrims' persistent ascent of the stony mountain indicate, he has not given up hope, and is searching for symbols to show that beyond man's calamity, a different, higher plane of existence may one day be reached.

The only other recent work to address the religious issue in an explicit manner is Jürg Amann's play *Ach, diese Wege sind sehr dunkel.* One scene shows how, in appropriately childlike fashion, Kaspar formulates a multitude of questions to help him understand his puzzling world. His stream of queries about mundane and abstract problems is punctuated three times by a question which differs from the rest, and may be the most significant question of all: "Warum sagt Gott kein Wort?" (19, 20). Needless to say, he does not find the answer. In one of the subsequent scenes, the hero tries to comprehend what he is taught about God and his ways, but finds that reason is an inadequate way to get to the root of the mystery: "Da habe ich wieder darüber nachge-dacht. Aber ich bin mit dem Nachdenken darüber nicht fertig geworden"

---

[16] Timothy Corrigan, *New German Film: The Displaced Image* (Austin, Texas: University of Texas Press, 1983), 128.

(23). A later episode, entitled "Der Gekreuzigte," also demonstrates that the intellect alone is not enough to cope with man's spiritual needs. Here Kaspar faces a cross, "an das einer mit einer Dornenkrone genagelt ist" (33). The neutrality of this description can of course convey the hero's unfamiliarity with the icon. But since we are dealing with a stage instruction rather than the hero's own reaction, and since, as the latter's words will make clear, it is obviously not his first encounter with a crucifix, the scene also implies that the conventional interpretation of the image is not necessarily unequivocal. Contemplating the image of the crucified Christ, Kaspar comments:

> Ich weiß ja, daß es nicht wirklich ist. Und ein Bild. Und ein Gleichnis. Und lange vorbei. Und vielleicht ein Gerücht. Aber er. Er hat es erlitten. (33)

Sober knowledge, and the demythologization of the sacred image, are evidently unsatisfactory. The unspoken implication is that Kaspar yearns for a spiritual explanation of Christ's suffering, which might justify his innate empathy with the emblem of suffering. Man reaches out, but is unable to make the connection.

In the very next scene, Amann follows some of his literary predecessors by directly equating the hero with the 'man of sorrows'. In the delirium of a deathbed monologue, Kaspar Hauser intermingles facts of his own reputed biography with details of Christ's death as recited in the liturgical creed:

> Ich. Sagen sie. Prinz. Sagen sie. Tot und lebendig. Gekreuzigt, gestorben und begraben worden. Auferstanden am wievielten Tag? Geboren am. Hab ich vergessen. (45)

Yet the interjection "sagen sie," repeated several times throughout the monologue, leaves the equation with Christ in the realm of uncertainty, on a par with the rumor of royal parentage in the worldly sphere. As in previous works, Kaspar Hauser is directly likened to Christ, but the author hesitates to draw explicit conclusions from this equation. It is up to the reader or viewer to draw the relevant inferences.

In fact, all the writers who turn Kaspar Hauser into a Christlike figure stop short of a truly confident assertion of his role as a redeemer of mankind. Several hint of his potential to change man for the better by describing the foundling's ability to awaken remorse in sinners like Wassermann's Stanhope, who under Kaspar's questioning gaze feels as though he were facing God's messenger ("als sei ein Gesandter Gottes neben ihn hingestellt"; 195), or, in Mann's "Legenden," the prostitute. But in the overall confrontation between Kaspar Hauser and the world, these instances are negligible. Only the anthroposophical school of thinking has completed the mythologization of Kaspar Hauser, investing him with the status of a prophet unfortunately unrecognized in his own time, and thus prevented from unfolding "those spiritual impulses necessary for the progressive development of mankind."[17] A literary demonstration of the anthroposophical mythologization of the figure can be found in an English play by the Rudolf Steiner disciple Carlo Pietzner, *Who was Kaspar Hauser?*. Its finale interprets Kaspar Hauser as the beacon of "a great conspiracy" for the betterment of the world. He is the "uncrowned king" (reminiscent of Hofmannsthal's *Kinderkönig*), leading a "children's crusade" into a presumably brighter future.[18]

In German literature, the regret for an unheeded opportunity is there as well, clearest perhaps in Wassermann's and Röttger's novels. A forward-looking need and longing for a savior are also very much apparent in the many attempts to resurrect Christ's image through the figure of Kaspar Hauser. But the optimism with regard to the future is not nearly as tangible. It appears only obliquely, in the promise of salvation we involuntarily associate with any evocation of the Messiah. Kaspar's vision of the nomads in the Sahara desert in Herzog's film probably symbolizes the situation best: With the right guidance, it may be possible to get out of the desert. But exactly where the path ends, and what comes next, the foundling is unable to visualize.

II. Pantheistic Approaches

The quest for a spiritual renewal is not restricted to the Christian framework in its narrower, conventional sense. Several authors also experiment with pantheistic notions in various forms. A revival of cosmic pantheism is, of course, very much in keeping with the general attempt to return to the ideas of Romanticism which we had noted at the beginning of this chapter. In fact, it is even more compatible with it than a reassertion of conventional Christian beliefs. After all, the idea that God is everything, and everything is God, had colored the religiosity of many a Romantic poet. Together with a fundamental longing for a return to simplicity, it had inspired the Romantic love of Nature, since it was thought to animate all of Nature's manifestations. In the modern context, a pantheistic outlook certainly contained some ingredients which, given the present dearth of spiritual comfort, seemed to make a revival worthwhile. The belief in an all-encompassing entity could reduce the scale and significance of current suffering. It could also

---

[17] Editorial comment [dust-cover] to the publication of Wassermann's novel in English by Rudolf Steiner Publications (New York, 1973). For an exposition of the anthroposophical view of Kaspar Hauser, see Peter Tradowsky's account, *Kaspar Hauser; oder, Das Ringen um den Geist* (Dornach: Philosophisch-Anthroposophischer Verlag, Goetheanum, 1980).

[18] Carlo Pietzner, "... and from the night, Kaspar," *Who was Kaspar Hauser?* (Oxford: Oxford University Press, 1983), 77, 76.

deprive death of much of its terror, for the concept that each individual would eventually return to an everlasting harmony provided more comfort than Nietzschean nihilism, and at least as much, if not more comfort than the biblical concept of a final judgment day. A quotation from Hölderlin's *Hyperion* exemplifies the pantheistic ideal of Romanticism, in which "der Schmerz der Einsamkeit" dissolves "ins Leben der Gottheit":

> Eines zu sein mit allem, das ist Leben der Gottheit, das ist der Himmel des Menschen.... Eines zu sein mit allem, was lebt, in seliger Selbstvergessenheit wiederzukehren ins All der Natur, das ist der Gipfel der Gedanken und Freuden, das ist die heilige Bergeshöhe, der Ort der ewigen Ruhe.[19]

What Hyperion describes is man's longing rather than his actual experience. Yet Hölderlin, like most Romantics, was still firmly convinced that the true writer or poet had access to that invisible universe in a very special way, and that it was his calling to interpret it for less gifted mortals. As amplified earlier on, by the twentieth century social realities had undermined such confidence, and the belief in the poet's priestlike function had become very fragile. Indeed it was precisely the resulting void which now posed a major problem for many writers.

To those reluctant to give up the notion of man's potential to connect with an unseen universe, Kaspar Hauser offered some positive evidence, and therefore, one suspects, a glimmer of hope that was worth exploring. Through his extraordinary abilities, this strange youth seemed to prove that man was capable of communing with the mysterious forces of the natural universe, and, ergo, that a mysterious realm did in fact exist beyond the prosaic existence of ordinary men.

According to the historical accounts, the foundling himself was initially fully convinced that the phenomena of Nature had a life and will of their own. He insisted that apples voluntarily jumped from their trees and hid in the grass to evade potential captors; that the snow 'bit' his hand; and that the thunder threatened him in a personal way — interpretations not inconsistent with the uncanny animation of Nature in the Romantic *Kunstmärchen*. But such assertions were rightly dismissed and smiled upon as manifestations of childish naivety, the symptoms of Kaspar's retarded development. Less easily explained, and more intriguing, was the fact that he showed — at least for a limited period — remarkable sensory perceptions. The fact that he could reputedly sense the emanation of the dead without being aware that a cemetery existed nearby, or that he could detect and distinguish metals without seeing or touching them, attested the existence of another dimension, unattainable to those around him. These strange endow-

---

[19] Friedrich Hölderlin, "Hyperion," I, *Werke, Briefe, Dokumente*, ed. Pierre Bertaux (Munich: Winkler, [1969]), 224.

ments caused much comment and wonder at the time, and were of special interest to proponents of animal-magnetism as popularized earlier by Franz Mesmer (1734–1815), who had tried to prove the existence of a so far unknown sphere of Nature.

Interestingly, the particular time-span in which the foundling's unusual gifts were at their most acute, and were intensely examined, is rarely referred to in twentieth-century literature. When mentioned at all, the reference serves mainly to illustrate the insensitivity and cruelty of his examiners. Much as similar stories of extraordinary powers may still be treasured by today's general public, the connotation of freak shows adherent to such displays has apparently made them unacceptable topics for serious literature, except as a vehicle for social concerns.[20] Kaspar Hauser's unusual ability to relate to an unseen dimension was, however, not forgotten; it was merely transferred into other contexts. In Wassermann's novel, for instance, the hero, for all his realistic traits, repeatedly experiences strange visions and premonitions. On one occasion, his awakening self-perception (through a chance encounter with his mirror image) is linked with the intuition or memory of another self in an irrational sphere:

> ... nun schien ihm, als ob hinter seinem Bild im Spiegel sich das Licht zerteile und als ob ein langer, langer Pfad nach rückwärts lief, und dort, in der weiten Ferne, stand noch ein Caspar, noch ein Ich, das hatte zugeschlossene Augen und sah aus, als wisse es etwas, was der Caspar hier im Zimmer nicht wußte.... Er verließ den Platz vor dem Spiegel und ging wie geistesabwesend zum Fenster. Dort stand er besinnend, beugte sich besinnend vor, immer weiter, völlig selbstvergessen, ganz vom Willen des Suchens erfüllt, bis die Brust auf dem Sims lag und seine Stirn in die Nacht tauchte. (57–58)

Later in Wassermann's work, when the hero becomes aware of his misery, his longing for refuge takes on a distinctly pantheistic coloration. He begins to sense God's presence in Nature, feels gratitude towards the earth itself, and equates Nature's phenomena with the divine, as we can see from the fact that he prays to the sun as well as to an oak tree in the forest. To escape from distress, he does not seek realistic hiding-places, but fantasizes about merging with a flower:

> Er wünschte sich das Angesicht einer Blume, um keinen Blick eines Menschenauges erwidern zu müssen. Oder er wünschte wenigstens sich im Schoß einer Blume bergen zu können ... dort könnte man stille sein und warten. (319)

---

[20] In this context, Leslie A. Fiedler makes some germane observations; see *Freaks: Myths and Images of the Secret Self* (New York: Simon & Schuster, 1978), esp. 256–73.

But the recurrence of this image at the end of the novel takes a form that reveals the futility of such hope. The mortally wounded boy tries to lift "den wie einen gebrochenen Blumenkelch seitwärts gesenkten Kopf" (437).

Lewandowski's Kaspar Hauser expresses a similar longing to merge with Nature in poetic form: "Blühen möcht ich, Sternen zugewendet, / als ein Baum, der tief die Wurzeln sendet," reads one of the entries in his purported diary. Another, written in premonition of his death, carries the idea of a union with the rest of the universe even further: "Ich wage es kaum noch, mich selbst / zu ahnen, Und schwimme, aufgelöstes Licht, im / Raum."[21]

Trakl's poem also contains a pantheistic element, in spite of the biblical ambience of its initial verse. The fact that "Tier und Busch" follow Kaspar into the uncongenial region of the city not only denotes the hero's fraternity with a purer realm, but also signals the continued ability to communicate with the forces of Nature. The plant and animal world is still available to provide a measure of divine comfort, at least for those who have not severed their ties to the larger context of existence.

Arp's firm belief in the healing powers of Nature and in the interrelationship of all of Nature's manifestations is not always evident in his works, but "kaspar ist tot" is an exception. His lament for Kaspar conveys that it is desirable, though not given to everyone, to understand this interrelationship. Kaspar, as remembered by those who now mourn his absence, had apparently known about that secret connectedness of all things. That knowledge had given him access to the various realms of Nature, and allowed him to control the elements. His use of that gift may appear to be capricious, but it must have been congruous with man's needs, since it is looked back upon with such regret. The fact that Kaspar may have turned into a star, or into a chain of water, also conforms to the pantheistic concept of the unity of all of Nature's phenomena.

Hofmannsthal's *Turm* expresses the co-existence of two worlds mainly through the hero's own position and attitude. As discussed previously, one of the aims of the Sigismund-plays was to test the idea whether the poet should and could still function in the role of priestly mediator between the unseen and the mundane realm. The figure of Sigismund, once it had transcended the model set by Calderón and absorbed the features of the mysterious Kaspar Hauser, certainly appears capable and likely to fulfil that function. It is worth remembering, however, that while in the preliminary sketches for his play Hofmannsthal portrays his (still incarcerated) hero in clearly pantheistic terms, he qualifies that picture with the epithet "Stadium der Megalomanie":

---

[21] *Das Tagebuch Kaspar Hausers*, 59, 87.

Der Wind ist ein Stück von ihm, und die Vögel sind er, auch die
Mäuse.... Auch seine Eßschale, sein Lagerstroh, seine Mordlust werden
jetzt Emanationen seiner Göttlichkeit.[22]

Evidently, the author here equated the pantheistic notion with the stage
of 'pre-existence', a stage one had to (regretfully) leave behind in order
to cope with the vicissitudes of modern life. It is no doubt for this
reason that in the actual plays the infusion with the divine is not that
explicit. Nevertheless, from the very beginning Sigismund seems to
straddle the borderline between his own grim reality and another world
he can barely sense. For him, as they once did for Kaspar Hauser,
natural phenomena can assume a life of their own. "So hab ich das
Feuer gesehen und das Feuer hat mich gesehen," he asserts on one
occasion.[23] His difficulties in determining which world he belongs to
only partially still relate to the Calderón-based dichotomy between
appearance and reality. That particular aspect of the drama now revolves
mainly around the magic potion he is forced to drink, and how it affects
his relationship with his father, the King. Instead, the author invests his
hero with an instinctive awareness of another world, which constantly
threatens his equilibrium and perspective on life. "Ich brings nicht
auseinander, mich und das andere," he says.[24] Recalling the slaughter
of a pig he had once witnessed, he wonders whether his soul has
entered the dead animal, and, in an almost blasphemous fusion of the
image of Christ on the cross, the memory of the butchered pig, and his
own anguish, he imitates the position of the crucified Christ and states:
"Ich brings nicht auseinander, mich mit dem und aber mich mit dem
Tier, das aufgehangen war an einem queren Holz."[25]

Of course on one level, this unusual three-way comparison of
suffering can be read, once again, as simply an attempt to reinforce the
impression of Sigismund's past and future ordeal. Or we can construe
it as a metaphorical equivalent of Röttger's assertion that in principle all
suffering is the same: "Ob Tierlein oder Kind ... oder Christ selber, der
Gottessohn: die Verlassenheit der gemordeten Seele ist immer dieselbe"
(352). But the hero's inability to separate his private sphere from that
of Nature and religion also reflects the writer's perception that the
borderlines between these spheres are vague and artificial. In addition,
the hero's self-identification with the crucified animal and the crucified
Christ lets us anticipate that he may have a greater mission to fulfil, one
of metaphysical rather than political importance, which may unite the

---

[22] Hugo von Hofmannsthal, "Aufzeichnungen und Entwürfe," *Dramen*, vol. 3 of
Gesammelte Werke in Einzelausgaben, ed. Herbert Steiner (Frankfurt a. M.: S.
Fischer, 1957), 429.

[23] *Turm* I, 84; omitted in *Turm* II.

[24] *Turm* I, 86; omitted in *Turm* II.

[25] *Turm* I, 87, 88; *Turm* II, 375, 376.

different realms. In both versions of *Der Turm*, the prince falls short of that expectation. But he does gain access to another, inner world, which can safeguard his integrity, whilst the eyes of Julian and the others remain "vermauert,"[26] unable to perceive this means of escape.

Röttger's contribution to the motif is to show that the belief in the existence of another dimension is an experience not easily shared. His hero reserves it for his innermost thoughts, which he confesses in a dream encounter with his former tutor, Daumer. Only in this unreal situation is he safe from ridicule, and can reveal his eerie feeling that everything around him possesses a soul. "Und das Laub an den Bäumen lebte nicht minder und hatte eine Seele und schwankte im Wind und raschelte und erschreckte mich ebenso," Kaspar relates, "am meisten, wenn ich allein war, wenn ich ging oder ritt vor der Stadt. Es erschien mir alles wie ein Wunder, obwohl es doch keines war." Daumer's reply confirms the unity of all creation: "Alles ist wunderbar, alles, was geschieht. Das Schöne und das Üble. Das Gute und das Schlechte. Die ganze Welt, die wir kennen oder nicht kennen" (195). Undoubtedly, the reticence about voicing pantheistic notions mirrors the author's own awareness that such views were out of tune with the materialistic climate of his time, and that it required courage to pronounce them.

We note, too, that the above examples all stem from the earlier part of the century. Whether the younger generation of writers did not have the necessary courage to enunciate such views, or whether they could in fact no longer muster the faith in pantheistic solutions, the flirtation with the idea of an unseen but reachable world is markedly less pronounced in the more recent Kaspar Hauser literature. Härtling's early poems and Höllerer's "Gaspard" might be cited as exceptions, since they refer to spirits which could bridge the gap between the real and the unreal world. In Herzog's film, the already mentioned initial quotation borrowed from Büchner's *Lenz*, ("Hören Sie denn nicht das entsetzliche Schreien ringsum, das man gewöhnlich Stille nennt?") also implies that a secret realm exists and shares in man's distress. In contrast, the incomplete dream visions of Herzog's Kaspar Hauser merely portray the longing for, not the actual existence of another sphere.

Like the attempts to revert to conventional Christian beliefs, or to mythologize Kaspar Hauser into a new redeemer figure, the endeavor to place the figure into a pantheistic context suggests the general need for a new direction rather than certainty and conviction, the search rather than the discovery. The explorations in this regard are too hesitant, too quickly abandoned, or suppressed by other imagery, to signal a true revival of pantheistic beliefs. There is indeed strong evidence that writers tested, through Kaspar Hauser, whether a metaphysical framework with some of the distinct hallmarks of Romanticism could be reestablished. But this undertaking lacks the Romantics' ardent conviction.

---

[26] *Turm* I, 158; omitted in *Turm* II.

6

The Attempt to Go Forward

I. Kaspar Hauser as 'tabula rasa'

CONCURRENTLY WITH THE VARIOUS attempts to deal with the predicament of modern man by returning to remedies of the past, or by going beyond the rational sphere of existence, twentieth-century literature also manifests the desire for a brand-new start through the creation of a 'new man'. We can term this aspect 'the attempt to go forward', since it concerns itself with the here and now, as a foundation for a better future.

We commonly associate the concept of the 'new man' with the Expressionist movement, which proclaimed his existence or potential existence as an article of faith. But the topic is also relevant to the literature about Kaspar Hauser. As the proverbial 'tabula rasa', the foundling presented his contemporaries with a unique opportunity not only to observe man's development, but to mold him according to the current ideals. It is therefore germane to ask how the writers under discussion viewed this particular facet of the story, and what conclusions they drew for their own time. We know that most admired the foundling's purity and innocence. But did they also see in this figure someone potentially capable and worthy of dealing with the demands of the future? Or, given the undeniably negative development of the events, did they at least recognize a lesson to be learned from the mistakes made in the historical case?

Like most phases of his life, Kaspar Hauser's development and education allow for diverse, even conflicting interpretations. We are told that within the few years available, he changed from someone who was like a two or three year old child into someone who could be described, "mit gewissen Einschränkungen, als ein vernünftiger, verständiger, sittlicher und gesitteter Mensch."[1] Yet even discounting the skeptics who declared him to be a common swindler from the start, he had detractors who downgraded his achievements. In particular his last teacher, Meyer, perceived only a superficial adjustment, which he felt masked a stubborn resistance against society's well-meant efforts to turn him into an upright citizen. Advocates like his first tutor, Daumer, on the

---

[1] Feuerbach, *Verbrechen am Seelenleben*, 147.

other hand, saw great promise in Kaspar Hauser. They continued to praise his receptivity, prodigious memory, and unfailing good nature. But overanxious to make the pupil conform to their standards of perfection, and lacking precedents, they, too, overburdened their ward with unreasonable demands. There is no doubt that Kaspar's rate of progress levelled off considerably. Whether he had simply reached the limit of his potential, or whether misguided teaching methods caused him to withdraw, remains open to questions.

Of course, seen objectively, the foundling was never quite the 'tabula rasa' he was thought to be when he was found in 1828. Earlier and present-day theories tend to agree that he must have had at least a few years of human contact and training in order to develop his subsequent abilities.[2] His own later record of memories and dreams, scanty as these were, confirms that his beginning in Nuremberg was not quite the zero-mark it appeared to be. And if we accept that the mysterious violent interventions in his fate were the consequence of his particular family background rather than mere coincidence, his past certainly shaped the course of his life in drastic ways. But much as speculations about his background dominated public attention, the idea of Kaspar Hauser as "ein weißes unbeschriebenes Blatt,"[3] with the chance for a fresh start in life, continued to hold its appeal.

As in the celebration of Kaspar Hauser as a paradigm of innocence, Rousseau's influence also infused the general interest in the idea of the 'tabula rasa'. In his *Émile*, Rousseau had set practical guidelines on how one might go about raising a 'new man' for the betterment of society. In the wake of these theories, the motif had already been explored in German literature prior to Kaspar Hauser's appearance. Jean Paul's *Die unsichtbare Loge* (1793), for instance, follows the path of a hero who is deliberately sequestered from the world for the first eight years of his life in order to shield him from corrupting influences. Unlike Kaspar Hauser, however, this innocent cave-dweller is accompanied by a well-meaning tutor of almost supernatural virtues, the *Genius*, who carefully prepares him for his entry into society.[4]

Following Kaspar Hauser's life and death, in fact closely modelled on the earlier part of his circumstances, the idea of the 'tabula rasa' reappeared as the leitmotif of Gutzkow's already mentioned *Die Söhne*

---

[2] See Lakies and Lakies-Wild, *Das Phänomen*, 219.

[3] Hofmannsthal, *Turm* I, 78; *Turm* II, 370.

[4] Although this mentor seems to represent a blueprint for the ideal tutor, of the kind Rousseau advocated in *Émile*, other interpretations have been advanced. Max Kommerell (in an evident effort to play down Rousseau's influence on Jean Paul) regards the figure as a symbol of the hero's better self: "Wir müssen im Genius mehr erblicken als eine weise, lenkende Menschenhand: er ist unmittelbare Weisung einer höheren Macht, eine Versinnlichung des schon im Kinde sich regenden höheren Ich." *Jean Pauls Verhältnis zu Rousseau* (Marburg a. L.: N. G. Elwert & G. Braun, 1924), 114.

Pestalozzis (1870). Like Jean Paul's work, this novel belongs to the popular but respectable genre of the German *Bildungsroman*, which traces the hero's social and spiritual growth through experience. In this case, however, the teachers are not ideal; they have to undergo a learning experience as much as their pupil. Gutzkow set out to explore the benefits and pitfalls of educating an ingenue. While not as optimistic as Rousseau about the potential of his 'tabula rasa', he steers the novel's course towards a positive outcome. The hero weathers the initial mistakes made in his upbringing, and finds success and contentment. Seen from today's vantage point, he may not seem like the 'new man' who will bring about a brighter tomorrow. But Gutzkow obviously approved of the end product of the interaction he outlined, and thus still showed confidence in the possibilities of education.

The Kaspar Hauser literature of the twentieth century presents a different picture. The quality of the educators remains an important concern, but the confidence has evaporated. None of the modern writers invented an ideal scenario, at least not in the German-speaking area.[5] In varying degrees and with different emphases, those who raise the issue indict the educational process, and implicitly hold it responsible for much of society's ills. One way of doing this is to concentrate on the shortcomings of Kaspar Hauser's teachers, or to portray them as downright malevolent. Physical appearance alone can reflect the author's negative judgement. In Martens' *Kaspar Hauser*, the teacher is "fett, plump, hämisch, [ein] Apoplektiker."[6] In Wassermann's novel, the professor from Leipzig who assesses the foundling's progress is described as follows:

> Er sprach mit ihm wie von Turmeshöhe herunter. Auch ließ er keinen Blick von ihm, und die gelblichen Augen hinter den kreisrunden Brillengläsern schimmerten bisweilen boshaft. (85)

Ebermayer's play includes two insensitive teachers, 'Professor Busch' and 'Lehrer Findeisen', who together with their students come to observe Kaspar's "außerordentlich primitive Struktur" (24) and, when he cries, comment on "[die] klagenden Kehlkopflaute" (23) with callous detachment.

Only Daumer, the boy's first mentor, is occasionally granted some redeeming qualities, perhaps as a reward for stalwartly defending his

---

[5] In contrast, François Truffaut's film *The Wild Child* (*L'Enfant Sauvage*, 1970), which examines the concept of the 'tabula rasa' by fictionalizing the story of the 'wolf boy of Aveyron', rewards the patient efforts of the teacher, Itard, with a happy ending. This is a deliberate amelioration of the historical reality, in which Itard tired of his struggle, and the pupil, less gifted than Kaspar Hauser, lived out his life in semi-retardation.

[6] Kurt Martens, *Kaspar Hauser: Drama* (Berlin: F. Fontane, 1903), 11. Where appropriate, further references to this play will be given after quotations in the text.

former protégé after the latter's death. In Wassermann's work, for example, he initially shows devotion beyond the call of duty. In Röttger's novel, Kaspar remembers him in his deathbed visions as a positive force, as someone who had taken his side against the scoundrel Stanhope. Much later, Herzog's film portrays this tutor as a kind old man, who unfortunately lacks the imagination to understand his ward. Nevertheless, even this figure does not escape criticism. In works which refer to the larger historical background (mainly those by Wassermann, Hofer, and Röttger), Daumer is blamed for the insensitivity of his experiments with Kaspar, and for abandoning him to less caring hands. In Wassermann's novel, this high-minded teacher lets egoism get the upper hand. Inconvenienced by the disruptions Hauser's notoriety entails, he detaches himself from the foundling, resolved, in future "die Kräfte des Geistes nur dort zu opfern, wo im Frieden der Erkenntnis und des Forschens jede Gabe sichtbar bezahlt wird" (110). Very likely, this tutor also served as model for Julian, the mentor of Hofmannsthal's prince. In him, too, signs of integrity and concern are outweighed by ambition. Julian is proud of having educated his prisoner, so that in spite of his miserable condition the prince is said to know Latin, and can deal with a book "wie wenns a Speckseiten wär," in his keeper's graphic description.[7] Yet Julian neglects to teach his pupil how to deal with reality, leaving him unprepared for the task ahead, and he uses the prince as a pawn in his own search for power.

But it is the figure of Meyer, Hauser's last tutor, who becomes the chief target for the literary resentment against the educational system and its functionaries. Wassermann (who rechristened his teacher 'Quandt' in order to avoid legal action by Meyer's descendants), Hofer, Schaumann, Ebermayer and Röttger all devote considerable space to the torment this outwardly respectable educator inflicts on his pupil. Röttger's figure is a downright sadistic schemer, who thinks that being able to denounce Hauser as a swindler will give him even greater pleasure than whipping his pupils ("als wenn man einem Bengel den Steiß verhaut"; 255). For the most part, however, these writers denounce a narrow-minded adherence to rules, the 'ossification of the soul', which can negate even well-meant efforts. Wassermann makes it clear that Meyer is not a unique case, but part of a much larger picture: "For all the Meyers, alias Quandts, for all these schoolmasters who can neither be educated nor taught, the formula 'slothfulness of heart' holds good."[8]

It looks as though the course of decades and presumable improvements in the educational system did nothing to change the cynical perception of educators, for more recent works still vent their spleen on

---

[7] *Turm* I, 22; *Turm* II, 333.

[8] Wassermann's "Introduction to the English Edition," *Caspar Hauser: The Enigma of a Century* (New York: Rudolf Steiner Publications, 1973; first publ. 1928), xvi, xvii.

this figure. In Forte's play, the teacher outdoes his fellow guests in the fatuity of his remarks. It is he who is made to extol the virtues of the censorship of which the author so obviously disapproves. "Man weiß, was man liest," he pontificates, "vorher wußte man es nicht. Irgendeiner' schrieb etwas, und man las es. Jetzt ist es amtlich" (40). In Trafic's presentation of Kaspar Hauser's life, it is Meyer's pedantic pettiness which finally drives the hero to open rebellion. Even Reinhard Mey's ballad turns the — this time nameless — guardian into a stern school-master, who unlike his neighbors may have shown charity to the stranger, but who is surly ("mürrisch"), and more concerned with punc-tuality than with Kaspar's well-being.

In Handke's *Kaspar*, the by now longstanding distrust of the educational process and what it can do to its gullible recipients is more than a side issue. It becomes a central theme of the play and takes on universal significance, by querying the whole process of socialization and its effect on society as a whole. In his stylized demonstration of the hero's progression from innocence to the enforced eradication of his personality, and then from pseudo-achievement to disillusionment and disintegration, Handke uses the historical model to show "was *möglich ist* mit jemandem" (7; emphasis Handke's). The perceived menace of enforced training is all the greater since it is now directly linked with the threat of modern technology, reflecting the widespread present-day phobia about the increasing mechanization of all aspects of life. Anonymous, robot-like voices have taken the place of tutors with human failings. Their methods are scientifically efficient, their intensity adjusts automatically to match the pupil's resistance: "Je heftiger [Kaspar] sich wehrt, desto heftiger wird auf ihn eingesprochen und desto heftiger zuckt das magische Auge zusammen" (7). Confronted by a depersonal-ized system of socialization such as this, the individual appears to be doomed.

In spite of this pessimistic scenario, one can argue that Handke's parable holds at least a glimmer of hope for the future of man. For even though the hero is driven into a cul-de-sac, he does arrive at a point where he is not only able to control his body and his physical environ-ment, but also gains an insight into his condition, if only for a brief moment. More importantly, he is able to express this insight even within the restrictive, stale idiom provided by his prompters. His comments, "Jeder Satz ist für die Katz" (92), or, "Schon mit meinem ersten Satz bin ich in die Falle gegangen" (98), may contain clichés, but are nevertheless appropriate evaluations of his situation. The capacity for self-awareness could not be totally circumvented, even under the most detrimental circumstances, and this makes a turning-point thinkable.

It is the educational system and its conveyors who in the eyes of the writers are at fault, not the recipient. In the context of Kaspar Hauser's situation, presenting the official functionaries in a negative light brings the innocence and goodness of the foundling into even sharper focus; the untrustworthiness of those he was forced to trust underlines his role as a victim. Taking a more universal view of the foundling as a paradigm for modern man, to cast blame on untrustworthy teachers — all those responsible for allowing ethical values and traditions to crumble and to be replaced with questionable new guidelines — is of course a convenient method of self-justification, but not a solution to the problem. A constructive reformation of the educators is not even envisaged. Yet without them it is a lonely and difficult existence.

Occasionally, there is a suggestion that the tables might be turned, and that Kaspar Hauser himself, the untaught and reluctant pupil, could serve as our teacher and guide. But it is worth noting that this hypothesis is never fully explored, and is mainly presented as a bygone or missed opportunity. Arp's hero in "kaspar ist tot" had evidently been capable of fulfilling the function of 'teacher', but he is no longer with us ("wer erklärt uns nun die monogramme in den sternen"). In Forte's drama, Kaspar Hauser's lack of social conditioning is credited with a clearer vision of life which could conceivably serve as a model. But again, the opportune moment has passed, and the idea of the foundling as teacher is couched in the subjunctive: "Man hätt von ihm lernen können" (11).

It would be a bleak picture indeed were it not for the foundling's own endurance and potential. As depicted in literature, he can outlast the damaging work of his educators without relinquishing his inner integrity, and may yet teach us something even in his absence. So we may have to put our hopes on hold, but do not have to relinquish them altogether.

II. *Sprachskepsis*

The development from 'tabula rasa' to civilized man, by whatever method and regardless of how we judge its results, is of course intimately linked with the acquisition and use of language. Paying special attention to this factor in the literature under discussion can help us understand another aspect of the problems these writers perceived, as well as illuminate their attempts to solve these problems.

The preoccupation with language and its development is in itself not a new phenomenon, but has a long history. An early example of particular relevance to Kaspar Hauser's situation is an experiment attributed to Friedrich II, ruler of the Holy Roman Empire in the thirteenth century. In order to study the origin and nature of language, the Emperor reputedly isolated a group of motherless infants, and had them raised by nursemaids who were forbidden to speak. The aim of this project was to determine beyond doubt whether the test objects would develop a common language spontaneously, and whether this language would be Hebrew, Greek, Latin, Arabic, or of an unknown kind. Sadly, these hapless children are reported to have died before any conclusions could be drawn.[9] Theories about the existence of a primary, untaught language continued to surface from time to time. One persistent notion, already raised by Vico in the eighteenth century, was that this first language was the language of imagination and constituted true or 'natural' poetry, since of necessity it had to be based on sensory experience. The conversion of sight and sound into verbal equivalents was thought to have created a language which was "poetic, musical, rhythmical, visual, gestural, and emotive."[10] The theory was that with the development of the human intellect, this kind of language gradually made way for linguistic artifice.

The thinkers of the Romantic movement revived the speculation about the origin of language. Rousseau, who as shown above had great influence on the evaluation of Kaspar Hauser in other respects, also believed in the existence of a natural language, a language based on emotions, and hence of poetic quality: "D'abord on ne parla qu'en poésie; on ne s'avisa de raisonner que longtemps après."[11] His thoughts on this matter once again show that he elevated the importance of the child over that of the adult: he was certain that in the original order of things it was the child who taught the adult how to communicate, rather than vice versa.[12]

In Germany, it was mainly Hamann and Herder who continued the discourse about a poetic, now irrevocably extinct *Ursprache*. "Was war diese erste Sprache," wrote Herder, "als eine Sammlung von Elementen der Poesie? Nachahmung der tönenden, handelnden, sich regenden Natur!" Taking issue with Rousseau's theory that the origin of language could be traced to a child's "Geschrei der Empfindungen," Herder argued that the imitation of the sounds of Nature needed a degree of reflection which was absent in the voice of instinct. To him, language was an innate, fundamental human trait which distinguishes man from other species: "Erfindung der Sprache ist ihm also so natürlich, als er ein Mensch ist."[13]

---

[9] For a review of the historical reports on this experiment, see Ernst Kantorowicz, *Kaiser Friedrich der Zweite* (Berlin: Georg Bondi, 1927), 325; also Kantorowicz, *Kaiser Friedrich der Zweite: Ergänzungsband. Quellennachweis und Exkurse* (Berlin: Georg Bondi, 1931), 156.

[10] Allan Megill, "Aesthetic Theory and Historical Consciousness in the Eighteenth Century," *History and Theory* 17, no. 1 (1978): 58.

[11] Jean-Jacques Rousseau, *Essai sur l'origine des Langues*, (1755), ed. Angèle Kremer-Marietti (Paris: Aubier Montaigne, 1974), 97. See also Rousseau's assertion, 144, that poetry, music, and natural language, all based on "les passions," emerged together.

[12] See *Discours sur l'origine et les fondements de l'inégalité parmi les Hommes*, ed. F. C. Green (Cambridge: University Press, 1941), 42.

[13] Gottfried Herder, "Abhandlung über den Ursprung der Sprache," *Frühe Schriften: 1764–1772*, ed. Ulrich Geyer (Frankfurt a. M.: Deutscher Klassiker Verlag, 1981), 740, 708, 722.

We note that it is the development and the mechanics of language rather than its usefulness and its meaning for those who transmit it which these reflections subject to scrutiny. It is an issue of scientific, historical interest rather than an existential matter. Man's inner need and desire to communicate with his fellowmen, and the role of language in society as a whole, were not seriously questioned until the end of the nineteenth century. At that time, *Sprachskepsis* became a conspicuous element in German literature, closely linked with the concept of alienation. In various forms and with fluctuating emphasis, a critical or ambivalent attitude towards language can be observed in many works, and in all genres, throughout our century. Perhaps the fact that so many theorists began to probe the nature and purpose of language in the twentieth century can also be seen as a symptom of modern doubt, rather than merely an expression of scientific curiosity and progress. More recent deconstructionist critics such as Jacques Lacan, for whom man's very entry into language signifies submission to the patriarchal order, gave the issue a further, political dimension and renewed importance.

The case of the historical Kaspar Hauser provided ample food for thought on the subject. Seen objectively, the rapidity and extent of the foundling's linguistic development seem to be more remarkable under the given circumstances than his shortcomings. They certainly set him apart from all other recorded cases of feral children, none of whom could boast such rate of progress and achievement. Yet it is mostly the foundling's initial incoherence, his inability to understand and make himself understood, and his perception of the messages from the outside world as physically painful,[14] which aroused the attention and empathy of modern writers. Evidently, these features struck a cord with their personal views of how intercommunication functioned, or malfunctioned, in their own age.

Of course the difficulty of finding the right word can be seen as part and parcel of a writer's work, independent of the problems of any particular era. Wassermann, for instance, freely admits that while he was always able to rely on an abundance of imagination, mastering the formal aspects of his craft could sometimes be a painstaking process. On occasion, he rewrote portions of his works up to twenty-two times before being satisfied with the result.[15] More recently, Wolf Biermann, with regard to the Kaspar Hauser song he presented at the Nuremberg 'Festival der Liedermacher' in 1986, attributes his feelings of kinship

---

[14] See Kaspar Hauser's own reports, e.g.: "... dan hat imer der Hieldel [= prison warden Hiltel] mich recht rasch an gesprochen und dieses hat mir im(m)er sehr weh gethan, in den Kopf," or: "Sie fingen zu sprechen an und so stark, daß es mir im ganzen Leib weh getan hat...." *Hausers erstes Auftreten in Nürnberg. Von ihm selbst beschrieben.* Reprint in Hörisch, ed., *Ich möchte ein solcher werden wie ... ,* 95, 107.

[15] See "Zur Charakteristik meiner Arbeitsmethode," *Lebensdienst* (Leipzig: Grethlein, 1928), 331.

with Kaspar Hauser specifically to the perennial difficulty of the poet's task of finding the right words for his thoughts: "Der Dichter ist immer in Kaspar Hausers elender Situation: er muß seine eigne Sprache neu lernen."[16]

But the problem had become more than just an occupational hazard. As discussed above, the social climate at the turn of the century had brought with it a widespread perception that the writer had, metaphorically speaking, 'lost his voice'. He was no longer accepted as the medium of truth, no longer listened to as he had been in previous eras. From his own point of view, the breakdown of traditions and the upheavals of the technological age admittedly made it more difficult to express cogent appraisals. Yet the desire of the artist to fulfil his former role did not simply vanish. Still wanting to be heard, yet seeing their message fall on deaf ears, it was only natural that some authors would see their own situation reflected in Kaspar Hauser's inarticulate state. They could commiserate with the feelings of helplessness this state induced, and identify with his longing to gain — or perhaps regain — the ability to speak. Thus the figure became, in Peter Handke's words, "das Modell einer Art von sprachlichem Mythos."[17]

Wassermann's novel contains a telling passage which beyond its specific context — Kaspar's initial struggle in learning to communicate — sums up the frustration of this situation:

> Es war ein langer Weg vom Ding bis zum Wort. Das Wort lief davon, man mußte nachlaufen, und hatte man es endlich erwischt, so war es eigentlich gar nichts und machte einen traurig. Gleichwohl führte derselbe Weg auch zu den Menschen; ja, es war, als ob die Menschen hinter einem Gitter von Worten stünden, das ihre Züge fremd und schrecklich machte; wenn man aber das Gitter zerriß oder dahinter kam, waren sie schön. (43)

The elusiveness of suitable words, and the disillusionment about what language per se can actually achieve, here appear as a barrier between people. But the last sentence of this paragraph also conveys that Wassermann saw it as a barrier that could and ought to be overcome.

Hofmannsthal also wavered between hope and despair about the potency of the poet's word in his own time. Critics usually cite his already mentioned Chandos-letter, in which his fictitious alter ego bemoans his doubts and inhibitions with regard to language, as a prime example of the poet's inner crisis at the turn of the century. Some regard Hofmannsthal's turning away from poetry to prose as a sign of surrender. In reality, his struggle continued throughout his lifetime, as the complex evolution of the two versions of *Der Turm* testifies. Man's

---

[16] Letter to author, 27 May 1987.

[17] Artur Joseph, "Peter Handke," in *Theater unter vier Augen* (Cologne: Kiepenheuer & Witsch, 1969), 35.

need to communicate, and the invisible barriers that frustrate this need, are one of the leitmotifs in these works. "Mit Reden kommen die Leut zusammen," observes Sigismund's astute factotum, Anton, early on in the play. One of the first things the King wants to know about the banished son he wants to call back from exile is what language he can expect from him. And when he finally meets him he urges: "Sprich, mein Sohn, laß mich deine Stimme hören." At the other end of the spectrum, the common people, expecting Sigismund's guidance, also repeatedly urge him: "Sprich zu uns!"[18] The prince certainly has the potential to comply, that is to say, he still has the poet's special gift. He can speak "wie vielleicht die Engel sprechen. Seine Sprache ist Zutagetreten des inwärts Quellenden."[19] But Hofmannsthal shows that the gift of *Engelszungen* is of little avail in the face of the brutal demands of reality. The prince becomes tongue-tied and displays a truly Kaspar-Hauser-like helplessness when confronted with the duplicity of his father, the king. "Sigismund kann nicht reden"; "Sigismund qualvoll ringend, stumm"; "Sigismund deutet durch Zeichen, er habe Furcht vor Gewalt," read the author's stage instructions.[20]

As Hofmannsthal presents it — and we may interpret this as a measure of self-defense — in this case the fault lies not so much with the originator of the potential message as with its recipients. We see that the insights the prince has gained through his suffering are lost on ruthless men like Oliver, and although the privations of the common people rouse Sigismund's pity and show him the need for action, he is unable to communicate with them. "Verdeutsch ihnen den Galimathias!" is Oliver's sarcastic advice in response to Sigismund's use of poetic imagery.[21] But the prince is unable to comply, and the danger of this is obvious: it leaves room for self-appointed (mis)interpreters like Jeronim, who seizes the opportunity to further his own, selfish aims by transforming what Sigismund sees as an existential experience into a political incitement to violence:

> Jeronim (mit schriller Stimme): Er sagt, sie haben ihn hungern und frieren lassen, und wenn sie vollgesoffen waren, haben sie ihn geprügelt wie einen störrischen Esel.[22]

---

[18] a) *Turm* I, 24; omitted in *Turm* II; b) *Turm* I, 117; in *Turm* II, 399, this passage reads: "Laß Uns deine Stimme hören, junger Fürst! Wir sind begierig nach ihr." c) *Turm* I, 164–65; *Turm* II, 446, 448.

[19] a) *Turm* I, 27; *Turm* II, 336. b) *Turm* I, 105; *Turm* II, 389 (text changed to: "Die vielleicht die Engel sprechen").

[20] a) *Turm* I, 118; *Turm* II, 399. b) *Turm* I, 118; omitted in *Turm* II. c) *Turm* I, 119; *Turm* II, 400.

[21] *Turm* I, 156 (omitted in *Turm* II).

[22] *Turm* I, 156 (omitted in *Turm* II).

Even with his friends and dependents, the prince often talks at cross purposes, not comprehending their advice, and precluding their efforts to help him with enigmatic pronouncements. Much as Hofmannsthal struggled to maintain his belief in the potency of language, the textual and subtextual evidence in both versions of *Der Turm* suggests that, like his hero Sigismund, and ultimately like Kaspar Hauser, he was in danger of losing the battle.

In the wake of World War II, many writers seem to have lost their trust in the efficacy of language — or, to be more precise, of traditional language — to an even greater extent. Handke's play *Kaspar* builds on the premise of man's desire to master language as a key to master life, only to unmask that whole concept as a delusion. Language acquisition is presented as the blueprint for the hero's education. Step by step, the prompters lure him to the point where — as the epitome of his linguistic achievement — he can express himself even in rhyme, and where he happily agrees with his mechanical mentors that "alles, was ich beim Namen nennen kann, ist nicht mehr unheimlich" (42). He thinks he has learned "alles was leer war / mit Wörtern zu füllen / ... und alles was schrie / mit Sätzen zu stillen" (83). Using Wittgenstein's theory as a point of departure, the author then reveals this belief in the trust-worthiness of language as a misconception. His hero comes to realize "wie viele Dinge mit der Sprache gedreht werden können,"[23] since there is no organic relationship between language and reality, and that the meaning of language lies exclusively in its actual use.[24]

While Handke's hero enjoys at least a passing illusion of having solved his problems through the mastery of language, the protagonist of Härtling's poem, "Kaspar Hauser," does not get beyond the stage of wishful thinking. Worse, he feels so incomplete, and has lost his self-confidence to such an extent, that he places his hope in finding an other who can make him whole, and speak for him and in his stead:

> Eine Liebste
> möchte er,
> die seinen Mund
> bewohnt

---

[23] Peter Handke, "Zur Tagung der Gruppe 47 in den USA," *Ich bin ein Bewohner des Elfenbeinturms* (Frankfurt a. M.: Suhrkamp, 1979), 30.

[24] "Ein Wort hat die Bedeutung, die man ihm gegeben hat." Ludwig Wittgenstein, *Das blaue Buch*, vol. 5 of *Schriften*, ed. G. E. M. Anscombe and G. H. von Wright (Frankfurt a. M.: Suhrkamp, 1970; orig. publ. Oxford: Basil Blackwell, 1958), 52. For a specific discussion of Handke's relationship to Wittgenstein, see e.g. Roger Bauer, "Peter Handke et le Paradoxe de Wittgenstein," *Revue d'Allemagne et des pays de langue allemande. Etudes littéraires* 12, no. 4 (Oct.–Dec. 1980): 629–42.

und aus ihm spricht.[25]

What he gets instead is the taste of death ("den Mund voll Blut"; ll. 28–29). Wenger's recent brief sketch, *magie der sprache* (1990), exudes similar pessimism, though in a less dramatic context. The 'magic' referred to in the title stands in ironic contrast to the impotence of the few words Kaspar uses "gegen alles, für alles." There is no communication with Nature, and his only human encounter is a dismal failure: "als er [dem Bauern] seinen satz sagte, rannte der mann davon."[26]

An interesting counterpoise to these works is Minnemann's apostrophe to a loved one in his brief poem "Kaspar":

> nimm mein wort
> wiege es in deinen armen
> sing dein lied
>
> und ich bin ein solcher
> wie nie ein anderer
> gewesen ist[27]

The author/narrator, evidently buoyed by the optimism of the student protest movement of the 1960s, shows confidence in his own identity, and in the potency of his word. He feels no need to echo the historical foundling's ostensible wish to become like his father, nor, as Handke's version reads, to become "wie einmal ein andrer gewesen ist" (13). He sees himself as unique, and lacks no 'other' who might speak on his behalf. His word is his gift, complementing his partner's song.

Minnemann's self-assured attitude represents a rare exception in the literature on Kaspar Hauser. Most writers are clearly wary about the efficacy of language transmission, if not necessarily about their own competence. The very essence of language was called in question, seen as contaminated by misuse. There seems to be a general consensus that this new distrust of language was fuelled by the discrepancy between the public presentation of social and political reality and the individual's — especially the artist's — perception of this reality. Early on in the century, Hofmannsthal commented on this corruption:

> Die Leute sind es … müde, reden zu hören. Sie haben einen tiefen Ekel vor den Worten. Denn die Worte haben sich vor die Dinge gestellt. … Die unendlich komplexen Lügen der Zeit, die dumpfen Lügen der

---

[25] *Die Mörsinger Pappel*, 19, ll. 1–5. The same motif, love as a healing force for the loss of speech, is the thematic backbone of another contemporary work, Siegfried Lenz's novel *Der Verlust* (Hamburg: Hoffmann & Campe, 1981).

[26] Wenger, "magie der sprache," 99.

[27] Joachim Minnemann, "Kaspar," in *Wir kommen: Literatur aus der Studentenbewegung*, ed. Franz Hutzfeldt (Munich: Damnitzverlag, 1976), 137.

Tradition, die Lügen der Ämter, die Lügen der einzelnen, die Lügen der Wissenschaften, alles das sitzt wie Myriaden tödlicher Fliegen auf unserem armen Leben.[28]

Arp's friend Hugo Ball, in defending the revolt of the Dada movement against the perceived corruption of language, laid the blame mainly on the doorstep of modern journalism, the transmitter of the official points of view. It had become necessary, he explained, to renounce "eine Sprache, die verwüstet und unmöglich geworden ist durch den Journalismus."[29] Since during the two World Wars that followed the misuse of language in the interest of social and political control increased rather than diminished, it is not surprising that the distrust of language persisted, perhaps even increased. It is precisely in this context that Härtling uses his reference to Kaspar Hauser in *Hugo; oder, Die Rückkehr nach Casablanca.* In the days of confusion that preceded the final collapse of Hitler's Third Reich in 1945, faced with the incompatibility of the evidence of his own eyes with the continuing war propaganda, the hero identifies with Kaspar Hauser's entrapment between appearance and reality:

Alles staute sich in ihm, wirr, und er fand keine Wörter dafür, keine Benennungen. In einer Zeitschrift las er über Kaspar Hauser, der gehalten worden war wie ein Tier und, als er unter Menschen kam, staunend lernte. Hubert dachte sich, daß für dieses Geschöpf jede Geste jeder Blick, jedes Wort zu Beginn unbeschreiblich rein gewesen sein müssen, bis er erschrocken merkte, wie verdorben sie waren durch ihre Geschichte und durch die Menschen. Er fragte sich auch, wie lange Kaspar brauchte, um zwischen Wahrheit und Lüge zu unterscheiden — oder ob es für ihn diese Unterscheidung nicht geben konnte.[30]

The confusing, grey area between public and private versions of truth also provides the background and pivot of Forte's play, *Kaspar Hausers Tod.* With their precarious set of values undermined by contemporary developments, and battered by untrustworthy messages, the characters on stage repeatedly compare themselves to the bewildered foundling. "Aber was soll ich mit der neuen Zeit, wenn ich sie nicht verstehe," is one comment, "ich komme mir langsam vor wie ein Kaspar Hauser" (53). Even the high-ranking official, whose job it is to implement the new modus vivendi, makes that comparison: "Manchmal kommt man

---

[28] Hugo von Hofmannsthal, "Eine Monographie. 'Friedrich Mitterwurzer', von Eugen Guglia," *Prosa*, vol. 1 of *Gesammelte Werke in Einzelausgaben*, ed. Herbert Steiner (Frankfurt a. M.: S. Fischer, 1951), 265.

[29] Cited by Hans Richter, "Erinnerungen und Bekenntnisse," in Hugo Ball, *Gesammelte Gedichte*, ed. A. Schütt-Hennings (Zurich: Arche, 1963), 120.

[30] Peter Härtling, *Hubert; oder, Die Rückkehr nach Casablanca*, paperback edition (Frankfurt a. M., 1980; orig. publ. Darmstadt: Luchterhand, 1978), 93.

sich wirklich vor wie ein Kaspar Hauser. Keine Erklärung stimmt mehr. Nichts ist von Bestand" (54).

But how should the writer himself react and function in this position? The most radical response, of course, would be to fall silent. It is a measure of the gravity of the problem that this option was indeed seriously considered. "Wer was zu sagen hat, trete vor und schweige," wrote Karl Kraus at the outbreak of World War I.[31] And at Hitler's ascent to power, with his journal shrunk from the customary two hundred or more pages to a mere four pages:

> Und Stille gibt es, da die Erde krachte,
> Kein Wort, das traf.
>
> ...
>
> Das Wort entschlief, als jene Welt erwachte.[32]

These lines might have been coined to describe the reaction of Hofmannsthal's Sigismund, when he is faced with the chaos created by Oliver and realizes the futility of his own commitment to society. "Mein Lehrer, warum sprichst du zu ihnen?" he advises Julian during their defeat, "Was zu sagen der Mühe wert wäre, dazu ist die Zunge zu dick."[33] He concludes that by choosing silence, one can at least save one's inner dignity. For Hofmannsthal, to show "den Anstand des Schweigens" was a respectable option, a victory of sorts, even though in the eyes of some critics — who had the benefit of hindsight knowledge about the world events which soon followed — this view deserves much approbation.[34]

It appears that at the end of his life Kurt Tucholsky, realizing that wit and words were no match for the ruthlessness of the Nazis, also came to the conclusion that silence might be the highest point of valor. Before committing suicide, he wrote this ascending scale into his private notebook, as his last entry:[35]

---

[31] "In dieser großen Zeit," *Die Fackel*, no. 404 (Dec. 1914): 2.

[32] Untitled poem, *Die Fackel*, no. 888 (Oct. 1933): 4. Significantly, the only other item in this issue is a funeral address (dedicated to Adolf Loos, the Viennese master-builder).

[33] *Turm* II, 447.

[34] Hugo von Hofmannsthal, "Ad me Ipsum," *Aufzeichnungen: Gesammelte Werke in Einzelausgaben*, ed. Herbert Steiner (Frankfurt a. M.: S. Fischer, 1959), 215. For a critical view of Hofmannsthal's conclusion, see, e.g. Michael Hamburger, *Hofmannsthal: Three Essays* (Princeton, N.J.: Princeton University Press, 1972), 106; or Gerhart Pickerodt, *Hofmannsthals Dramen: Kritik ihres historischen Inhalts* (Stuttgart: J. B. Metzler, 1968), 262.

[35] Heinrich Schröder, "Kurt Tucholsky: Polemik und Satire im Kampf um eine Weltanschauung" (Ph.D. diss., University of Vienna, 1958), 33.

Schweigen
Schreiben
Sprechen

Decades later, "Ausbrechen in die Freiheit des Schweigens"[36] still seems to be an honorable option. When in "nachricht von kasper" Härtling says of his hero: "ihm ist der kasperatem ausgegangen," we cannot be sure whether the ensuing silence is voluntary or caused by an outside force. In the case of Handke's protagonist, the evidence is more convincing. As Bekes rightly observes, the hero uses his brief moment of awareness about his past and present to reject his linguistic achievement and opt for silence: "Ich weiß jetzt, was ich will: ich will still sein." Three times he returns on stage, "tut, als hätte er noch was zu sagen," but opts for silence.[37] One may query whether the hero's final linguistic disintegration happens by choice or force. Most critics make little distinction between the completion of Kaspar's training and his final breakdown, judging both as the symptoms of total defeat. It is possible, however, to see signs of at least passive resistance in the undeniably negative course of events. According to Held, the evidence of such resistance transpires already during the training process itself. Comparing Kaspar to the folk hero-soldier Schwejk, he comments on the former's irrational verbal responses to his prompters: "Scheinbar pariert er weiter, unversehens schleicht sich aber der Hohn des allmählich zur Besinnung kommenden ein: Kaspar ironisiert die Satzmodelle seiner Einsager, indem er die Funktion der Syntax unangetastet läßt, lediglich die semantischen Teile auswechselt."[38] In view of Kaspar's later delight in his apparent mastery of the language, followed by consternation when he recognizes his entrapment, such early cunning is not very plausible. But perhaps one can interpret the final relapse into incoherence as a voluntary retreat rather than the ultimate triumph of pernicious forces. After all, if the latter's goal had been to train obedient tools to perpetuate the system, we would have to regard their effort as a dismal failure. While Kaspar's real aims have indeed been thwarted, and the compatibility between reality and language proves to be illusory, he has at least rendered himself — like Hofmannsthal's hero had done in the second version of *Der Turm* — "nicht verwendbar" for potential misuse.[39]

---

[36] From Wolfgang Bächler's poem "Ausbrechen," in *Ausbrechen: Gedichte aus 30 Jahren* (Frankfurt a. M.: S. Fischer, 1976), 193.

[37] *Kaspar*, 69–70; for the comment referred to, see Peter Bekes, *Peter Handke: "Kaspar." Sprache als Folter* (Paderborn: Ferdinand Schöningh, 1984), 85.

[38] Wolfgang Held, "Kaspar Hauser und die Kritik der Sprache," in *Beiträge zu den Sommerkursen 1969*, ed. Goethe-Institut (Munich: Goethe-Institut, 1969), 49.

[39] See Hofmannsthal, *Turm* II, 457.

Even as late as 1988, Lange-Müller's hero Amica, alias "Kasper Mauser," responds to the uncongenial messages he receives from his social environment by choosing to turn his back on language. Having first established several external parallels with the historical foundling in order to direct our attention to the more important thematic correlation, the author presents the hero's retreat into total silence as the only way in which he can register his protest and defend his identity, affirming as a voluntary stance what had, for the real Kaspar Hauser, not been a matter of choice:

> Von nun an wort-, ja sprachlos, wie weiland — erst mal — Caspar Hauser, würde er darauf bestehen, die Unperson, die jeder ist — in *solcher* Lage — auch gänzlich zu sein *und* zu *bleiben*. [emphasis Lange-Müller's][40]

Throughout the narrative, Lange-Müller's style exudes her own distrust in the reliability of language. Idioms and proverbs are dissected and inverted to examine them for other possible meanings. The train of thoughts in sentences and paragraphs is constantly interrupted by diverging, perhaps opposite hypotheses, asides, or puns, as, for instance, in this elaboration on why Amica adopts his new name 'Kaspar Mauser', as a tribute to Kaspar Hauser and other outsiders:

> Er nur wußte noch und wollte — o wie bald schon — es vergessen. daß je er jener andere gewesen, der 'gebohren' einst in Weimar und dessen Held war und Idol und Star … der historische Caspar Hauser (und der eines Jakob Wassermann) den er so sehr bewunderte, wie andere Mimen oder Schlagersänger, und der nun sich nannte: Kasper Mauser. Wohl wegen möglicher Assoziationen zur Kasper-Puppe, zum Suppen-Kasper, zu Müllers/Brechts 'Mauser', der Mauser der kanarischen Vögel, der Pistole gleichen Namens.[41]

Yet for a writer to turn away from words is surely a contradiction in terms. If taken seriously by all, it would bring about the 'death of literature', which has indeed been prophesied in recent years as a logical development in the realm of letters. Luckily, it has not happened, and shows no sign of happening in the near future, because writers also found other methods to cope with the problem of language, and to preserve their self-esteem.

One of these methods was to invent new ways of expression. If the problem lay in the actual usage of words, maybe a determined change of this usage could break the vicious cycle and redress the damage? We remember that even in the depth of his depression about his linguistic

---

[40] Lange-Müller, *Kasper Mauser*, 63.

[41] Ibid., 62.

impotence, Hofmannsthal's Lord Chandos speculated about the possible existence of a brand-new language,

> in welcher nicht nur zu schreiben, sondern auch zu denken [ihm] vielleicht gegeben wäre ... eine Sprache, von deren Worten [ihm] auch nicht eines bekannt ist, eine Sprache, in welcher die stummen Dinge zu [ihm] sprechen, und in welcher [er] vielleicht einst im Grabe vor einem unbekannten Richter [sich] verantworten werde.[42]

Some writers resolutely embarked on a search for such a new language. Hence, in a Dada poem like Arp's "kaspar ist tot," the deliberate flouting of poetic conventions, the unexpected, seemingly random juxtaposition of ideas and expressions, and the creation of new word combinations and puns, such as "glockenscheune" or "heufische." For all their playful and nonsensical ingredients, poems of the Dada movement, such as "kaspar ist tot," were part of a serious crusade, designed, as Arp put it, "das gelobte Land des Schöpferischen zurückzugewinnen."[43] The Dadaist flavor of Meret Oppenheim's later poems (and ipso facto of her "Ohne mich ohnehin," with its allusion to Hauser) may no longer convey that earlier militant tenor, but the mere title of the relevant edition, *Husch, husch, der schönste Vokal entleert sich*, speaks of the concern with language and its flux of meaning. Trakl's esoteric codification of symbols and colors is another vivid example of this approach, although in his case it was a very private struggle. In more recent days, Höllerer's and Härtling's poems (as indeed most modern poetry), as well as Handke's search for unique modes of presentation — of which his *Kaspar* is merely one example — can be seen as attempts to escape the corruption of language through innovations in its formal aspects. The rejection of rhyme and capitalization are all part of this picture up to today (as for instance in Wolfgang Wenger's "magie der sprache," [1990]), although by now the flouting of conventions has lost much of its former shock value, indeed has almost become a convention itself.

Herzog tried a different approach, by inventing a language of pictures which allowed him to economize, and partially even to dispense with the conventional dialogue of film. As he articulates it:

> Zentrum vielleicht von dem, was ich mache, ist eine Sucherei. ... ich versuche, Bilder zu artikulieren, die wir unbedingt haben müssen, weil wir mit unseren Bildern hinter unserem Zivilisationsstand herhinken. Und wenn wir nicht eine adäquate Sprache beziehungsweise adäquate Bilder für unseren Zivilisationsstand finden, dann ist das eine ernste

---

[42] "Ein Brief," *Prosa*, vol. 2 of *Gesammelte Werke in Einzelausgaben*, ed. Herbert Steiner (Frankfurt a. M.: S. Fischer, 1951), 22.

[43] Hans Arp, "Dada war kein Rüpelspiel," *Unsern täglichen Traum: Erinnerungen, Dichtungen und Betrachtungen aus den Jahren 1914–1954* (Zurich: Arche, 1955), 21.

Sache, weil eine Zivilisation dann wegstirbt wie die Dinosaurier weggestorben sind.[44]

In some cases, the desire for a language other than the worn-out tool of a civilization gone awry appears in thematic rather than stylistic attributes. The various instances in which Kaspar Hauser's reputed gift for music is magnified into a mysterious, wordless form of communication fall into this category. So do the repeated references (particularly noticeable in Wassermann's and Röttger's work) to the intuitive understanding the foundling arrives at with women and children, that is to say with those members of society who presumably have little part in the process of corruption. A third example is Kaspar Hauser's ability to communicate with animals, already discussed above as an aspect of his interrelationship with Nature. The fact that he can calm a rabid dog by his mere presence (Wassermann), make the deer of the forest follow him into the city (Trakl), or easily command spirited horses (Wassermann, Arp, Hofmannsthal, Schaumann), is proof that he has a different kind of language at his disposal.

Even when Kaspar Hauser is shown to make use of human speech, the emphasis is not on his growing sophistication. Instead, writers stress a continued simplicity of expression, which sets the foundling apart from those around him. In Trakl's poem, the hero's "dunkle Klage" is more than adequate to convey his misery. In Röttger's novel, Kaspar affects a childlike, naive dialect even at the very end of his learning process. When Amann lets Kaspar Hauser recite from his memoirs, he deliberately reverses the progression of his writing style: Kaspar begins with the rhetorical flourishes of his latest entry, only to dismiss it and revert to the earlier, simpler versions, presumably because the simplest words give the most accurate portrayal of the truth.

Thus with regard to language, the picture is not entirely negative. In spite of *Sprachskepsis* and ambivalence, writers retained various options, and they were and still are exploring alternative ways of expression. One might say that in this respect, Kaspar Hauser's hardiness reflects their own. Therefore, we find in the works on Kaspar Hauser not only critical assessments of the educational process, but also attempts to salvage something from the given situation. With very few exceptions, Kaspar Hauser's teachers are shown in a negative light. Even Daumer and pastor Fuhrmann certainly do not qualify as role models for tutors of the kind Rousseau had in mind. In other words, one must not look to the educational system — as nineteenth-century writers still tended to do — to produce the 'new man' who could safeguard the future. Nevertheless, the outlook is not totally gloomy. Kaspar Hauser, as 'tabula rasa', is generally shown to have an innate resilience which allows him to

---

[44] Herzog, cited by Pflaum, "Interview," in Hans Günther Pflaum and others, *Werner Herzog*, Reihe Film 22, ed. Peter W. Jansen and Wolfram Schütte (Munich: Carl Hanser, 1979), 68.

weather even the most misguided intervention in his life. In terms of the situation of modern man, this implies that new beginnings are still possible, and that corruption is not always inevitable.

With regard to language, the vehicle of the process of socialization, an ambiguous attitude prevails. Having lost his former role as mouthpiece of wisdom and truth, the writer usually sympathizes with Kaspar Hauser's inarticulate endeavors to join the mainstream of society. But much of the Kaspar Hauser literature also reflects the widespread *Sprachskepsis* of our century, which holds the corruption of language responsible for many of our present-day ills. Yet here, too, a glimmer of hope exists. Various writers have used the figure of Kaspar Hauser to test alternative ways of expression, either in the formal aspects of their work, or by concentrating on the foundling's mysterious abilities to communicate without the use of words. Or else they simply invest his linguistic incompetence with positive overtones, and thus, by proxy, are able to rescue some of their self-respect.

7

The Attempt to Rejoin Society:
Kaspar Hauser as a Tool for Social Criticism

I. The Writer as Social Critic

As WILL HAVE BECOME apparent by now, much of the uneasiness and even despair in the literature under discussion centered on the individual human being and the invasion of his or her personal sphere. Were those who turned Kaspar Hauser into an emblematic figure a breed apart, more ready than others to withdraw from society to mourn man's fate, and content to accept their outsider status as permanent? Or do their works also contain signals of remaining or renewed commitment to society as a whole? There is evidence that at least some of the writers in question widened their concern about the present and future to encompass society as a whole.

With Germany's turbulent history in mind, the charge is sometimes leveled that writers on the whole have not been vigorous enough in the defense of socio-political values, and that too often they have recoiled from involvement in everyday matters when they should have spoken out in protest. With one particular aspect of literature in mind, Wolfgang Körner perceives this dichotomy as a fundamental, typically German trait:

> Es ist eine bekannte Tatsache, daß bei uns Deutschen Poesie und Politik als entschiedene und durchaus unversöhnbare Gegensätze betrachtet werden, und daß demgemäß politische Poesie bei uns meist für ein Ding gilt, welches entweder als unmöglich, nicht existiert, oder als unberechtigt, doch nicht existieren sollte.[1]

The implication of such charges is that more political vigilance and vigor on the authors' part are called for, and, had they existed throughout the century, might have made a difference in the course of recent history, an assumption which in spite of its negativity still reveals a belief in the power of the writer. But the situation is more complex. It is true that participation in 'art for art's sake' at the beginning of the century, in the *Innere Emigration* of the Hitler years, and in the *Neue Subjektivität* of

---

[1] "Ist Handke romantisch?", *Egoist* 4, no. 14 (1968): 10.

more recent years constitutes a refusal to become involved in the sordid business of current affairs which can be interpreted as silent approval. Conversely, it is also not difficult to refute the above accusation by citing the individual efforts of politically committed writers such as Toller or Brecht, or the combined efforts of those who grappled with the malfunction of society in publications like *Die Weltbühne,* such as Tucholsky or Otto Flake. More recently, following the years of student unrest in the 1960s, there was a veritable onus on writers to become part of the *Außerparlamentarische Opposition* (APO), and to demonstrate their social commitment through their works. For those who subscribed to the idea of historical determinism, the distinction between desirable and undesirable writing seemed easy. "Weil Geschichte ... bisher ein Prozeß der Befreiung ist," writes Martin Walser confidently, "ein Prozeß der Annäherung an die Demokratie, deshalb kann man ungeniert von Fortschritt sprechen und, zur Kritik, Literatur einteilen in fortschrittliche und konservative."[2] In this framework of thinking, to use poetry as a weapon (e.g.: "Mein Gedicht ist mein Messer"), even to be knowledgeable about "Fahrpläne" rather than "Oden,"[3] was the decree of the mainstream of literature at that time.

Yet even such resolute engagement never totally eliminated all qualms about the place and purpose of the writer, and there is evidence that Körner's charge of literary ambivalence is not entirely unjustified. For instance, as Last has pointed out, in the earlier part of the century there is a curious inconsistency between the militant titles of journals such as *Der Sturm, Der Brenner,* and *Die Aktion,* and the aesthetic exclusiveness of much of their contents.[4] Hofmannsthal consciously sacrificed aesthetic exclusiveness, but never quite came to terms with the burden of social commitment. On the one hand, he deplored in the writers of his generation "ein Sich Wegwenden von dem, was die lautesten Fragen der Zeit zu sein scheinen," which in his view showed "wie wenig sich die Dichter ihres Amtes zu erinnern scheinen."[5] On the other hand, he himself struggled for decades with the perceived task, but — as the outcome of both versions of *Der Turm* reveals — finally had to concede, if not personal defeat, at least the temporary impossibility of effective intervention in the course of public events. Klaus Mann, in his more mature years, threw himself wholeheartedly into the literary

---

[2] *Wie und wovon handelt Literatur?* (Frankfurt a. M.: Suhrkamp, 1973), 120.

[3] See *Mein Gedicht ist mein Messer,* ed. Hans Bender (Munich: Paul List, 1961); the title refers to Wolfgang Weyrauch's poem of the same name. The second reference is to Hans Magnus Enzensberger's well-known poem "ins lesebuch für die oberstufe," in *Gedichte* (Frankfurt a. M.: , 1962), 28.

[4] See Rex W. Last, *German Dadaist Literature: Kurt Schwitters, Hugo Ball, Hans Arp* (New York: Twayne Publishers, 1973), 73.

[5] "Der Dichter und diese Zeit," *Prosa,* vol. 2 of *Gesammelte Werke in Einzelausgaben,* ed. Herbert Steiner (Frankfurt a. M.: S. Fischer, 1951), 288.

crusade against Hitler, yet he worried that the involvement with politics might contaminate his vision as a writer. "I am sometimes afraid," he confessed at one point, "the constant preoccupation with politics might eventually corrupt or obfuscate my mind, and in the end distract me from the problems and pleasures which really are my natural métier."[6] Similar fears may well have prevented others from joining the fray from the very start, quite apart from the threat to life and liberty they would have had to face during the years of the Nazi regime.

Even in the activist climate of more recent times, one can still discern signs of hesitation about the social function of literature. The fact that writers now shy away from the title of *Dichter*, referring to themselves, like Brecht, as *Stückeschreiber*, or, like Martin Walser, as "dichtende Schreiber" or "sogenannte Künstler,"[7] may have as much to do with a continued lack of confidence in the role of the *Dichter* as with solidarity with the working class, or with the rejection of tradition. Also, the frequency with which latter-day authors feel obliged to theorize on the issue seems more like a case of 'protesting too much' than an expression of certainty. Martin Walser, for example, one of the prominent spokesmen for the generation of socially committed authors after the Second World War, sees the writer as indispensable for "Ideologie-Pflege," but at the same time evidently considers his work as inferior to practical involvement in politics: "Verglichen mit dem unmittelbaren politischen Handeln wird Schreiben unter allen Umständen eine mindere Art des Handelns bleiben."[8] Handke's theoretical reflections on his work also reveal that he had not resolved the tension between writer and society. He vigorously defends his right to remain the apolitical "Bewohner des Elfenbeinturms" which his more left-wing colleagues had accused him of being, stating that he does not feel qualified to hand out blueprints for the future.[9] Yet he regards his work as "nichts Gegensätzliches ... zu der aktionistischen oder rein begrifflichen Auffassung von Gesellschaft," indeed as something that could contribute to a correction of the latter.[10] He expects of literature "ein Zerbrechen aller gültigen Weltbilder," and adds: "Und weil ich erkannt habe, daß ich selber mich durch die Literatur ändern konnte ... , bin ich auch überzeugt, durch meine

---

[6] *The Turning Point: Thirty-five Years in this Century* (London: Victor Gollancz, 1944), 280–81.

[7] *Wie und wovon handelt Literatur?*, 121, 132.

[8] Ibid., 136–37.

[9] See e.g. his comment: "Ein engagierter Autor kann ich nicht sein, weil ich keine politische Alternative weiß zu dem, was ist, hier und woanders, (höchstens eine anarchistische). Ich weiß nicht, was sein soll." *Ich bin ein Bewohner des Elfenbeinturms*, 26.

[10] Heinz Ludwig Arnold, "Gespräch mit Peter Handke," *Text und Kritik* 24/24a (Sept. 1974): 32.

Literatur andere ändern zu können."[11] Thus for him, subjective writing is not necessarily incompatible with participation in social change.

Dieter Forte, questioned about his views on the role of the author in society, also refuses to draw clear dividing lines. To him, the very act of putting pen to paper counts as a kind of political commitment: "Schon indem ich eine Zeile hinsetze, engagiere ich mich."[12] Peter Härtling in turn, who as co-editor of *Der Monat* and in his campaign for the SPD has paid his political dues in practical terms, considers explicit commitment as inherently futile, and therefore not part of his task as a writer.[13] Such patent ambivalence in literary circles, coupled with the inability of the committed faction to bring about tangible changes, may account for the recent return of a more tolerant climate, which accommodates a wider spectrum of writing. Under the label of *Neue Innerlichkeit*, the pendulum even began to swing in the opposite direction, away from social activism and back to more self-centered concerns.

Where does the literature on Kaspar Hauser fit into this perennial vacillation between the rejection and acceptance of communal responsibility? Certainly, none of the works under discussion exhibits the militancy which characterizes the vanguard of radical social commitment, and which is usually associated with the left-wing critics of society. Possibly Kaspar Hauser's passive acceptance of his fate and the reputation of his aristocratic descent (which, though not nearly as important as it used to be, still clings to his name even today) disqualified him from becoming a suitable hero in these quarters.[14] There is no doubt that it was, above all, the foundling's exclusive nature and his suffering which provided the major literary inspiration, and which were lovingly explored, especially in the earlier part of the century. But most of those who took up the material also show some form of general social awareness in their work. Some go further than that, and clearly demonstrate that they are not content to remain in isolation, but wish to participate in the pragmatic business of shaping the future. As can be expected, the wide range in the form and content of their works is matched by an equally wide range in the degree of commitment they exhibit, and in the aim of their criticism.

---

[11] *Ich bin ein Bewohner des Elfenbeinturms*, 20.

[12] See *Butzbacher Autorenbefragung*, ed. Hans-Joachim Müller (Munich: Franz Ehrenwirt, 1973), 48.

[13] See his pessimistic comment: "Da der Schriftsteller heute in der Gesellschaft kaum mehr einen 'Stellenwert' hat, ist er auch kaum mehr in der Lage, die Gesellschaft zu beeinflussen." *Butzbacher Autorenbefragung*, 67–68.

[14] Perhaps, as a pawn and victim of political intrigues, Kaspar Hauser should have warranted attention even in left-wing circles. In fact, Horst Martin relates Kaspar Hauser to Brecht's figure 'Apfelbök', and to the poem "Vom armen BB." See "Kaspar Hauser und Sigismund," 245, n. 57.

We had noted previously that most nineteenth-century plays and novels revolved not around the foundling himself, but around invented misdeeds of the aristocracy which could account for his fate. Although these works patently exploited the public's appetite for sensationalism, they also contained an implicit disapproval of the ruling elite, which in the contemporary climate of social unrest and official censorship must count as a form of social criticism. In the twentieth century, the aristocracy could no longer be targeted as the sole scapegoat for society's ills. If a writer now wanted to use the Kaspar Hauser material as an instrument for social criticism, he had to send his barbs in another direction, or at least widen his aim. The greater part of the Kaspar Hauser literature does not even concern itself with the aristocracy, and works that still include the so-called *Prinzentheorie* now give it far less prominence. It is true that where writers do incorporate emissaries of royal courts (e.g. Martens, Wassermann, Röttger, and Schäfer), they invariably still cast them in the role of the villain. Lord Stanhope in particular is usually judged very harshly, or, especially in Schäfer's play and Herzog's film, ridiculed as a foppish buffoon. But by far the most frequent modern object of criticism is the community as a whole.

Analyzing the reasons behind the historical Kaspar Hauser's continued isolation, Hörisch argues that the society of that era had in fact no choice but to exclude the strange youth from its midst, if it wanted to preserve its hard-won and precarious sense of self-esteem.[15] Masche, in an investigation of four other outsider figures in German literature, sees the confrontation between outsider and society in the same light. "One of the functions observed," he concludes, "is that the outsider helps the group to find some identity as a group, and to confirm this group-identity."[16] This view implies that, as in Aristotelian tragedy, one may well pity the hero but in the final analysis ought to side with the excluding group. Interestingly, the Kaspar Hauser literature presents us with the reverse situation, since without exception, the authors under discussion side with the excluded, and view the excluding group as the culprit who disturbs the natural order and harmony. This unanimous support for the odd individual can be seen as a measure of the extent to which the faith in society had eroded. Kaspar Hauser's own shortcomings, insignificant as they may have been, are invariably ignored, or excused as necessary measures of self-defense.[17] He is either presented as a paragon of virtue, or at least as someone who

---

[15] Hörisch, "Die Sprachlosigkeit des Kaspar Hauser." See esp. 272.

[16] U. Masche, "Zum Problem des Außenseiters; Muschgs 'Schwarze Spinne,' Kleists 'Michael Kohlhaas,' Goethes 'Werther' und Döblins 'Biberkopf'" (Ph.D. diss., University of Basel, 1971). See Masche's summary in *Dissertation Abstracts International*, 38 (1978), 537.

[17] "Wer nicht körperlich fliehen kann, flieht in das Gestrüpp der Verstellung," is the explanation for Kaspar's white lies in Röttger's *Kaspar Hausers letzte Tage*, 34.

behaves as man ought to behave. And while it is fair to say that the real Kaspar Hauser was *not* treated with deliberate cruelty, and certainly not with indifference (in fact, considering his initial unkempt and inarticulate state, society reached out to him in a way no ordinary vagrant of that time could hope for), the standard modern portrayal is that of an innocent victim of a cruel and heartless community.

The negative evaluation of society in this constellation began already at the turn of the century, with the influence of Verlaine's "Gaspard Hauser chante." Verlaine's own exclusion from society had prompted him to depart from the prevailing pattern of nineteenth-century literature on Kaspar Hauser, which strained to find explanations for his confinement. By subtly engaging the reader's sympathy for the protagonist's simplicity and fate, and with the aid of just a few cryptic details, the poem succeeds in casting the military and city people, who cast out this orphan, in a critical light. The German transcribers of the poem, finding their own skeptical view of society confirmed, all perpetuated the stance, as did those who in turn were inspired by the transcriptions to deal with the figure in a manner of their own.

Where the chosen form demanded an economy of words, as in poetry, the writer's negative view of society may only transpire indirectly, through his choice of imagery. Trakl's "Kaspar Hauser Lied," for instance, contains no explicit condemnation. The poet evokes the uncaring aspect of Kaspar Hauser's world through the emptiness and darkness of the city, and through the bleak imagery of winter. The hero's "dunkle Klage" resonates with an accusation, and confirms his loneliness. Härtling's poem "kasper" uses the metaphor of a separating wall of glass to convey a distorting distance between the hero and his fellowmen.

As many writers recognized, Kaspar Hauser's own innocence about the ways of the world was potentially a very effective device for social criticism. This is of course a well-worn literary technique; we need only think of figures like Grimmelshausen's Simplizissimus, or Voltaire's Candide. From the foundling's point of view, and through his naive eyes, the discrepancy between life as it is and as it ought to be could be made apparent. For like the boy in the tale of the emperor's new clothes, he was not fooled by conventions, and could still see the essence of things. Lewandowski, after giving his version of Kaspar Hauser's life, sums up this recognition in the following words:

Kaspar Hauser konnte, da er so unvoreingenommen der Kultur seiner Zeit gegenübertrat, vieles beobachten und denken, was den meisten seiner Mitmenschen gar nicht auffiel, weil sie von Kind an daran gewöhnt waren.[18]

---

[18] *Das Tagebuch Kaspar Hausers*, 41.

Thus by presenting Kaspar's own view of the world, and by relying on the reader's or viewer's recognition of dramatic irony, writers could question the perception of what is normal, or even reverse it. In an interview about his work, Herzog once articulated this very process:

> Ein Mann wie der Kaspar Hauser in dem Film *Jeder für sich und Gott gegen alle*, das ist wohl einer, der scheinbar wie von einem fremden Planeten auf unsere Erde gefallen ist, aber wenn man genau hinsieht — und das zeigt der Film von der ersten bis zur letzten Minute: Die gesamte bürgerliche Gesellschaft benimmt sich da so absonderlich, daß der Kaspar Hauser als Mensch, der noch unberührt ist von Gesellschaft-lichem und Erlerntem, auf einmal zu fragen und hinterfragen anfängt. Und man sieht auf einmal, daß das ja die ganzen Exzentriker sind. Der einzige Mensch, der da Sinn gibt, der menschlich ist und einen anrührt, das ist der Kaspar.[19]

The naive perspective, already embedded in the deliberately artless diction of Verlaine's early poem, often determines the choice of style in the works that followed. Röttger, for example, may interrupt the neutral style of his third-person account with a halting syntax when he enters the foundling's thoughts: "O, alles so schwer! ... Alles so schwer — zu lernen" (383). The presentation of the world through the foundling's own eyes is, of course, most appropriate where the author mimics the foundling writing his diary, or where he enters his dreams. Schaumann relies on this approach for the diary segments of her story. Wassermann and Röttger also include portions of Kaspar's putative diary for the sake of dramatic irony.[20] Röttger, in these instances, switches to a Fran-conian dialect, which contrasts with the standard German of those around Kaspar Hauser who presumably taught him to speak, but which can give added simplicity and thus an aura of wholesomeness to the conveyed thoughts.

In a more abstract context, Handke applies the naive point of view to expose the detrimental mechanism beneath man's social adaptation. The world, represented by simple, everyday objects, is a frightening place, only tameable, it seems to Kaspar, if he learns how to impose a specific linguistic meaning on all its manifestations. But the price for this peace of mind turns out to be too high, and — as in the other kinds of Kaspar Hauser literature — the initial, naive perception proves to be the correct one, the one endorsed by the writer.

Herzog's film also devotes considerable attention to Kaspar's own perceptions, and includes them in various ways. Optically, the camera interrupts the narrative from time to time to switch from the perspective

---

[19] Werner Herzog, cited by Hans-Günther Pflaum, "Interview," *Werner Herzog*, 68.

[20] Lewandowski's *Tagebuch* is an exception, since the view it presents, and its language, are far too sophisticated to be accepted by the reader as the foundling's own; congeniality of spirit is all this hero can claim.

of those who find and manipulate the foundling to his own field of vision. Verbally, the hero shares his evaluations of the world around him, and, on one occasion, succeeds in upstaging the learned men who want to test his faculty of logic with a simple aperçu, much to the amusement of the audience. Herzog abandoned his initial idea (still recorded in the film's script) to let Kaspar Hauser give a first-person, retrospective commentary on the events of his life. This would have provided a further opportunity to describe the world from the outsider's perspective. But although the planned voice-over was patterned after the relatively unrefined style of Hauser's historical autobiography, Herzog must have recognized that the required level of fluency and sophistication was still high enough to conflict with the visual depiction of the hero's perceptions.

Appropriate as the employment of the naive point of view may be, as a tool of criticism it did have its limitations. It is significant that in all cases Kaspar's field of vision is restricted. While his 'uncivilized' perception illuminates details in unexpected ways, and can give fresh insights into some of the absurdities of life, he never grasps the whole picture, the totality of life, and he — and by implication: Everyman — remains puzzled by his fate. As Herzog shows figuratively in the dream sequences of his film, an unspoilt individual like Kaspar may discern more than those around him, but the final meaning, "wie der Traum ausgeht," stubbornly eludes him right up to his death.

Relying entirely on the foundling's naivety to convey social criticism was also insufficient and frustrating for those writers whose pent-up anger required a more vigorous response. Tucholsky found this out in his use of the alias 'Kaspar Hauser'. While the pen name allowed him to show a gentler side of himself, and now and again promoted a very effective 'tongue-in-cheek' approach (as, for example, in the purported school essay by Kaspar Hauser, entitled "Der Mensch"),[21] it put certain restraints on his attacks on the hypocrisies of his time. He therefore was inconsistent in his employment of the pseudonym, occasionally using strident tones that were inconsistent with Kaspar Hauser's naive persona.

Tucholsky was not the only one who felt compelled to castigate society more openly. Novels and plays had, of course, the greatest scope to elaborate on civic shortcomings, and they catalogued a variety of vices and weaknesses. The denunciation of outright malice stands out most clearly. A pertinent example is the figure of Oliver in Hofmannsthal's *Turm*, the antagonist and opposite of the Kaspar-Hauser-like prince. He is evil personified. War and chaos are his natural milieu, and human pity is foreign to him. Hofmannsthal also illustrates, through Oliver's obedient followers, how easily people can be led and misled, and that evil can be contagious. In works with stronger affinities to the historical

---

[21] *Die Weltbühne* 27/I (1931).

source, true malice is often attributed to the schoolteacher Meyer, under whose demanding and petty regime Kaspar Hauser is said to have suffered the most. He is regarded as someone who, in Röttger's words, carries "das Böse als einen Dämon in sich" (297). As we have seen in the preceding chapter, writers used him to embody the perversion of educational values and traditions that can account for much of the misery of our time. Several authors, however, notably Wassermann and Hofer, take pains to explain this character's meanness in terms of his own social conditioning. In these cases, the antagonist is as he is because he himself has been caught in a vicious circle, and he merely does his duty as he perceives it. While this may have diffused his guilt in the eyes of the readers at the time of publication, cruelty in the line of duty has obviously become much more difficult to excuse after the experiences of the Second World War; it is not an extenuating circumstance that has stood the test of time. In his *Kaspar*, Handke raises the same issue. Acceptance of brutality is unthinkingly passed on to the unwary pupil by agents who, one must assume, have been conditioned to this task in a similar manner. Images of violence gradually infiltrate the willingly accepted lessons:

> Beim Dreinschlagen
> ist man
> nie so ruhig wie beim Teppich-
> klopfen
>
> (75)

> ...
> ein Schluck Säure in den Mund
> oder ein Tritt in den Magen
>
> (76)

The identity of those who initiate and oversee the conditioning process is left deliberately nonspecific; Handke is adamant that he did not intend to criticize any particular social model.[22] Be that as it may, the implication is that unthinking obedience tends to lead to brutality.

Malice coupled with stupidity is repeatedly attributed to civil servants. As an outward symbol of the state's power and injustice, and its most accessible representative, this class has traditionally been a popular target for literary ridicule and criticism. So it is not surprising that in the climate of heightened unease about society and its leadership, the civil servant is subjected to special disdain. Tucholsky never tired of satirizing the mindless bureaucrat. Sometimes physical attributes express the writer's contempt for the state official. "Er reibt öfters die Hände und hat das komische Kreuz, das so Leute haben, die immer bei Hofe sind": thus

---

[22] "Kein konkretes gesellschaftliches Modell wird im *Kaspar* kritisiert, weder das kapitalistische noch auch das sozialistische." Handke, cited by Joseph, "Peter Handke," 27–39 (38).

Schäfer's Feuerbach describes an official, encapsulating the mixture of eagerness and obsequiousness that is seen as typical of civil servants. Herzog finds a visual equivalent for the latter's inner disfigurement in the shrunken, deformed figure of his clerk, who with bureaucratic zeal classifies the details of Kaspar Hauser's life and death, and in the last scene of the film limps away in triumph, having succeeded in reducing a human being to a tidy protocol, no longer a threat to the bureaucratic order ("ein schönes Protokoll, ein ordentliches Protokoll").[23] Both Wassermann and Ebermayer turn the historical figure of police sergeant Hickel into an arch-villain, and thus, by association, indict the keepers of law and order as a whole. They portray this character as vain, corruptible, and spiteful, and hold him responsible for much of Kaspar Hauser's misery.[24] Against the historical background of the repressive Metternich era, the civil servant is also denounced in his capacity of official watchdog and informer. Röttger and Schäfer attack this sinister ingredient of communal life merely in passing, by depicting the fear created by censorship, and the power it gives to the informer.[25] More recently, Forte's play *Kaspar Hausers Tod* revives the motif more emphatically, in order to voice his repugnance at the contemporary government-imposed restrictions in the wake of the 1968 student revolt. In his work, the trepidation of the funeral guests that they might trespass on forbidden topics and be reported to the authorities is exaggerated to comic proportions, and the recurring need for a deliberate *Themawechsel* punctuates the play. In Handke's *Kaspar*, the fact that electronic machinery has taken over the surveillance and control of the individual adds an even more sinister note, and provides an ironic comment on the technological 'progress' of our age. But regardless of the medium, the effect on the object of surveillance is always the same: a feeling of bewildered helplessness. "Man hat mich in der Hand," acknowledges Handke's Kaspar. "Ich bin aufgeknackt" (100).

Equally threatening in its potential effect on mankind is professional or scientific self-centeredness. Since it ignores the feelings of its test objects, and is oblivious to the consequences of research beyond a narrow aim, it contributes to the dehumanization of society. Kaspar's tutor Daumer and the physicians who tested and retested his reflexes without regard for his wishes are all indirectly accused of this fault in the earlier novels by Wassermann, Hofer, and Röttger. More recently, Herzog found a pertinent image for this motif. His script summarizes the scene of the foundling's autopsy towards the end of the film as follows: "Fünf Ärzte beugen sich über den Leichnam und weiden ihn aus, wie die

---

[23] *Jeder für sich*; sound track.

[24] In Schäfer's *Richter Feuerbach*, the character of Hickel, while not evil, is tempted to yield to corruption, and unwittingly plays a part in the betrayal of Feuerbach. But the author also grants him some redeeming qualities.

[25] See Röttger, *Kaspar Hausers letzte Tage*, 387; Schäfer, *Richter Feuerbach*, 17, 42.

Geier. Ruhige, geschäftige, sachliche Gier" (192). In the context of the Kaspar Hauser story, with its focus on only one particular victim, this motif may not appear very momentous, but it anticipates (in the earlier novels) and illustrates (in Herzog's film) the larger debate of this century about scientific responsibility towards mankind.

Social arrogance and snobbery earn similar derision. Wassermann, in following the stages of Kaspar Hauser's life, describes in detail how the upper classes vied with each other to obtain the foundling as an exhibit for their social entertainments. They prized the foundling as a means to enhance their social prestige, and dismissed him when he had served that purpose. Forte uses his stage gathering of upper-class burghers as an opportunity to lampoon their pretensions more directly. He exaggerates their indignation at the lack of proper deference by the workers who meet next door, and ridicules their attempts to keep up appearances even when intoxicated. Appropriately, "dröhnendes Gelächter" from the adjoining room coincides with some of their pompous pronouncements, as a mocking comment.[26] Unseemly snobbishness can even interfere with the bourgeois acceptance of material progress. The mayor's wife recoils at the very idea of travelling on the soon-to-be-opened railroad,[27] since it may force people of her standing to mingle with the socially inferior: "Kostspielig ginge ja noch an, gefährlich finde ich, daß man gezwungen wird, mit Gevatter Schneider und Handschuhmacher zu fahren" (32). Conceit of this sort accounts for at least some of the fissures which rend society.

The railway project also provides a convenient pretext to introduce the subject of materialist greed. As the potential shareholders in this gathering debate the merits and disadvantages of the railroad, it becomes clear that in this venture, as in most aspects of their lives, the profit motive will override all other social considerations. The lack of moral principles in capitalism is of course a very topical and popular theme in modern literature, a theme which Forte had already expounded with more vigor in previous works. In a more timeless guise, greed also plays a role in Herzog's film. It is the townspeople's reluctance to use their assets for Kaspar Hauser's upkeep which prompts the decision to exhibit him in a freak show for profit, together with other unfortunates. But the faults of materialism are not only confined to the bourgeoisie. Where Lord Stanhope still makes an appearance, the historical rumor that he yielded to bribes is usually taken for granted.[28] The monetary temptation of Schäfer's otherwise upright adjutant Hickel has already been

---

[26] *Kaspar Hausers Tod*, 26; see also 31, 34.

[27] A realistic touch by Forte, in line with his mentioned predilection for 'documentary theatre', since the first German railway began to operate between Nuremberg and Fürth in 1835, i.e. two years after Hauser's death.

[28] See Martens, *Kaspar Hauser*, 61, 67; Wassermann, *Caspar Hauser*, 190–93; Röttger, *Kaspar Hausers letzte Tage*, 278–79; Schäfer, *Richter Feuerbach*, 24, 25.

mentioned, although in this case loyalty finally prevails. Schäfer extends the motif of greed and envy to include some of the 'simple people', as in this commentary on Kaspar Hauser's existence:

> Ich sage, so ein Leben sollte eins haben, der sitzt in seinem Zimmer, da kommen die Leute und er lässt sich anschauen, er redet ein wenig und dafür kriegt er sein Essen, und was für ein Essen, Durchlaucht! (20)

While the topic of Kaspar Hauser offered many opportunities to single out explicit faults which can undermine the social fabric, Wassermann in particular showed that the absence of active goodness, the simple omissions due to "Trägheit des Herzens," are equally pernicious. As we see in his parade of Kaspar's mostly well-meaning but self-centered patrons, it does not always need evil to create the conditions in which an individual can wither and perish.

Much of the social censure outlined above emerges from descriptions of deplorable behavior which are integral parts of the narrative or dramatic discourse. Not satisfied with these measures, the authors of the longer works of the earlier century, still indebted to nineteenth-century techniques of writing, occasionally resort to their omniscient point of view to add comments of disapproval. In one such instance, Wassermann denounces the hypocrisy of teacher Quandt as follows:

> Es war nämlich mit diesem Mann derart beschaffen, daß er in einer merkwürdigen Zweiheit existierte. Der eine Teil war die öffentliche Person, der Bürger, der Steuerzahler, der Kollege, das Familienoberhaupt, der Patriot; der andere Teil war sozusagen der Quandt an sich. Jener war ein Heros der Tugend, eine wahre Mustersammlung von Tugenden; dieser lag versteckt in einer stillen Ecke und belauerte die liebe Gotteswelt. (274)

Hofer similarly interrupts her story from time to time in order to scold her past and present fellowmen. The writers of recent decades no longer resort to such blunt interventions, but leave no room for doubt that they, too, evaluate their social environment with critical eyes.

II. The Search for Solutions

As we have seen, many authors demonstrated an intuitive and acute awareness of social failings, and were adept at voicing their disapprobation. Furthermore, as the preceding chapters have shown, the correlate of criticism, namely the perception of ideal conditions, can be discerned at least in tentative forms. This concern in itself indicates a continued willingness to remain involved in social matters. But it is of course far easier to take stock and criticize than to come up with concrete recommendations for change. Insight may well be a first step towards

improvement ("der erste Weg zur Besserung," as the German proverb
asserts), but the goal is evidently so nebulous, or the negative impres-
sions are so overwhelming, that few of these writers suggest in their
work how to proceed from their present position. Nor is there any
evidence that the path into the future became clearer in the course of
time. What recommendations we find in these works are almost evenly
distributed throughout the century.

One important step in the direction of change is the recognition that
it is not enough to distance oneself from the perceived corruption of
social standards, but to *share* in the communal responsibility. Both
Wassermann and Röttger openly advocate this point of view. The novel
of the former ends with Kaspar Hauser's friend Clara von Kannawurf,
distraught by the foundling's death, denouncing the population as a
whole as guilty ("Schuldig sind wir alle"; 446). Having experienced the
panorama of varying degrees of social misconduct from the foundling's
point of view, the reader is likely to agree. Röttger arrives at the same
verdict. In his epilogue to Hauser's death, a ballad-singer sums up the
past events and ends with the stanza:

> Wer hat ihn gemordet? Wer hat es getan?
> Menschen stehn. Einer sieht den andern an.
> Sie wissen es: j e d e r hat es getan,
> Verhüllt's Gesicht, schaut euch nicht an,
> (383)

whereupon we read: "... da war eine namenlose Stille ... bis eine Frau
aufschrie: 'Die Wahrheit ist am Tag! Alle haben's getan!'" (387).

It is worth pointing out that in these instances the actual recognition
of communal guilt is ascribed to women, who in both novels are
consistently described as more sensitive and spontaneous, and to a
wandering minstrel, who presumably represents the artist per se and can
accordingly be credited with a greater than average intuition. In other
words, contrition is so far limited to only that part of society which in
the eyes of the author possesses the needed positive qualities, but,
unfortunately, little power to change the present-day predicament. It is
not *their* insight that can make a difference in this world, but that of the
recalcitrants. Of these, only Wassermann's Lord Stanhope comes to
recognize and regret his failings. But the form of his atonement, suicide,
can obviously not be advocated as a fruitful, generally valid social
response.

Yet in several cases there is no doubt that the writer felt the duty, in
his capacity as *Dichter*, at least to attempt the conversion of those
responsible for society's predicament. Wassermann's recipe was to
advocate more humanitarian principles, although his later *Selbstbetrachtungen* reveal that he came to see these efforts as largely un-
rewarded:

Ethisch angesehen ist das Ergebnis zum Verzweifeln. Nicht, als ob es nicht da und dort Ergriffene gäbe, Reuige und der Verwandlung Fähige, aber am Lauf der Welt ändert sich nichts, am Haß, an der Lüge, am Mißverständnis, am Wahn und an der Ungerechtigkeit nichts.[29]

Tucholsky, who had hoped that his satire of the culpable segment of society — the military, the bureaucrats, the profiteers — would help to bring about a "geistige Revolution," came to similarly pessimistic conclusions. "Pathos tuts nicht und Spott nicht und Tadel nicht und sachliche Kritik nicht," he agonized, "sie wollen nicht hören."[30] Hofmannsthal was another tenacious idealist who reluctantly had to concede defeat as far as the betterment of society is concerned. His Sigismund conquers the reluctance of his naive and peaceful Kaspar-Hauser-persona sufficiently to confront the enemy, but comes to realize that he is outmatched by the forces of evil. All he can hope for, on the pragmatic level, is that his resistance will one day be remembered as an inspiring example: "Gebet Zeugnis, ich war da. Wenngleich mich niemand gekannt hat."[31] Schäfer's Judge Feuerbach, in his role as Kaspar Hauser's champion, pleads for moral courage. Even in the expectation of defeat, he finds it worthwhile to risk his life for what he sees as the cause of social justice: "Es lohnt sich doch, dafür zu sterben, dass es ein bisschen anständiger in der Welt wird" (43).

Since the events of their time and the nature of the Kaspar Hauser material were not exactly suited to show the victory of high moral principles, some authors simply withhold a prognosis, or retrench their position to advocate more modest goals. Röttger recommends "die große Solidarität aller wahren, nicht bösen Menschen" as a force of passive resistance against the forces of evil. "Laßt uns nicht böse sein! Noch auch böse werden," concludes Feuerbach's daughter in his novel, "daran hängt die Rettung der Welt" (269). Other works place their hopes on the future generation. In Hofmannsthal's first version of *Der Turm*, for instance, Sigismund hands on the task of saving the world from itself to the *Kinderkönig*, who has so far escaped the contamination of his purity. Schäfer also passes the torch from the present generation to the descendants. In his play, Feuerbach exhorts his children: "Ihr seid jetzt dran, Ihr werdet es schaffen, oder die nächsten."

As the above examples show, the advocated solutions to the modern predicament were all, as Theisz says with specific reference to Wassermann, "noch humanistisch befangen."[32] They were appeals to the better nature of man, appeals for individual insight and inner change,

[29] *Selbstbetrachtungen* (Berlin: S. Fischer, 1933), 105.

[30] Kurt Tucholsky, cited by Hans Prescher, "Klagerufe und Prophezeiungen," *Text und Kritik* 29 (Jan. 1971): 25.

[31] *Turm* I, 207; *Turm* II, 463.

[32] R. D. Theisz, "Kaspar Hauser im zwanzigsten Jahrhundert," 172.

and, if all else failed, appeals for patience. As already stated in the beginning of this chapter, so far, the Kaspar Hauser material seems to have held little attraction to writers of a more militant social commitment. Even a work like Handke's *Kaspar*, whose whole raison d'être was, after all, to expose the traps of the process of socialization, was denounced by this faction as sadly inadequate for the social struggle. "[Handke] unterstellt ... was er deduzieren sollte, erhöbe er den Anspruch, kritischer, nicht scheinkritischer Theoretiker zu sein," comments Henisch.[33] Uwe Timms is equally deprecatory: "Wichtiger als die neutrale Sprachstruktur ist ... , wer über sie verfügt, mit welchen Inhalten er sie füllt und mit welchem Zweck er sie einsetzt."[34]

Literary activists would indeed have to look very closely to find anything in the Kaspar Hauser literature which would merit their wholehearted approval. Nevertheless, some portrayals of the foundling denote a more militant attitude, and the readiness to fight for a change. In fact, we find the first distinct example of a more radical stance in one of the earliest relevant works of the twentieth century, Kurt Martens's play, *Kaspar Hauser*. In this case, the hero exhibits none of the passive resignation which marks so many of his successors. Although the plot, following the historical model, requires the final downfall of the protagonist, Kaspar resists his enemies every step of the way, mentally and physically. The fact that at one point he even threatens to make common cause with the lower-class rabble to achieve his aim ("Geht's mit den großen Herren nicht, so ruf' ich das Volk!"; 119) looks promising in the context of our discussion, but Martens does not pursue this motif to influence the course of his play.

Arp's Kaspar is another exception in our line of rather passive heroes. We know nothing about the circumstances of his departure, since the poem freely diverges from the traditional ingredients of the story. But as the poem's narrative voice describes him in retrospect, Kaspar's wilfulness and ability to take charge do not agree with the popular notion of the gentle victim. He had served as a role model and teacher to those who now mourn his absence, and thus fulfilled a useful social function. Evidently, he was not afraid to flout conventions — an important pre-condition for any new beginning. But what finally matters is that he is no longer available. There is also nothing in the poem to indicate the hero's own view of society, so that we cannot exclude the possibility that he left of his own free will for a more congenial environment. Utterly different as Hofmannsthal's work is in form and style, in certain respects we might put the hero of *Der Turm* in the same category as Arp's Kaspar. He, too, is seen as a charismatic leader, who can break with conventions, and is potentially capable of reversing the

---

[33] Peter Henisch, "Späte Überlegungen zu Handke," *Neues Forum*, 17, no. 194/1 (1970): 120.

[34] "Peter Handke; oder, Sicher in die 70er Jahre," *Kürbiskern* 4 (1970): 611–21 (617).

given situation. In his case, however, the influx of Kaspar Hauser's reputed passivity and peacefulness gained the upper hand in the author's mind, and it is this side of his character which causes Sigismund to fail his people when they need him most. He is painfully aware of his social obligation, but unable to fulfil it.

Wassermann's Kaspar Hauser demonstrates signs of a social conscience through small acts of charity. On the whole, however, he is oblivious to social differences, and in the end passively resigns himself to his fate. Only once does he muster the initiative to try actively to stem the flow of events, when he persuades his guard to desert his duty and carry a letter to the woman he believes to be his mother. But that mission fails, and with it the foundling's courage.

In the literature of more recent years, we find two examples in which the general indictment of society is combined with at least the possibility of an active revolt against existing conditions. In *Kaspar Hausers Tod*, Forte uses the pretext of the funeral gathering to expose and criticize the stultifying social atmosphere of Metternich's time. But he clearly had his own time in mind rather than a slice of history. The debut of the play came at a time when many writers were chafing under various restrictive laws, which the (West) German government had decreed in the name of the country's *Verfassungsschutz*, to counteract remnants of student unrest and left-wing terrorism. Therefore, most contemporary viewers would (and undoubtedly were intended to) interpret the criticism of Metternich's restrictions as barbs against the government of their own time. The analogy confirms Forte's belief that history tends to repeat itself. "Es gibt anscheinend Konstellationen," he stated on a previous occasion, "die sich modellhaft wiederholen."[35] The strategy meeting of the proletariat offstage, which intrudes upon the middle-class gathering in the center of the play, carries at least undertones of an active struggle to come. The workers' belligerence grows in step with the burghers' division and confusion, and they progress from nonchalantly helping themselves to the furniture of their social superiors to confining the latter physically in their room. The time for the final confrontation has obviously not yet arrived, since the guests can all still make their escape. But a warning has been sounded, as Forte confirms in the double entendre of the night-watchman's call, the final lines of the play: "Löscht das Feuer und das Licht, / daß bei euch kein Brand ausbricht!"

The most interesting example of incipient social rebellion, however, can be found in Trafic's drama, *Kaspar Hauser* (1983). Like most works on the foundling, this play concerns itself with society's effect on the individual, rather than with the impact of the individual on society. It depicts the by now traditional stages of the protagonist's bewilderment, development, suffering, and endurance. But when this stage hero, rather than resigning himself to further victimization, seizes the newborn child

---

[35] Dieter Forte, *Martin Luther & Thomas Münzer; oder, Die Einführung der Buchhaltung* (Frankfurt a. M.: S. Fischer, 1971), 140.

of his malevolent landlord, and fires a pistol at his oppressor as the final curtain falls, he marks a new departure in the relevant literature. We do not know how Trafic envisaged the continuation of this story. But his Kaspar Hauser is a new breed, willing to defend not only his own rights, but, more importantly, determined to protect the child in his arms (representative of the future generation) "vor dem Zugriff der V-Erwach-senen,"[36] even by drastic means. Whether this rebellious Kaspar Hauser is the harbinger of a pattern for future works remains to be seen.

[36] The pun, with its dual meaning, stems from Johannes Wacker, the actor who played the role of Kaspar Hauser in the 'Schauspielhaus' Nuremberg, in 1983. Letter to author, 30 August, 1988.

Summary and Conclusion

THE MOST SIGNIFICANT LINK between the disparate works we have classified as Kaspar Hauser literature is not the story itself, but the figure's emblematic function in a universal sense. The literary interest in Kaspar Hauser intensified at a time when many traditional values seemed to be outmoded or under serious threat, and when feelings of social and existential alienation had become very pervasive, especially in literary circles. Kaspar Hauser was admirably suited to embody the artist's sense of loss, insecurity, and malaise, for he, too, had been deprived of something precious, of the very mainstays of his life. He had been as writers now began to see themselves: a quintessential victim of his time and place, and a social outsider. Yet at the same time, the foundling's aura of mystery and dignity could compensate, at least in part, for the perceived disenfranchisement, and thereby salvage a measure of the writer's self-respect. At least vestigial remains of this stance can be observed throughout this century, indicating that the concept of the writer's social task and status is still in flux, and still a matter of great concern.

But increasingly the equation of Kaspar Hauser with the *Dichter* per se went side by side with, and gradually gave way to, his depiction as Everyman, who is seen as no less a victim, and as no less disenfranchised in the given social circumstances, than the artist, but who may lack the ennobling attributes which characterized the portrayal of the latter.

While distress about existing conditions suffuses the majority of works, there are also signs that writers were not content with self-pity and lament, whether on a personal or universal level. Although the gentle and passive figure of Kaspar Hauser was clearly not regarded as a suitable vehicle for the more tendentious literary attempts to influence social and political developments, there is multiple evidence, from the very beginning, of a search for ways to overcome the existential isolation of modern man.

One particularly prominent path in this quest leads back into the past. Many works revive and explore Rousseauistic notions, as if to test whether the Romantic antidotes against threats to the individual's sense of self-worth and security can still be applicable in the twentieth century. The idea that man is inherently good, and a marked degree of nostalgia for the pre-civilized way of life, repeatedly surface in both earlier and later works. In most cases, Kaspar Hauser is celebrated not for the unusual abilities he showed when he first appeared, nor for his astonishingly fast adaptation, but for his simplicity and innocence, and because he had the unencumbered vision of a child. In some of the works whose length and form allowed the elaboration on details of the story — such as Wassermann's and Röttger's novels, and, more recently,

Herzog's film — the Rousseauistic *Zivilisationspessimismus* is particularly evident in the fact that the gradations of inner corruption are proportional to the degree of sophistication in those around Kaspar Hauser. Invariably, however, writers relativize the ideal of the noble savage, and subvert its prospects by not glossing over, indeed emphasizing the fact that in the foundling's case the forces of civilization triumph.

Vestiges of Romanticism also imbue the many attempts to re-establish Nature as an ally of man, and as a counterweight to the forces of materialism and technological progress, which are blamed for many of society's ills. Kaspar Hauser (who in reality had a very tenuous relationship to Nature due to his long confinement) is frequently endowed with close ties to the animal and plant world. This intimate bond with Nature can vouch for his continued purity, and even provide remnants of magical powers, as shown, for instance, in the exaltation of Kaspar Hauser's supposedly innate horsemanship. On the other hand, one can discern a hesitancy in the endeavors to test whether Nature can still provide sanctuary in an uncongenial world. The general conclusion seems to be that it can no longer do so. Some writers undermine their own effort to establish Nature as a positive force by showing how the foundling turns to it in vain. Others, prefiguring or echoing the current concern with the environment, describe Nature as debilitated and thus powerless, or enumerate the ravages it has suffered in the name of progress.

A similar tension between wishful thinking and sober perception of reality governs the various attempts to overcome the void of the modern age by resurrecting metaphysical and religious values. If successful, such a venture might help the *Dichter* regain his previous status as mediator between the everyday world and the irrational sphere beyond. In these particular efforts, Kaspar Hauser serves to reaffirm traditional but recently eroded Christian values. Or he himself is portrayed as a Christlike redeemer figure, who can serve as an example and point others in the right direction. We also find the figure linked with various pantheistic notions, another manifestation of nostalgia for the age of Romanticism. But like the idea of the noble savage, these attempts at establishing a new mythology do not really succeed, or rather, are voluntarily aborted, for most authors are too aware of reality to carry them through to a triumphant conclusion. With very few exceptions — such as the apotheoses in Trakl's "Kaspar Hauser Lied" and Klaus Mann's "Legenden" — the relevant imagery experiments with the idea of potential salvation, but is then abandoned.

In what we have termed "the attempt to go forward," many works explore how Kaspar Hauser fared in his role as a 'tabula rasa', and as a potential 'new man'. Invariably, very negative views of education, the transmitter of culture and tradition, transpire throughout the whole period in question. Wherever writers refer to the foundling's socialization, they are highly critical of the shortcomings of educators. This sweeping condemnation expresses a contemporary cynical distrust of all those who were and still are supposed to supply society with the guidelines for the present and future. It is safe to say that any help from these quarters is completely ruled out. If we can discern a ray of hope in this situation, it is the fact that Kaspar Hauser — and, by implication, Everyman — is shown to have the resilience to maintain his integrity and good nature even in adverse conditions, and in spite of misguided and harmful educators.

The issue of Kaspar Hauser's problematic language acquisition also assumes a multivalent metaphorical significance in many works. The foundling's initial inability to communicate serves to symbolize the poet's 'loss of voice' in the twentieth century, the prolonged "*Sprachskepsis*" which arose from the perceived misuse and unreliableness of language, as well as man's existential isolation. But here, too, writers do more than take stock of insufficiencies. They attempt to overcome the predicament, whether by passive resistance to contemporary pressures, through fresh approaches to language, emphasis on alternative, non-verbal means of communication, or by simply declaring the foundling's linguistic handicap a positive trait, thereby removing its stigma.

The last chapter investigated the extent to which writers show social commitment. While probably none of these works on Kaspar Hauser would pass muster with the proponents of the more militant strands of literature, which emerged particularly strongly in the wake of the student revolt in the 1960s, most nevertheless contain unmistakable signs of social awareness. There is an almost unanimous concern about the social outsider. Writers identify with him, and many subject the excluding group to criticism and condemnation.

The widespread disillusionment with society notwithstanding, many works imply that membership in the group is still regarded as a desirable goal. Understandably, the negative ending intrinsic to the original material — not to mention the negative experiences of the historical events in Germany — narrowed the writers' scope for including an optimistic outlook. Social prospects appear to be in a 'holding pattern': patience, self-improvement, solidarity of all those of good will, and trust in the next generation are the major recommendations.

From a diachronic point of view, one curious and surprising finding is that while stylistically the treatment of the material keeps pace with the times, the underlying attitude of writers and the tenor of their works undergo comparatively little change. It is true that the celebration of the poet diminishes in the course of the century. After World War II, we no longer encounter descriptions of Kaspar Hauser as a youth of shining beauty. In the few instances in which he still has magical powers, these are limited, and of no avail to humanity. There is some evidence, admittedly still tenuous, that latter-day writers find the foundling's passive acceptance of his fate uncongenial. Future Kaspar Hauser figures might therefore present a more militant demeanor.

Perhaps the most notable attitude shared by these works as a whole is the coupling of an evident desire to return to prescientific modes of thinking with the sober recognition that such a return is no longer possible. Thus we cannot term the preoccupation with Kaspar Hauser as merely a form of escapism. Writers show the courage to examine reality, and perhaps even more courage to admit that they have not yet found an answer. And there is an evident and continued willingness to search for solutions to the malaise of modern man. For both the inventory of modern man's state and the quest for remedies, Kaspar Hauser's life and fate yield appropriate metaphors. Undoubtedly, we have not heard the last of this figure.

Sources Consulted

Details of publication refer to the editions used in this study. In the case of later editions or reprints, references to the original publication have been added in brackets where available.

A. Primary Material

Amann, Jürg. "Ach, diese Wege sind sehr dunkel: Ein Kaspar Hauser-Stück." *Ach, diese Wege sind sehr dunkel: Drei Stücke.* Munich: R. Piper, 1985. 9–35.

Arp, Hans. "kaspar ist tot." *Gedichte 1903–1939.* Vol. 1 of *Gesammelte Gedichte.* Wiesbaden: Limes, 1963 (orig. publ in *Dada-Almanach*, ed. Richard Huelsenbeck, Berlin, 1920). 6–27.

———. "kaspar ist tot." In *Lyrik der Zeit.* Pfullingen: Günther Neske, n.d. Gramophone recording.

Biermann, Wolf. "Kaspar Hauser singt" (nach Verlaine). *Affenfels und Barrikade: Balladen.* Cologne: Kiepenheuer & Witsch, 1986. 111.

Bihacht, Victor Curt. "Kaspar Hauser: Ein Spiel." *Spiele.* Munich: E. W. Bonsels & Co., 1911. 5–32.

Colombo, John Robert. "The Child of Europe." *The Sad Truth.* Toronto: Peter Martin Press, 1974. 64–69.

Constantine, David. "Under that bag of soot." In *The Poetry Book Society Anthology.* Vol. 1, n.s., ed. Frazer Steel. London: Hutchinson, 1990. 70.

Dehmel, Richard. "Lied Kaspar Hausers." *Erlösungen: Gedichte und Sprüche.* Vol. 1 of *Gesammelte Werke.* Berlin: S. Fischer, 1918 (orig. publ. 1913). 50.

Ebermayer, Erich. *Kaspar Hauser: Dramatische Legende.* Leipzig: Philipp Reclam, Jr., 1929 (orig. publ. Leipzig: Schauspiel-Verlag, 1926).

Evers, Franz. "Kaspar Hausers Lied." *Die Insel* 1, no. 3 (Dec. 1899): 254.

Flake, Otto. *Kaspar Hauser: Vorgeschichte — Geschichte — Nachgeschichte.* Mannheim: Kessler, n.d. [1949].

Forte, Dieter. *Kaspar Hausers Tod: Ein Theaterstück.* Reihe: Theater, Film, Funk, Fernsehen, no. 1. Frankfurt a. M.: S. Fischer, 1979.

George, Stefan. "Kaspar Hauser singt." *Zeitgenössische Dichter: Übertragungen.* Vol. 2 of *Gesamt-Ausgabe der Werke.* Berlin: Georg Bondi, 1929. 29.

Gielen, Sibylle. "Ein Mensch wie Kaspar Hauser." Performance Theater (1989).

Gutzkow, Karl. *Die Söhne Pestalozzis.* 3 vols. Berlin: Otto Janke, 1870.

Härtling, Peter. *Hubert; oder, Die Rückkehr nach Casablanca*. Darmstadt: Luchterhand, 1978.

———. "Kaspar Hauser." *Die Mörsinger Pappel: Gedichte*. Darmstadt: Luchterhand, 1987. 19–20.

———. "kasper." *Mein Gedicht ist mein Messer: Lyriker zu ihren Gedichten*, ed. Hans Bender. Munich: Paul List, 1961. 164–65.

———. "nachricht von kasper." *Mein Gedicht ist mein Messer: Lyriker zu ihren Gedichten*, ed. Hans Bender. Munich: Paul List 1961. 165.

Handke, Peter. *Kaspar*. 5th ed. Frankfurt a. M.: Suhrkamp, 1967.

Herzog, Werner. "Jeder für sich und Gott gegen Alle." Vol. 2 of *Drehbücher*. Munich: Skellig, 1974. 103–94.

———. *Jeder für sich und Gott gegen Alle*. Munich: Werner Herzog, 1974.

Hoechstetter, Sophie. "Das Totenhemdlein des Kaspar Hauser." *Mein Freund Rosenkreutz*. Dachau: Einhorn, n.d. [1917]. 321–26.

———. "Die Damen von Irmelsleben: Eine verschollene Kaspar-Hauser-Geschichte." *Das Herz: Arabesken um die Existenz des George Rosenkreutz*. Dresden: Carl Reißner, 1913. 1–24.

Höllerer, Walter. "Gaspard." *Mein Gedicht ist mein Messer: Lyriker zu ihren Gedichten*, ed. Hans Bender. Munich, Paul List, 1961. 100–101.

Hönig, Matthias. "kaspar hauser: theaterimprovisation." Lützelflüh, 1985.

Hofer, Klara [Klara Höffner]. *Das Schicksal einer Seele: Die Geschichte von Kaspar Hauser*. Nuremberg, J. L. Schrag, 1925.

Hofmannsthal, Hugo von. "Das Leben ein Traum." *Dramen*. Vol. 3 of *Gesammelte Werke in Einzelausgaben*, ed. Herbert Steiner. Frankfurt a. M.: S. Fischer, 1957. 339–425.

———. "Der Turm" (1925). *Dramen*. Vol. 4 of *Gesammelte Werke in Einzelausgaben*, ed. Herbert Steiner. Frankfurt a. M.: S. Fischer, 1958. 7–208.

———. "Der Turm" (1927). *Dramen*. Vol. 4 of *Gesammelte Werke in Einzelausgaben*, ed. Herbert Steiner. Frankfurt a. M.: S. Fischer, 1958. 321–463.

Kalckreuth, Wolf Graf von. "Caspar Hauser singt." *Gedichte und Übertragungen*, ed. Hellmut Kruse. Heidelberg: Lambert Schneider, 1962. 109.

Kempowski, Walter. *Ein Kapitel für sich*, 5th ed. Hamburg: Albrecht Knaus, 1980 (orig. publ. Munich: Hanser, 1975).

———. *Herzlich Willkommen*. Munich: Knaus, 1984.

Klabund [Alfred Henschke]. "Der arme Kaspar." *Das heiße Herz: Balladen, Mythen, Gedichte*. Berlin: Erich Reiss, 1922. 29.

———. "Kaspar Hauser." *Das heiße Herz: Balladen. Mythen. Gedichte*. Berlin: Erich Reiss, 1922. 7.

Kunze, Wilhelm. "Das Kaspar-Hauser-Hörspiel." Unpubl. manuscript, [1930s]. City Archives Ansbach, Germany.

Lange-Müller, Katja. *Kaspar Mauser: Die Feigheit vorm Freund.* Cologne: Kiepenheuer & Witsch, 1988.

Lerner, Laurence. "Kaspar Hauser." *The Man I Killed.* London: Secker & Warburg, 1980. 22.

Lewandowski, Herbert. *Das Tagebuch Kaspar Hausers: Eine Gabe für einsame Menschen.* Utrecht: Pfeil, 1928.

Mann, Klaus. "Kaspar-Hauser-Legenden." *Vor dem Leben.* Hamburg: Enoch, 1925. 161–91.

Marheineke, Philipp Konrad. *Das Leben im Leichentuch: Enthüllungen eines argen Geheimnisses.* Berlin: August Mylius, 1934.

Martens, Kurt. *Kaspar Hauser: Drama.* Berlin: F. Fontane, 1903.

Mey, Reinhard. "Kaspar." *Ankomme Freitag den 13.* LP recording. Leinfelden: Intercord, 1968.

———. "Kaspar." *Ich wollte wie Orpheus singen. Chansons.* Bonn: Voggenreiter, n.d.. 19.

Minnemann, Joachim. "Kaspar." Für Elisabeth. In *Wir kommen: Literatur aus der Studentenbewegung,* ed. Franz Hutzfeldt. Munich: Damnitzverlag, 1976. 137.

Oppenheim, Meret. "Ohne mich ohnehin" [1969]. *Husch, husch, der schönste Vokal entleert sich: Gedichte, Zeichnungen,* ed. Christiane Meyer-Thoss. Frankfurt a. M.: Suhrkamp, 1984. 83.

———. *Kaspar Hauser; oder, Die Goldene Freiheit: Textvorlage für ein Drehbuch* [1944]. Bern: Gachnang & Springer, 1987.

Pietzner, Carlo. "… and from the night, Kaspar" (a play in seven scenes). *Who was Kaspar Hauser?* Oxford: Oxford University Press, 1983. 31–78.

Pütz, Wilhelm. *Der alte Garten.* Augsburg/Traunstein: Brücken Verlag, 1963.

Rilke, Rainer Maria. "Der Knabe" (1902/3). *Das Buch der Bilder. Sämtliche Werke,* ed. Ernst Zinn. Wiesbaden: Insel Verlag, 1955. 386.

Röttger, Karl. *Kaspar Hausers letzte Tage; oder, Das kurze Leben eines ganz Armen.* Berlin: Paul Zsolnay, 1938.

Schäfer, Walter Erich. *Richter Feuerbach: Schauspiel.* Berlin: Chronos, 1929.

Schaumann, Ruth. *Ansbacher Nänie.* Berlin: G. Grote, 1936.

Schmidt-Rogge, Carl. "Es ist nicht gut, dass der Mensch allein ist: Das Schicksal Caspar Hausers." [Broadcast 29.4.1961, West-deutscher Rundfunk, Cologne]. Unpubl. typescript. City Archives, Ansbach, Germany.

Schoenhals, Albrecht. "Lied Kaspar Hausers." *Erinnerungen an französische Verse.* Stuttgart: Deutsche Verlags-Anstalt, 1968. 169.

Scoper, Ludwig [Georg Karl Ludwig Schöpfer]. *Kaspar Hauser; oder, Die einge-mauerte Nonne: Wahrheit und Dichtung.* Nordhausen: Ernst Friedrich Fürst, 1834.

Seybold, Friedrich. *Caspar Hauser; oder, Der Findling.* Stuttgart: P. Balz, 1834.

Trafic, Carlos, and Wolfgang Trevisany. *Kaspar Hauser.* Unpubl. play. Städtische Bühnen, Nuremberg, 1983

Trakl, Georg. "Kaspar Hauser Lied." *Die Dichtungen. Gesamtausgabe,* ed. Kurt Horwitz. Zurich: Arche, 1946. 109.

Tucholsky, Kurt. Publications under the pseudonym "Kaspar Hauser." *Die Weltbühne* 1918–1932. Reprint. Königstein, Ts.: Athenäum, 1978.

Vega, Suzanne. "Casper Hauser's Song." *Solitude Standing.* A & M Records, Inc., 1987. Sound cassette.

Verlaine, Paul, "Gaspard Hauser chante." Vol. 1 of *Oeuvres Complètes,* ed. Albert Messein. Paris: Albert Messein, 1911 (orig. publ. in Paul Verlaine, *Sagesse.* Paris: Société Générale de Librairie Catholique, 1881). 270–71.

———. "Scénario pour ballet." Vol. 1 of *Oeuvres Complètes.* Paris: Le Club du meilleur livre, 1959. 739–44.

Vesper, Guntram, "Kinder." *Kriegerdenkmal ganz hinten.* Frankfurt a. M.: Fischer Taschenbuch Verlag, 1985. 38–41.

———. "Licht in das Leben." *Die Inseln im Landmeer und neue Gedichte.* Frankfurt a. M.: Fischer Taschenbuch Verlag, 1984. 11.

———. *Nördlich der Liebe und südlich des Hasses.* Frankfurt a. M.: Fischer Taschen-buchverlag, 1981 (orig. publ. Munich: Hanser, 1979).

Wassermann, Jakob. *Caspar Hauser; oder, Die Trägheit des Herzens.* Zurich: Carl Posen, 1947 (orig. publ. in serial form, 1907).

———, Jacob [sic]. *Caspar Hauser: The Enigma of a Century,* trans. C. Newton. New York: Rudolf Steiner Publications, 1973.

Wenger, Wolfgang. "magie der sprache." *weit weg in den filmen.* Salzburg: Residenz Verlag, 1990. 99.

Wolfenstein, Alfred. "Kaspar Hauser singt." *Armer Lelian: Gedichte der Schwermut, der Leidenschaft und der Liebe.* Berlin: Paul Cassirer, 1925. 18.

B. Secondary Material (Published)

Ackermann, Irmgard, ed. *Kurt Tucholsky: Sieben Beiträge zu Werk und Wirkung.* Munich: Edition Text und Kritik, 1985.

Adam, Antoine. *The Art of Paul Verlaine,* trans. Carl Morse. New York: New York University Press, 1963.

Andrian, Leopold. "Erinnerungen an meinen Freund." *Hugo von Hofmannsthal: Die Gestalt des Dichters im Spiegel der Freunde*, ed. Helmut A. Fiechtner. Vienna: Humboldt, 1949. 52–64.

Arnold, Heinz Ludwig. "Gespräch mit Peter Handke." *Text und Kritik* 24/24a (Sept. 1976): 15–37.

————. "Innovation und Irritation als Prinzip: Zu Peter Handkes 'Kaspar.'" In *Über Peter Handke*, ed. Michael Scharang. Frankfurt a. M.: Suhrkamp, 1972. 246–55.

Arnold, Heinz Ludwig, ed. *Westdeutsche Literatur von 1945–71*. Vol. 3 of *Geschichte der deutschen Literatur aus Methoden*. Frankfurt a. M.: Athenäum, 1973.

Aron, Albert W. "A Key to Jakob Wassermann." *Germanic Review* 3 (1928): 46–54.

Arp, Hans. *On my Way: Poetry and Essays. 1912–1947.* New York: Wittenborn, Schultz, 1948.

————. "Dada war kein Rüpelspiel." *Unsern täglichen Traum: Erinnerungen, Dichtungen und Betrachtungen aus den Jahren 1914–1954.* Zurich: Arche, 1955. 20–28.

————. "Dadaland." *Unsern täglichen Traum: Erinnerungen, Dichtungen und Betrachtungen aus den Jahren 1914–1954.* Zurich: Arche, 1955.

Babbitt, Irving. *Rousseau and Romanticism.* Austin, Texas: University of Texas Press, 1977 (orig. publ. 1919).

Bächler, Wolfgang. "Ausbrechen." *Ausbrechen: Gedichte aus 30 Jahren.* Frankfurt a. M.: S. Fischer, 1976, 193.

Baedeker, Peer, and Karl Lemke, eds. *Erich Ebermayer: Buch der Freunde.* Lohhof-Munich: Karl Lemke, 1960.

Ball, Hugo. *Die Flucht aus der Zeit.* Lucerne: Stocker, 1946.

Bance, A. F. "The Kaspar Hauser Legend and its Literary Survival." *German Life & Letters* 28 (1974/75): 195–210.

Bapst, Edmond. *À la Conquête du Trône de Bade.* Paris: A. Lahure, 1930.

Basil, Otto. *Georg Trakl in Selbstzeugnissen und Bilddokumenten.* Reinbek bei Hamburg: Rowohlt, 1965.

Batt, Kurt. "Leben im Zitat. Notizen zu Peter Handke." *Sinn und Form* 26, no. 3 (1974): 603–23.

Batts, Michael S., Anthony W. Riley, and Heinz Wetzel, eds. *Echoes and Influences of German Romanticism.* New York: Peter Lang, 1987.

Bauer, Roger. "Peter Handke et le paradoxe de Wittgenstein." *Revue d'Allemagne et des pays de langue allemande. Études Littéraires* 12, no. 4 (Oct.–Dec. 1980): 629–42.

Beiss, Adolf. "Nexus und Motive." *Deutsche Vierteljahrsschrift für Literaturwissenschaft und Geistesgeschichte* 36, no. 2 (1962): 248–76.

Bekes, Peter. *Peter Handke: "Kaspar." Sprache als Folter.* Modellanalysen: Literatur, 7, ed. Werner Zimmermann and Klaus Lindemann. Paderborn: Ferdinand Schöningh, 1984.

Beller, Manfred. "Von der Stoffgeschichte zur Thematologie: Ein Beitrag zur komparatistischen Methodenlehre." *Arcadia* 5 (1970): 1–38.

Bellmann, Werner. "Zeugnisse zu Hofmannsthals 'Turm.'" *Wirkendes Wort* 35, no. 5 (1985): 253–56.

Benjamin, Walter. "Dialog über die Religiosität der Gegenwart." *Frühe Arbeiten zur Bildungs- und Kultur-Kritik.* Vol. 2 of *Gesammelte Schriften,* ed. Rolf Tiedemann and Hermann Schweppenhäuser. Frankfurt a. M.: Suhrkamp, 1977. 16–35.

———. "Hugo von Hofmannsthals 'Turm.' Anläßlich der Uraufführung in München und Hamburg." Vol. 3 of *Gesammelte Schriften,* ed. Hella Tiedemann-Bartels. Frankfurt a. M.: Suhrkamp, 1972. 98–101.

Bing, Siegmund. *Jakob Wassermann: Weg und Werk des Dichters.* Berlin: S. Fischer, 1933.

Blanke, Mechthild. "Zu Peter Handkes 'Kaspar.'" *Über Peter Handke,* ed. Michael Scharang. Frankfurt a. M.: Suhrkamp, 1972. 256–94.

Blass, Regine. *Die Dichtung Georg Trakls: Von der Trivialsprache zum Kunstwerk.* Berlin: Erich Schmidt, 1968.

Blumer, Arnold. *Das dokumentarische Theater der sechziger Jahre in der Bundesrepublik Deutschland.* Hochschulschriften: Literaturwissenschaft. no. 32. Meisenheim a. G.: Anton Hain, 1977.

———. "Peter Handkes romantische Unvernunft." *Acta Germanica* 8 (1973): 123–32.

Bormann, Alexander von. "Politische Lyrik in den sechziger Jahren." *Die deutsche Lyrik der Gegenwart: Aspekte und Tendenzen,* ed. Manfred Durzak. Stuttgart: Philipp Reclam Jr., 1971. 170–91.

Bosch, Manfred. "Ein blinder Passagier steigt zu." *Die Horen* 25 (1980): 204–5.

Brinkmann, Richard. "Hofmannsthal und die Sprache." *Deutsche Vierteljahrsschrift für Literaturwissenschaft und Geistesgeschichte* 35, no. 1 (1961): 69–95.

Brinkmann, Richard, ed. *Romantik in Deutschland.* Sonderband der Deutschen Vierteljahrsschrift für Literaturwissenschaft und Geistesgeschichte. Stuttgart: J. B. Metzler, 1978.

Brod, Max. "In memoriam Jakob Wassermann." *Die Sammlung* 1 (1934): 282–85.

Büchner, Georg, "Lenz." *Werke und Briefe,* ed. Fritz Bergemann. Wiesbaden: Insel Verlag, 1953. 81–108.

———. "Woyzeck." *Werke und Briefe,* ed. Fritz Bergemann. Wiesbaden: Insel Verlag, 1953. 143–67.

Burckhardt, Carl. J. *Erinnerungen an Hofmannsthal und Briefe des Dichters.* Munich: Hermann Rinn, 1948.

Calderón de la Barca. *Das Leben ein Traum.* Vol. 2 of *Calderóns ausgewählte Werke in drei Bänden.* Trans. A. W. Schlegel and J. D. Gries. Stuttgart: J. G. Cotta, n.d. 93–192.

Carter, A. E. *Paul Verlaine.* New York: Twayne Publishers Inc., 1971.

Casey, T. J. *Manshape that Shone: An Interpretation of Trakl.* Modern Language Studies. Oxford: Basil Blackwell, 1964.

Claydon, Leslie F., ed. *Rousseau on Education.* London: Collier-MacMillan, 1969.

Conradt, Marcus. *Fünfeinhalb Jahre unter Menschen.* Stuttgart: Ernst Klett, 1983.

Corrigan, Timothy. *New German Film: The Displaced Image.* Austin, Texas: University of Texas Press, 1983.

Daumer G. F. *Enthüllungen über Kaspar Hauser.* Frankfurt a. M.: Meidinger, Sohn & Co., 1859.

——. *Kaspar Hauser: Sein Wesen, seine Unschuld, seine Erduldungen und sein Ursprung.* Regensburg: A. Coppenrath, 1873.

Dede, Hans Ewald. "Die Politisierung der Literatur in der Bundesrepublik seit 1968." *Kontext 1, Literatur und Wirklichkeit,* ed. Uwe Timms and Gerd Fuchs. Munich, C. Bertelsmann, 1976.

Dierks, Manfred. *Autor — Text — Leser: Walter Kempowski.* Munich: Francke, 1981.

Dietz, W. "Erich Ebermeyer [sic]: 'Kaspar Hauser.' Uraufführung Hamburger Kammerspiele." *Die literarische Welt* 3, no. 9 (4 March 1927): 7.

Dixon, Christa K. "Peter Handkes 'Kaspar': Ein Modellfall." *German Quarterly* 46 (1973): 31–46.

Döhl, Reinhard. *Das literarische Werk Hans Arps, 1903–30: Zur poetischen Vorstellungswelt des Dadaismus.* Stuttgart: J. B. Metzler, 1967.

——. "Hans Arp: 'Kaspar ist tot.' Beispiel einer Parodie." *Deutschunterricht* 18 (June 1966): 51–62.

Doehlemann, Martin. "Zur gesellschaftlichen Rolle des heutigen Schriftstellers." *Poesie und Politik: Zur Situation der Literatur in Deutschland.* Stuttgart: W. Kohlhammer, 1973. 32–42.

Dostoevski, Fedor Mikhailovich. *Der Idiot.* Trans. Arthur Luther. 8th ed. Munich: Deutscher Taschenbuch Verlag, 1985 (orig. publ. Petersburg, 1868/69).

Dücker, Burckhard. *Peter Härtling.* Munich: C. H. Beck, 1983.

Durzak, Manfred. "Einleitung." *Die deutsche Literatur der Gegenwart: Aspekte und Tendenzen,* ed. Manfred Durzak. Stuttgart: Philipp Reclam, Jr., 1971. 7–12.

——. *Peter Handke und die deutsche Gegenwartsliteratur: Narziß auf Abwegen.* Stuttgart: W. Kohlhammer, 1982

Ebermayer, Erich. *Denn heute gehört uns Deutschland ... : Persönliches und politisches Tagebuch. Von der Machtergreifung bis zum 31. Dezember 1935.* Hamburg: Paul Zsolnay, 1959.

―――. "Mein erster Erfolg — Mein erster Mißerfolg." *Die literarische Welt* 8, no. 43 (1932): 4.

―――. Untitled Homage to Klaus Mann, *Klaus Mann zum Gedächtnis*, ed. Erika Mann. Amsterdam: Querido, 1950. 33–45.

Eichendorff, Joseph von. *Gedichte.* Vol. 1 of *Werke in vier Bänden.* Re-edited and expanded by René Strasser. Zurich: Stauffacher, 1965.

Fahrner, Rudolf. *Dichterische Visionen menschlicher Urbilder in Hofmannsthals Werk.* Publications of the Faculty of Philosophy, no. 100. Ankara: Ankara University, 1956.

Faulstich, Werner, and Ingeborg Faulstich. *Modelle der Filmanalyse.* Munich: Wilhelm Fink, 1977.

Feuerbach, Paul Johann Anselm. *Kaspar Hauser: Beispiel eines Verbrechens am Seelenleben des Menschen.* Reprint. In Jochen Hörisch, ed. *Ich möchte ein solcher werden wie ... : Materialien zur Sprachlosigkeit des Kaspar Hauser,* 119–93. Frankfurt a. M.: Suhrkamp, 1979 (orig. publ. Ansbach: J. M. Dollfuß, 1832).

Fiechtner, Helmut A. "Nachwort." In *Hugo von Hofmannsthal: Der Dichter im Spiegel seiner Freunde,* ed. Helmut A. Fiechtner, Vienna: Humboldt, 1949. 367–71.

Fiedler, Leslie A. *Freaks: Myths and Images of the Secret Self.* New York: Simon & Schuster, 1978.

Finger, Ellis. "Kaspar Hauser Doubly Portrayed: Peter Handke's 'Kaspar' and Werner Herzog's 'Every Man for Himself and God against All.'" *Literature/Film Quarterly* 7 (1979): 235–43.

Fischer, Brigitte B. *Sie schrieben mir; oder: Was aus meinem Poesiealbum wurde.* Munich: Deutscher Taschenbuch Verlag, 1985.

Forte, Dieter. "Sprachspiel." *Neue Rundschau* 92, no. 4 (1981): 5–24.

―――. Untitled contribution. In *Butzbacher Autorenbefragung,* ed. Hans-Joachim Müller. Munich: Franz Ehrenwirt, 1973. 67–69.

Frenzel, Elisabeth. *Stoffe der Weltliteratur.* Stuttgart: Alfred Kröner, 1963.

―――. *Stoff- Motiv- und Symbolforschung.* Sammlung Metzler. Realienbücher für Germanisten, no. 28. Stuttgart: J. B. Metzler, 1963.

Frenzel, Herbert A., and Elisabeth Frenzel. *Daten deutscher Dichtung: Chronologischer Abriß der deutschen Literaturgeschichte.* Vol. 2, 11th ed. Munich: Deutscher Taschenbuch Verlag, 1975 (orig. publ. Cologne, Kiepenheuer & Witsch, 1953).

Fried, Erich. "Klage über die Doppeldeutung." *Die bunten Getüme.* Berlin: Klaus Wagenbach, 1977. 12–13.

Furness, Raymond. "Modernism and 'Sprachkrise.'" *The Twentieth Century: 1890–1945.* London: Croom Helm, 1978.

Furst, Lillian R. *Romanticism in Perspective*. 2nd ed. London: MacMillan Press, 1979.

George, Stefan. "Verlaine." *Tage und Taten: Aufzeichnungen und Skizzen. Gesamt-Ausgabe der Werke*. Endgültige Fassung, XVII. Berlin: Georg Bondi, 1933. 56–59.

Görtz, Franz Josef. "Nachwort." In Guntram Vesper. *Landeinwärts: Prosa und Gedichte*, ed. Franz Josef Görtz. Stuttgart: Philipp Reclam, Jr., 1984. 83–90.

Goldschmit, Rudolf. *Hugo von Hofmannsthal*. Friedrichs Dramatiker des Welttheaters, 43, Velber, Hannover: Friedrich, 1968.

Grimm, Reinhold. "Die Sonne: Bemerkungen zu einem Motiv Georg Trakls." *Deutsche Vierteljahrsschrift für Literaturwissenschaft und Geistesgeschichte* 35 (1961): 223–46.

————. "Georg Trakls Verhältnis zu Rimbaud." *Germanisch-Romanische Monatsschrift*. Neue Folge 9 (1959): 288–315.

————. "Werk und Wirkung des Übersetzers Karl Klammer." *Neophilologus* 44 (1960): 20–36.

Grimsley, Rolf. *The Philosophy of Rousseau*. Oxford: Oxford University Press, 1973.

Haas, Willy. *Hugo von Hofmannsthal*. Köpfe des XX. Jahrhunderts, no. 34, Berlin: Otto H. Hess, 1964.

Härtling, Peter. "Auf der Linie im Kreis." In *Mein Gedicht ist mein Messer: Lyriker zu ihren Gedichten*, ed. Hans Bender. Munich: Paul List, 1961. 161–65.

————. "Literatur als Revolution und Tradition." *Akzente* 14 (1967): 221–23.

————. "Kuttel Daddeldu grüßt Anna Blume: Eine Galerie literarischer Geister vorgestellt von Peter Härtling." Radio essay, Süddeutscher Rundfunk (30 Dec. 1960).

————. *Palmström grüßt Anna Blume: Essay und Anthologie der Geister aus Poetica*. Stuttgart: Henry Goverts, 1961.

————. "Peter Härtling. 1948." *Als ich fünfzehn war: Schriftsteller der Gegenwart erzählen*, ed. Eckart Kroneberg. Gütersloh: Gerd Mohn, 1969. 21–26.

————. *Protokoll zur Person: Autoren über sich und ihr Werk*, ed. Ekkehart Rudolph. Munich: Paul List, 1971.

————. *Spielgeist, Spiegelgeist: Gedichte*. Stuttgart: Henry Goverts, 1962.

Härtling, Peter, and Hellmut Jaesrich. Preliminary "Editorial." *Der Monat* 17, no. 200 (May 1965).

Hamburger, Michael. *Hofmannsthal: Three Essays*. Princeton, N. J.: Princeton University Press, 1972.

Handke, Peter. "Die Literatur ist romantisch" [1966]. *Ich bin ein Bewohner des Elfenbeinturms*. Frankfurt a. M.: Suhrkamp, 1972. 35–50.

————. "Horváth und Brecht" [1968]. *Ich bin ein Bewohner des Elfenbeinturms*, Frankfurt a. M.: Suhrkamp, 1972. 62–64.

————. "Ich bin ein Bewohner des Elfenbeinturms" [1967]. *Ich bin ein Bewohner des Elfenbeinturms*. Frankfurt a. M.: Suhrkamp, 1972. 19–28.

————. "Jemand anderer: Hermann Lenz." *Als das Wünschen noch geholfen hat.* Frankfurt a. M.: Suhrkamp, 1974. 81–100.

————. *Über die Dörfer: Dramatisches Gedicht*. Frankfurt a. M.: Suhrkamp, 1981.

Hartung, Harald. "Stich ins Herz: Guntram Vespers neue Gedichte." *Frankfurter Allgemeine Zeitung*, 5 Feb. 1983, 30.

Haug, Gerhart. *Verlaine: Die Geschichte des armen Lelian. Leben, Dichtung, Bekenntnisse, Briefe*. Basel: Benno Schwabe, 1944.

Heinrich, Karl Borromäus. "Die Erscheinung Georg Trakls." *Georg Trakl: Die Dichtungen*, ed. Kurt Horwitz. Zurich, Arche, 1946. 204–8.

Heißenbüttel, Helmut. "Peter Handke." In *Westdeutsche Literatur von 1945–71*. Vol. 3 of *Geschichte der deutschen Literatur aus Methoden*, ed. Heinz Ludwig Arnold. Frankfurt a. M.: Athenäum, 1973. 206–13.

Held, Wolfgang. "Kaspar Hauser und die Kritik der Sprache." *Beiträge zu den Sommerkursen 1969*, ed. Goethe-Institut. Munich: Goethe-Institut, 1969. 38–50.

Heller, Erich. *The Disinherited Mind: Essays in Modern German Literature and Thought*. 3rd ed. London: Bowes & Bowes, 1971.

Henisch, Peter. "Späte Überlegungen zu Handke." *Neues Forum* 17, no. 194/1 (1970): 120.

Herder, Gottfried. "Abhandlung über den Ursprung der Sprache." *Frühe Schriften: 1764–1772*, ed. Ulrich Geyer. Frankfurt a. M.: Deutscher Klassiker Verlag, 1981. 695–810.

Hermand, Jost. "Fortschritt im Rückschritt: Zur politischen Polarisierung der westdeutschen Literatur seit 1961." *Deutsche Gegenwartsliteratur: Ausgangspositionen und aktuelle Entwicklungen*, ed. Manfred Durzak. Stuttgart: Philipp Reclam Jr., 1981. 299–313.

————. *Synthetisches Interpretieren: Zur Methode der Literaturwissenschaft*. Munich: Nymphenburger Verlagsbuchhandlung, 1968.

Hern, Nicholas. *Peter Handke: Theatre and Anti-Theatre*. Modern German Authors: Texts and Contexts, no. 5. London: Oswald Wolff, 1971.

————. *Peter Handke*. New York: Frederick Ungar, 1971.

Herzog, Werner. *Was ich bin sind meine Filme*. Television documentary, directed by Christian Weisenborn and Erwin Keusch (1978).

Hesse, Günter. "Kaspar Hauser und sein Schlüssel." *Deutsches Ärzteblatt: Kulturmagazin* 81, no. 6 (10 Feb. 1984): 365–68.

Hinderer, Walter. "Wittgenstein für Anfänger? Anmerkungen zu Peter Handkes linguistischem Theater." *Jahrbuch der Deutschen Schillergesellschaft* 26 (1982): 467–88.

Hinton Thomas, R., and Keith Bullivant. *Literature in Upheaval: West German Writers and the Challenge of the 1960s.* Manchester: University Press, 1974.

Hirsch, Rudolf. "Unbekannte Äußerungen Hofmannsthals zum 'Turm.'" *Literatur und Kritik* 14 (1979): 257–59.

Hoffer, Peter T. *Klaus Mann.* Boston: Twayne Publishers, 1978.

Hölderlin, Friedrich. "Hyperion." I. *Werke. Briefe. Dokumente,* ed. Pierre Bertaux. Munich: Winkler, n.d. [1969]. 219–95.

Höllerer, Walter. "Fortgang." In *Mein Gedicht ist mein Messer: Lyriker zu ihren Gedichten,* ed. Hans Bender. Munich: Paul List, 1961. 96–100.

Hörisch, Jochen. "Die Sprachlosigkeit des Kaspar Hauser." In *Ich möchte ein solcher werden wie ...* : *Materialien zur Sprachlosigkeit des Kaspar Hauser,* ed. Jochen Hörisch. Frankfurt a. M.: Suhrkamp, 1979. 265–301.

Hofmannsthal, Hugo von. "Ad me ipsum." *Aufzeichnungen. Gesammelte Werke in Einzelausgaben,* ed. Herbert Steiner. Frankfurt a. M.: S. Fischer, 1959. 211–44.

———. "Anmerkungen." *Dramen.* Vol. 3 of *Gesammelte Werke in Einzelausgaben,* ed. Herbert Steiner. Frankfurt a. M.: S. Fischer, 1957. 501–4.

———. "Aufzeichnungen und Entwürfe." *Dramen.* Vol. 3 of *Gesammelte Werke in Einzelausgaben,* ed. Herbert Steiner. Frankfurt a. M.: S. Fischer, 1957. 426–38.

———. "Briefe und Aufsätze für amerikanische Zeitschriften." *Aufzeichnungen. Gesammelte Werke in Einzelausgaben,* ed. Herbert Steiner. Frankfurt a. M.: S. Fischer, 1959. 265–349.

———. "Der Dichter und diese Zeit." *Prosa.* Vol. 2 of *Gesammelte Werke in Einzelausgaben,* ed. Herbert Steiner. Frankfurt a. M.: S. Fischer, 1951. 264–98.

———. "Ein Brief." *Prosa.* Vol. 2 of *Gesammelte Werke in Einzelausgaben,* ed. Herbert Steiner. Frankfurt a. M.: S. Fischer, 1951. 7–22.

———. "Eine Monographie. 'Friedrich Mitterwurzer', von Eugen Guglia." *Prosa.* Vol. 1 of *Gesammelte Werke in Einzelausgaben,* ed. Herbert Steiner. Frankfurt a. M.: S. Fischer, 1951. 265–70.

Holthusen, Hans Egon. *Der unbehauste Mensch: Motive und Probleme der modernen Literatur.* Munich: R. Piper, 1951.

Horn, Peter. "Vergewaltigung durch die Sprache: Peter Handkes 'Kaspar.'" *Literatur und Kritik* 51 (1971): 30–40.

Hüppauf, Bernd. "Peter Handkes Stellung im Kulturwandel der sechziger Jahre." In *Handke: Ansätze — Analysen — Anmerkungen,* ed. Manfred Jürgensen. Bern: Francke, 1979.

Huizinga, J. *Jean-Jacques Rousseau: The Making of a Saint.* London: Hamish Hamilton, 1976.

Jaspersen, Ursula. "Georg Trakl." *Deutsche Dichter der Moderne; ihr Leben ihr Werk,* ed. Benno von Wiese. Berlin: Erich Schmidt, 1965. 379–99.

Jean Paul [Jean Paul Friedrich Richter]. *Die Unsichtbare Loge*. Vol. 2 of *Sämtliche Werke*, ed. Eduard Berend. Weimar: Hermann Böhlaus Nachfolger, 1927 (orig. publ. 1793).

Jens, Walter. *Deutsche Literatur der Gegenwart: Themen, Stile, Tendenzen*. Munich: R. Piper, 1961.

Jolles, Andé. *Einfache Formen*, 2nd ed. Halle/Saale: Max Niemeyer, 1956 (orig. publ. 1929).

Joseph, Artur. "Peter Handke." In *Theater unter vier Augen*. Cologne: Kiepenheuer & Witsch, 1969. 27–39.

Jungmann, Otto. *Kaspar Hauser: Stoff und Problem in ihrer literarischen Gestaltung*. Würzburg: Konrad Triltsch, 1935 [Ph.D. diss., University of Frankfurt a. M., 1935].

Jurgensen, Manfred, ed. *Handke: Ansätze, Analysen, Anmerkungen*. Bern: Francke, 1979.

Kaiser, Gerhard R. *Einführung in die vergleichende Literaturwissenschaft: Forschungsstand — Kritik — Aufgaben*. Darmstadt: Wissenschaftliche Buchgesellschaft, 1980.

Kantorowicz, Ernst. *Kaiser Friedrich der Zweite*. Berlin: Georg Bondi, 1927.

———. *Kaiser Friedrich der Zweite: Ergänzungsband. Quellennachweise und Exkurse*. Berlin: Georg Bondi, 1931.

Kesting, Marianne. *Panorama des zeitgenössischen Theaters: 58 literarische Porträts*. Munich: R. Piper, 1969.

———. "Sprachterror oder dichterische Sondersprache: Zur Verwandlung der Kaspar-Hauser-Figur in Hofmannsthals 'Turm'-Dichtungen und Peter Handkes 'Kaspar.'" *Drama und Theater im 20. Jahrhundert: Festschrift Walter Hinck*, ed. Hans Dietrich Irmscher and Werner Keller. Göttingen: Vandenhoeck & Ruprecht, 1983. 365–80.

Killy, Walther. *Über Georg Trakl*. 3rd, expanded ed. Göttingen: Vandenhoeck & Ruprecht, 1967.

Kleist, Heinrich von. "Über das Marionettentheater." *Werke in einem Band*, ed. Helmut Sembdner. Munich: Hanser, 1966 (orig. publ. 1810). 802–7.

Klettenhammer, Sieglinde. "Unbekanntes Puppenspiel 'Kaspar Hauser' von Georg Trakl." *Mitteilungen aus dem Brenner-Archiv* 1 (1982): 50–56.

Kluckhohn, Paul. "Berufungsbewußtsein und Gemeinschaftsdienst des deutschen Dichters im Wandel der Zeiten." *Deutsche Vierteljahrsschrift für Literaturwissenschaft und Geistesgeschichte* 14, no. 1 (1936): 1–30.

———. *Das Ideengut der deutschen Romantik*. 2nd ed. Halle/Saale: Max Niemeyer, 1942.

Körner, Wolfgang. "Ist Handke romantisch?" *Egoist* 4, no. 14 (1968): 10.

Kommerell, Max. *Jean Pauls Verhältnis zu Rousseau*. Marburg a. L.: N. G. Elwert & G. Braun, 1924.

Kraft, Wetzel. "Interview." In Ulrich Gregor and others. *Herzog — Kluge — Straub.* Reihe Film 9, ed. Peter W. Jansen and Wolfram Schütte. Munich: Hanser, 1976. 113–30.

Kramer, Kurt. *Kaspar Hauser: Kein Rätsel unserer Zeit.* Ansbach: Ansbacher Verlagsgesellschaft, 1978.

Kramer, Sibylle. "Wer wir sind." *Frankfurter Rundschau,* 18 Sept. 1982, 4.

Kraul, Fritz. "Hilfsmittel zu Spielfilmbetrachtungen." *Deutschunterricht* 3 (1958): 32–45.

Kraus, Karl. "In dieser großen Zeit." *Die Fackel* 16, no. 404 (Dec. 1914): 1–20.

————. Untitled poem. *Die Fackel* 35, no. 888 (Oct. 1933): 4.

Kreuzer, Helmut. *Veränderungen des Literaturbegriffs.* Göttingen: Vandenhoeck & Ruprecht, 1975.

Kroll, Fredric, and Klaus Täubert. *1906–1927: Unordnung und früher Ruhm.* Vol. 2 of *Klaus-Mann-Schriftenreihe.* Wiesbaden: Blahak, 1977.

Krummacher, Hans-Henrik, Fritz Martini, and Walter Müller-Seidel. *Zeit der Moderne.* Stuttgart: Alfred Kröner, 1984.

Kunze, Wilhelm. *Mythos, Gestalt und Schicksal von Kaspar Hauser.* Nuremberg: September Verlag, 1931.

Lachmann, Eduard. *Kreuz und Abend: Eine Interpretation der Dichtungen Georg Trakls.* Salzburg: Otto Müller, 1954.

Lakies, Holger and Gisela Lakies-Wild. *Das Phänomen: Entwicklungspsychologisch bedeutsame Fakten des Hauser-Mysteriums.* Ansbach: Ansbacher Verlagsgesellschaft, 1978.

Lane, Harlan. *The Wild Boy of Aveyron.* Cambridge, Mass.: Harvard University Press, 1976.

Lassahn, Bernhard. *Dorn im Ohr: Das lästige Liedermacher-Buch.* Zurich: Diogenes, 1982.

Last, Rex W. *German Dadaist Literature: Kurt Schwitters, Hugo Ball, Hans Arp.* New York: Twayne Publishers, 1973.

————. *Hans Arp, the Poet of Dadaism.* Modern German Authors: Texts and Contexts, no. 1. London: Oswald Wolff, 1969.

————. "In Defence of Meaning: A Study of Hans Arp's 'Kaspar ist tot.'" *German Life & Letters* 12 (1968/69): 330–40.

Laubach, Jakob. "Hofmannsthals Turm der Selbstbewahrung." *Wirkendes Wort* 4 (1954): 257–68.

Lenz, Siegfried. *Der Verlust.* Hamburg: Hoffmann & Campe, 1981.

Leonhardt, Ulrike. *Prinz von Baden, genannt Kaspar Hauser.* Reinbek bei Hamburg: Wunderlich, 1987.

Levin, Harry. "Thematics and Criticism." In *Grounds for Comparison*, ed. Harvard University Press. Cambridge, Mass.: Harvard University Press, 1972. 91–109.

Limbach, Hans. "Begegnung mit Georg Trakl (1914)." *Georg Trakl: Die Dichtungen*, ed. Kurt Horwitz. Zurich: Arche, 1946. 208–13.

Lovejoy, A. O. "On the Discrimination of Romanticisms." In *English Romantic Poets*, ed. M. H. Abrams. Oxford: Oxford University Press, 1960. 3–24.

Lüthi, Max. "Motiv, Zug, Thema aus der Sicht der Volkserzählungsforschung." *Elemente der Literatur: Beiträge zur Stoff-, Motiv- und Themenforschung*. Vol. 1, ed. Adam J. Bisanz and Raymond Trousson. Stuttgart: Alfred Kröner, 1980. 11–24.

Lütkehaus, Ludger. "Kaspar Hauser; oder, Die Natur in der Gesellschaft." In Artin, Alexander Baron von. *Kaspar Hauser. Seine mysteriöse Ermordung. Sein hartnäckiges Weiterleben*, ed. Alfons Wiesinger. Zurich: Taja Gut, 1982–85.

MacKenzie, Paul A. "Kaspar Hauser in England: The First Hundred Years." *German Life & Letters* 35, no. 2 (Jan. 1982): 118–37.

Maclean, Charles. *The Wolf Children*. New York: Hill & Wang, 1977.

Mahrholdt, Erwin. "Aus einer Studie über Georg Trakl" [1925]. *Georg Trakl: Die Dichtungen*, ed. Kurt Horwitz. Zurich: Arche, 1946. 200–204.

Malson, Lucien. "Wolfchildren." In Malson, Lucien, and Jean Itard. *Wolfchildren: The Wild Boy of Aveyron*, trans. Edmund Fawcett, Peter Ayrton, and Joan White. London: Union Générale d'Editions, 1964. 9–88.

Mann, Klaus. *Anja und Esther: Ein romantisches Stück in sieben Bildern*. 2nd ed. Berlin: Oesterheld, 1925.

———. *Der fromme Tanz: Das Abenteuerbuch einer Jugend*. Hamburg: Enoch, 1926.

———. *Der Wendepunkt: Ein Lebensbericht*. Berlin: G. B. Fischer, 1958.

———. "Kaspar Hauser." *Die Weltbühne* 21, no. 1 (1925): 511.

———. *Kind dieser Zeit*. Munich: Nymphenburger Verlagsbuchhandlung, 1965 (orig. publ. 1932).

———. "Ödön von Horváth." *Deutsche Literaturkritik der Gegenwart: Vorkrieg, Zweiter Weltkrieg und zweite Nachkriegszeit*, ed. Hans Mayer, 174–77. Stuttgart: Goverts Krüger Stahlberg, 1971.

———. *The Turning Point: Thirty-five Years in this Century*. London: Victor Gollancz, 1944.

Mann, Thomas. "In memoriam Hugo von Hofmannsthal." *Das essayistische Werk*, ed. Hans Bürgin. Frankfurt a. M.: S. Fischer, 1960. 209–12.

———. "Jakob Wassermanns 'Caspar Hauser oder die Trägheit des Herzens.'" *Gesammelte Werke in zwölf Bänden*. Vol. 10, ed. Thomas Mann Archives Berlin and Zurich. Oldenburg: Gerhard Stalling, 1960. 553–55.

Marey, Suzanne. "Georg Trakl et Kaspar Hauser." *Aspects de la Civilisation Germanique*. Travaux VII, 12 (1975): 189–203.

Martens, Kurt. "Im Spiegel." *Das Litterarische Echo* [sic] 20 (1903): 1394–96.

——. *Literatur in Deutschland: Studien und Eindrücke*. Berlin: Egon Fleischel, 1910.

——. *Schonungslose Lebenschronik*. 2 vols. Vienna: Rikola, 1921–24.

Martin, Horst. "Kaspar Hauser und Sigismund: Über eine Quelle zu Hofmannsthals 'Turm.'" *Seminar* 12 (Nov. 1976): 236–58.

Martini, Fritz. *Was war Expressionismus? Deutung und Auswahl seiner Lyrik*. Urach: Port, 1948.

Marx, Reiner. "'Ich möchte einer werden so wie die ...': Zur Kaspar-Hauser-Allusion in Rilkes Gedicht 'Der Knabe.'" *Blätter der Rilke-Gesellschaft* 13 (1986): 107–20.

Masson, Michel. *Les Enfants Célèbres ou Histoire des Enfants de tous les siècles et de tous les pays*. Paris: Didier, 1845.

Mayer, Hans. *Aussenseiter*. Frankfurt a. M.: Suhrkamp, 1975.

——. "Kaspar, der Fremde und der Zufall: Literarische Aspekte der Entfremdung." *Text und Kritik* 24 (1969): 30–42.

Mayer, Johannes, and Peter Tradowsky. *Kaspar Hauser: Das Kind von Europa*. Stuttgart: Urachhaus, 1984.

Megill, Allan. "Aesthetic Theory and Historical Consciousness in the Eighteenth Century." *History and Theory* 17, no. 1 (1978): 29–62.

Melville, Herman, "Billy Budd." *Typee and Billy Budd*. London: Dent, 1958 (orig. publ., posthumously, 1924).

Mendelsohn, Peter de. *S. Fischer und sein Verlag*. Frankfurt a. M.: S. Fischer, 1970.

Mennemeier, Franz Norbert. "Dieter Forte: 'Martin Luther & Thomas Münzer; oder: Die Einführung der Buchhaltung' — Versäumte Vermittlung." *Geschichte als Schauspiel*, ed. Walter Hinck. Frankfurt a. M.: Suhrkamp, 1981. 371–79.

Metzler Literatur Lexikon, ed. Günther and Irmgard Schweikle. Stuttgart: Metzler, 1984.

Metzner, Ernst Erich. "Die dunkle Klage des Gerechten — Poésie Pure? Rationalität und Intentionalität in Georg Trakls Spätwerk, dargestellt am Beispiel 'Kaspar Hauser Lied.'" *Germanisch-Romanische Monatschrift* 24 (1974): 446–72.

Migand, J. F. "Trakl et l'Enfance angélique." *Etudes Germaniques* 27 (1972): 407–19.

Mitscherlich, Alexander. "Ödipus und Kaspar Hauser: Tiefenpsychologische Probleme der Gegenwart." *Der Monat* 3, no. 25 (Oct. 1950): 11–18.

Moeller, Bernhard. "Literatur und Film im medienüberschreitenden Produktionskontext." *Deutsche Literatur in der Bundesrepublik seit 1965*, ed. Paul Michael Lützeler and Egon Schwarz. Königstein, Ts.: Athenäum, 1980. 85–98.

Naef, Karl J. *Hugo von Hofmannsthals Wesen und Werk*. Zurich: Max Niehaus, 1938.

Naegele, Rainer. "Das Unbehagen in der Sprache: Zu Peter Handkes 'Kaspar.'" *Basis* 6 (1976): 78–96.

Naegele, Rainer, and Renate Voris. *Peter Handke*. Munich: C. H. Beck, 1978.

Overbey, David. "Werner Herzog's 'Everyman for Himself.'" *Sight and Sound* 44, no. 2 (Spring 1975): 73–75.

Paulsen, Wolfgang, ed. *Das Nachleben der Romantik in der modernen deutschen Literatur*. Poesie und Wissenschaft, no. 14. Heidelberg: Lothar Stiehm, 1969.

Peitler, Hans, and Hans Ley. *Kaspar Hauser: Über tausend bibliographische Nachweise*. Ansbach: C. Brügel & Sohn, 1927.

Pesch, Ludwig. *Die Romantische Rebellion in der modernen Literatur und Kunst*. Munich: C. H. Beck, 1962.

Peucker, Brigitte. "Werner Herzog: In Quest of the Sublime." In *New German Filmmakers: From Oberhausen through the 1970s*, ed. Klaus Phillips. New York: Frederick Ungar, 1984. 168–94.

———. "Literature and Writing in the Films of Werner Herzog." *Film und Literatur: Literarische Texte und der neue deutsche Film*, ed. Sigrid Bauschinger, Susan L. Cocalis, and Henry A. Lea. Bern: Francke, 1984. 156–68.

Pflaum, Hans Günther. "Interview." In Hans Günther Pflaum and others, *Werner Herzog*. Reihe Film 22, ed. Peter W. Jansen and Wolfram Schütte. Munich: Carl Hanser, 1979. 59–86.

Pickerodt, Gerhart. *Hofmannsthals Dramen: Kritik ihres historischen Inhalts*. Stuttgart: J. B. Metzler, 1968.

Pies, Hermann. *Die Wahrheit über Kaspar Hausers Auftauchen und die erste Nürnberger Zeit*. Saarbrücken: Minerva, 1956.

———. *Fälschungen und Tendenzberichte einer 'offiziellen' Hauserliteratur: Aktenmäßige Feststellungen*. Nuremberg: Schrag, 1926.

———. *Fälschungen, Falschmeldungen und Tendenzberichte*. Ansbach: Museumsverlag, 1973.

———. *Kaspar Hauser: Augenzeugenberichte und Selbstzeugnisse*. 2 vols. Stuttgart: Robert Lutz, 1925.

———. *Kaspar Hauser: Eine Dokumentation*. Ansbach: C. Brügel & Sohn, 1966.

Porché, François. *Verlaine, tel qu'il fut*. Paris: Ernest Flammarion, 1933.

Prescher, Hans. "Klagerufe und Prophezeiungen." *Text und Kritik* 29 (1971): 24–34.

Preu, Paul Siegmund Karl, and others. *Kaspar Hauser: Arztberichte*, ed. Peter Tradowsky. Dornach, Switzerland: Rudolf Geering, 1985.

Reinhold, Ursula. *Tendenzen und Autoren*. Berlin: Dietz, 1982.

Requadt, Paul. "Sprachverleugnung und Mantelsymbolik im Werk Hofmannsthals." *Deutsche Vierteljahrsschrift für Literaturwissenschaft und Geistesgeschichte* 29, no. 2 (1955): 255–83.

Rey, William H. "Hofmannsthal, 'Der Turm.'" *Das deutsche Drama vom Barock bis zur Gegenwart: Interpretationen* Vol. 2, ed. Benno von Wiese. Düsseldorf: Bagel, 1958. 265–83.

Richter, Hans. *Dada-Profile*. Zurich: Peter Schifferli; Arche, 1961.

Richter, Hans. "Erinnerungen und Bekenntnisse." In Hugo Ball. *Gesammelte Gedichte*, ed. A. Schütt-Hennings. Zurich: Arche, 1963. 110–22.

Ries, Klaus. "Peter Handke — Autor einer deutschen Nachmoderne?" *Boletin de Estudios Germanico* 9 (1972): 155–70.

Riessauw, Anne-Marie. *Catalogues des Oeuvres vocales écrites par des Compositeurs Européens sur des poèmes de Verlaine*. Gent: Rijksuniversiteit Gent, 1980.

Rilke, Rainer Maria. *Neue Gedichte*. Vol. 1 of *Sämtliche Werke*, ed. Rilke Archives with the aid of Ruth Sieber-Rilke and Ernst Zinn. Wiesbaden: Insel, 1955.

Rimbach, G. C. "Sense and Non-Sense in the Poetry of Jean-Hans Arp." *German Quarterly* 36 (1963): 152–63.

Rippere, Vicky. *Schiller and 'Alienation.'* Bern: Peter Lang, 1981.

Ritzer, Walter. *Neue Trakl Bibliographie*. Salzburg: Otto Müller, 1983.

Rolf, Peter Carl. "Dokumentarisches Theater." *Die deutsche Literatur der Gegenwart: Aspekte und Tendenzen*. Stuttgart: Philipp Reclam, Jr., 1971. 99–127.

Rosenhaupt, Hans Wilhelm. *Der deutsche Dichter um die Jahrhundertwende und seine Abgelöstheit von der Gesellschaft*. Bern: Paul Haupt, 1939.

Rotermund, Erwin. *Die Parodie in der modernen deutschen Lyrik*. Munich: Eidos, 1963.

Rousseau, Jean-Jacques. *Discours sur l'origine et les fondements de l'inégalité parmi les hommes*, ed. F. C. Green. Cambridge: University Press, 1941.

————. *Du Contrat Social*, ed. Ronald Grimsley. Oxford: Clarendon Press, 1972 (orig. publ. Amsterdam: Marc Michel Rey, 1762).

————. *Émile; ou, De l'Éducation. Oeuvres Complètes de Jean-Jacques Rousseau*. Vol. 1. Paris: Imprimerie de Découchant, 1831 (orig. publ. Amsterdam: Jean Néaulme, 1762).

————. *Essai sur l'origine des langues* (1755), ed. Angèle Kremer-Marietti. Reprint Paris: Aubier Montaigne, 1974.

Rutra, Arthur Ernst. "Erich Ebermeyer [sic]: 'Kaspar Hauser.'" *Die literarische Welt* 3, no. 9 (1927): 7.

Sandford, John. "Werner Herzog." *The New German Cinema*. London: Oswald Wolff Publishers, 1980. 48–63.

Schaeder, Grete. "Hugo von Hofmannsthals Weg zur Tragödie: Die drei Stufen der Turm-Dichtung." *Deutsche Vierteljahrsschrift für Literaturwissenschaft und Geistesgeschichte* 23, nos. 2/3 (1949): 306–50.

Scharang, Michael, ed. *Über Peter Handke*. Frankfurt a. M.: Suhrkamp, 1972.

Schaukal, Richard von. *Frühling eines Lebens*. Vienna: Herold, 1949.

Schaumann, Lore. "Dieter Forte: Klausur in Basel." *Düsseldorf schreibt: 22 Autorenporträts*. Düsseldorf: Triltsch, 1981. 47–53

Schlueter, June. "Kaspar." *The Plays and Novels of Peter Handke*. Critical Essays in Modern Literature. Pittsburgh: University of Pittsburgh Press. 1981. 41–50.

Schneditz, Wolfgang. "Georg Trakl: Versuch einer Deutung des Menschen und des Dichters." In *Nachlaß und Biographie*. Vol. 3 of *Gesammelte Werke*, by Georg Trakl, ed. Wolfgang Schneditz. Salzburg: Otto Müller, 1949. 66–126.

Scholz, Hans. *Kaspar Hauser: Protokoll einer modernen Sage*. Munich: Wilhelm Heyne, 1985 (orig. publ. Hamburg: Campe, 1964).

Schultz, Franz. "'Romantik' und 'romantisch' als literarhistorische Terminologien und Begriffsbildungen." *Deutsche Vierteljahrsschrift für Literaturwissenschaft und Geistesgeschichte* 2, no. 3 (1924): 349–66.

Schultz, Uwe. *Peter Handke*. Dramatiker des Welttheaters, 2nd ed. Velber, Hannover: Friedrich, 1974.

Schulz, Gerhard. "Die metaphorische Darstellung des Gegensatzes Einsamkeit — Öffentlichkeit in der deutschen romantischen Lyrik." In *Romantik in Deutschland*. Sonderband der Deutschen Vierteljahrsschrift für Literaturwissenschaft und Geistesgeschichte, ed. Richard Brinkmann. Stuttgart: J. B. Metzler, 1978. 611–24.

Schulze, Joachim. "Marginalien zur Methodologie: Geschichte oder Systematik? Zu einem Problem der Themen- und Motivgeschichte." *Arcadia* 10 (1975): 76–82.

Schwarz, Egon. *Hofmannsthal und Calderón*. 'S-Gravenhage: Mouton, 1962.

Sdun, Wilfried. *Probleme und Theorien des Übersetzens in Deutschland vom 18. bis 20. Jahrhundert*. Munich: Max Hueber, 1967.

Seelmann-Eggebert. "Der Dichter Walter Erich Schäfer: Zur Neuausgabe seiner 'Schauspiele' und 'Hörspiele'." *Stuttgarter Leben* 43, no. 1 (Jan. 1968): 25–27.

Sell, Anne-Liese. *Das metaphysisch-realistische Weltbild Jakob Wassermanns*. Bern: Paul Haupt, 1932.

Sengle, F. "Wunschbild Land und Schreckbild Stadt: Zu einem zentralen Thema der neueren deutschen Literatur." *Studium Generale* 16, no. 10 (1963): 619–31.

Sergoris, Gunther. *Peter Handke und die Sprache*, Bonn: Bouvier Verlag Herbert Grundmann, 1979.

Shattuck, Roger. *The Forbidden Experiment: The Story of the Wild Boy of Aveyron*. New York: McGraw-Hill Ryerson, 1980.

Silverman, Kaja. "Kaspar Hauser's 'Terrible Fall' into Narrative." *New German Critique* 24/25 (1981/82): 73–93.

Singh, J. A. L., and Robert M. Zingg. *Wolf-Children and Feral Man*. Denver: Archon Books, 1942.

Spiel, Hilde. "Jakob Wassermann: Zu einer Ausstellung in Wien." *Literatur und Kritik* 199/200 (Nov./Dec. 1985): 412–17.

Spoerri, Theod. *Georg Trakl: Strukturen in Persönlichkeit und Werk. Eine psychiatrisch-anthropographische Untersuchung*. Bern: Francke, 1954.

Stix, Gottfried. *Trakl und Wassermann*. Rome: Edizioni di Storia e Letteratura, 1968.

Strauß, Botho. "Anläßlich Kaspar." *Theater heute*. Sonderheft (1968): 68.

Szklenar, Hans. "Georg Trakl: Ein biographischer Abriß." *Text und Kritik* 4/4a (1973): 42–45.

Taraba, Wolfgang F. "Friedrich Nietzsche." *Deutsche Dichter der Moderne*, ed. Benno von Wiese. Berlin: Erich Schmidt, 1965. 11–26.

Theisz, R. D. "Kaspar Hauser im zwanzigsten Jahrhundert: Der Aussenseiter und die Gesellschaft." *German Quarterly* 49, no. 2 (March 1976): 168–80.

Thiele, Herbert. "Das Bild des Menschen in den Kaspar-Hauser-Gedichten von Paul Verlaine und Georg Trakl." *Wirkendes Wort* 14 (1964): 351–56.

Thorley, Wilfried. *Paul Verlaine*. London: Constable, 1914.

Timms, Uwe. "Peter Handke; oder, Sicher in die 70er Jahre." *Kürbiskern* 4 (1970): 611–21.

Toulmin, Stephen. "Introduction." In S. Morris Engel. *Wittgenstein's Doctrine of the Tyranny of Language: An Historical and Critical Examination of His Blue Book*, ix–xiii. The Hague: Martinus Nijhoff, 1971.

Tradowsky, Peter. *Kaspar Hauser; oder: Das Ringen um den Geist*. Dornach: Philosophisch-Anthroposophischer Verlag, Goetheanum, 1980.

Trakl, Georg. *Aus Goldenem Kelch. Die Jugenddichtungen*. Vol. 2 of *Gesamtausgabe*. 2nd ed., ed. Wolfgang Schneditz. Salzburg: Otto Müller, n.d. [1939].

———. *Dichtungen und Briefe*. Vol. 1, ed. Walther Killy and Hans Szklenar. Salzburg: Otto Müller, 1969.

———. *Die Dichtungen: Gesamtausgabe mit einem Anhang. Zeugnisse und Erinnerungen*, ed. Kurt Horwitz. Zurich: Arche, 1946.

———. *Nachlaß und Biographie*. Vol. 3 of *Gesammelte Werke*, ed. Wolfgang Schneditz. Salzburg: Otto Müller, 1949.

Trousson, Raymond. "Les Études de Thèmes: Questions de Méthode." *Elemente der Literatur. Beiträge zur Stoff-, Motiv- und Themenforschung*. Vol. 1, ed. Adam J. Bizanz and Raymond Trousson. Stuttgart: Alfred Kröner, 1980. 1–10.

————. "Plaidoyer pour la Stoffgeschichte." *Revue de Littérature Comparée* 38 (1964): 101–14.

Ullmann, Richard, and Helene Gotthard. *Geschichte des Begriffes 'Romantisch' in Deutschland*. Nendeln, Liechtenstein: Kraus Reprint, 1967 (orig. publ. Berlin: Matthiesen, 1927).

Usinger, Fritz. *Die dichterische Welt Hans Arps*. Akademie der Wissenschaften und der Literatur, no. 3. Wiesbaden: Franz Steiner, 1965.

Voegeli, Walter. *Jakob Wassermann und die Trägheit des Herzens*. Winterthur: P. G. Keller, 1956.

Voris, Renate. *Peter Handke: Kaspar. Grundlagen und Gedanken zum Verständnis des Dramas*. Frankfurt a. M.: Moritz Diesterweg, 1984.

Wackenroder, Wilhelm Heinrich, and Ludwig Tieck. *Phantasien über die Kunst*. Reprint. Stuttgart: Reclam, 1973 (orig. publ. as *Phantasien über die Kunst für Freunde der Kunst*. Hamburg: Friedrich Perthes, 1799).

Walser, Martin. "Engagement als Pflichtfach für Schriftsteller." *Poesie und Politik: Zur Situation der Literatur in Deutschland*, ed. Wolfgang Kuttenkeuler. Stuttgart: W. Kohlhammer, 1973. 304–18.

————. *Wie und wovon handelt Literatur: Aufsätze und Reden*. Frankfurt a. M.: Suhrkamp, 1973.

Wandrey, Uwe. *Das Motiv des Krieges in der expressionistischen Lyrik*. Geistes- und sozialwissenschaftliche Dissertationen, no. 23. Hamburg: Hartmut Lüdke, 1972.

Wassermann, Jakob. *Bula Matari: Das Leben Stanleys*. Berlin: S. Fischer, 1932.

————. *Christian Wahnschaffe*. 2 vols. Berlin: S. Fischer, 1923.

————. *Das Gänsemännchen*. Munich: Georg Müller, 1972.

————. *Der Fall Maurizius*. Hamburg: Rütten & Loening, n.d.

————. "Habt Mut zu euren Träumen." *Tagebuch aus dem Winkel: Erzählungen und Aufsätze aus dem Nachlaß*. Amsterdam: Querido, 1935. 118–40.

————. "Hofmannsthal der Freund." *Bekenntnisse und Begegnungen*, ed. Paul Stöcklein. Bamberg: Bamberger Reiter, 1950 (orig. publ. Zurich, Carl Posen, 1949). 9–31.

————. *Lebensdienst*. Leipzig: Grethlein, 1928.

————. *Mein Weg als Deutscher und Jude*. Berlin: S. Fischer, 1921.

————. "Selbstbetrachtungen." *Bekenntnisse und Begegnungen*. Bamberg: Bamberger Reiter, 1950 (also publ. separately, Berlin: S. Fischer, 1933). 32–61.

Webb, Karl E. "Trakl/ Schiele and the Rimbaud Connection: Psychological Alienation in Austria at the Turn of the Century." *Jahrbuch für Internationale Germanistik*. Reihe A: Kongressberichte, ed. Joseph P. Strelka. Bern: Peter Lang, 1984. 12–21.

Weber, Albrecht. *Trakl: Gedichte*. Selective interpretations. Munich: Kösel, 1961.

Weber, Carl Hans. "Kurt Martens." *Das Litterarische Echo* [sic] 20 (15 July 1903): 1387–94.

Weimann, Robert. "Past Significance and Present Meaning in Literary History." *New Directions in Literary History*, ed. Ralph Cohen, London: Routledge & Kegan Paul, 1974. 43–61.

Wittgenstein, Ludwig. *Das blaue Buch. Schriften*. Vol. V, eds. G. E. M. Anscombe and G. H. von Wright. Frankfurt a. M.: Suhrkamp, 1970 (orig. publ. Oxford: Basil Blackwell, 1958).

Witzeling, Klaus. "Torturen des Gehenlernens." *hamburger rundschau*, 17 Oct. 1985.

Wuthenow, Ralph-Rainer. *Das fremde Kunstwerk: Aspekte der literarischen Übersetzung*. Göttingen: Vandenhoeck & Ruprecht, 1969.

Ziolkowski, Theodore. "Das Nachleben der Romantik in der modernen deutschen Literatur." In *Das Nachleben der Romantik in der modernen deutschen Literatur*, ed. Wolfgang Paulsen. Heidelberg: Lothar Stiehm, 1969.

Zipes, Jack. *The Brothers Grimm: From Enchanted Forests to the Modern World*. New York: Routledge, 1988.

C. Secondary Material (Unpublished)

Amann, Jürg. Typescript of interview held at the 'Theater an der Winkelwiese', Switzerland. Sent to author by J. Amann on 18 May 1986.

————. Letter to author, 18 May 1987.

Biermann, Wolf. Letter to author, 27 May 1987.

Cierpka, Helga. "Interpretationstypen der Trakl-Literatur: Eine kritische Betrachtung der wissenschaftlichen Arbeiten über das Werk Georg Trakls." Ph.D. diss., Freie Universität Berlin, 1963.

Forte, Dieter. Letter to author, 18 Feb. 1989.

Härtling, Peter. Letter to author, 29 Feb. 1987.

Kempowski, Walter. Personal conversation with author, London-Richmond, 30 May 1986.

Masche, U. "Zum Problem des Außenseiters; Muschgs 'Schwarze Spinne' Kleists 'Michael Kohlhaas', Goethes 'Werther' und Döblins 'Biberkopf.'" Ph.D. diss., University of Basel, 1971.

Mey, Reinhard. Letter to author, 23 Nov. 1988.

Oft, Henrich. "Das Problem der Autonomie bei Hofmannsthal." Ph.D. diss., Freie Universität Berlin, 1976.

Richter, Ruth. "Der Einfluss F. M. Dostojevskijs [sic] auf die Werke Jakob Wassermanns." Ph.D. diss., University of Bonn, 1951.

Schröder, Heinrich. "Kurt Tucholsky: Polemik und Satire im Kampf um eine Weltanschauung." Ph.D. diss., University of Vienna, 1958.

Stern, Olga. "Kaspar Hauser in der Dichtung." Ph.D. diss., University of Frankfurt a. M., 1920.

Universum-Film-Aktiengesellschaft (UFA). Dramaturgische Abteilung. Letter 8 July 1933, City Archives, Ansbach.

Vesper, Guntram. Letter to author, 11 Feb. 1986.

Wacker, Johannes. Letter to author, 30 Aug. 1988.

Index